# ADAPTATIONAL PSYCHODYNAMICS:

## MOTIVATION
## AND CONTROL

# ADAPTATIONAL PSYCHODYNAMICS:
## MOTIVATION AND CONTROL

## by SANDOR RADO

EDITED BY
Jean Jameson, M.D.
Henriette Klein, M.D.

SCIENCE HOUSE · NEW YORK · 1969

Library of Congress Catalog Card Number: 70–82528
Standard Book Number: 87668 018 x

Manufactured by Haddon Craftsmen, Inc.
Scranton, Pennsylvania

# Table of Contents

# Author's Introduction

Over two hundred years ago Alexander Pope observed that the proper study of mankind is Man. But this insight had no immediate influence on the direction of mankind's quest for knowledge. Marching from triumph to triumph, the physical sciences left the study of Man far behind in development. Still worse, overspecialization has split human biology into a loose collection of isolated and self-contained sciences, less and less capable of capturing the infinite organizational complexity of the life of Man. The task, then, is to pool our resources and try to reach general agreement upon a suitable design for a unified science of human behavior.

The spectacular success of the physical sciences should not obscure the fact that biologically mankind is better equipped for exploring Man than for exploring the rest of the universe. We examine the world about us through our senses, chiefly by inspection. As Sir Arthur Eddington remarked, our picture of the physical world rests on our use of the yardstick and the clock; in the last analysis, on pointer-reading. However, the human organism can be examined by introspection as well as by inspection. The organism is directly aware of its thoughts, feelings and doings, and can communicate them to others. Thus, we can evolve two scientific pictures of the organism, one inspective, the other introspective. Should we succeed in making these two pictures truly complementary, then we could comprehend Man more fully than anything else. The proper study of mankind is indeed Man.

This volume is based on courses of lectures given by me annually from 1945 to 1955 at the Psychoanalytic Clinic for Training and Research, College of Physicians and Surgeons, Columbia University.

During these years, my investigative work aimed at the further development of the theory and practice of psychoanalysis. In this pursuit, the first task was the thorough reexamination and resystematization of Freud's psychoanalytic theories, now technically known as "classical psychodynamics." Combining Freud's original investigative procedure with a strict application of the scientific method, this work has led to the conceptual scheme of an *adaptational psychodynamics*. In this theory, the biological concept of adaptation serves as the overall framework for the interpretation of healthy and disordered behavior. By virtue of its biological framework, adaptational psychodynamics proposes to lay the foundation for a unified science of human behavior.

The Freudian psychoanalytic school, to which I belong, has taken little cognizance of these developments. Its exclusive preoccupation with Freud's formulations—which Freud himself continuously changed and always regarded as provisional—proves once again the accuracy of Goethe's observation.

> Every great idea as soon as it appears exerts a tyrannous
> influence. Hence the advantages that it produces are all
> too soon transformed into disadvantages.

In 1932, in a personal conversation, I asked Freud to write an article for publication in our Psychoanalytic Journal which was directed by Freud and edited then by me.

> *Es fällt mir nichts ein* (Nothing comes to my mind),
> he replied, and then added with a smile, *Falls ich etwas
> schreiben täte, würden es meine Schüller nicht germe
> haben.* (If I wrote something, my pupils wouldn't like it.)

*Sandor Rado*

# Sandor Rado, M.D., Dr. Pol. Sci.

# A Brief Biography

On January 8, 1890, five years before Freud's first publication, *Studies on Hysteria*, Sandor Rado was born in Hungary into a moderately prosperous family. By 1907 he entered the University of Budapest, intending to study political science and law. It was not until the late fall of 1910 that he reached the turning point in his life.

By accident a Hungarian pamphlet called "Analysis of the Soul" by Sandor Ferenczi fell into his hands. Rado was wildly enthusiastic. Here were answers to a question he had often pondered—Why do different people respond so differently? Here was Sigmund Freud, a man who had developed verbalized free association, an investigative method of studying the part of the brain that was the mind, the part that could not be scrutinized by the inspective methods of physiology.

A whole world of excitement lay before Sandor Rado and he could hardly wait to learn more. From the bookstore he ordered everything then in print by Sigmund Freud, and after devouring every word, Rado's mind was made up. At his first meeting with Ferenczi he told him he wanted to become a doctor and specialize in psychiatry and psychoanalysis. For the sake of his family he decided to finish his political science courses while beginning his medical studies. Nothing seemed too much for this eager young man who had found the work he was enamored of and to which he would then dedicate his life.

Rado's psychoanalytic training from 1911 to 1915 followed the pattern of the day. He also joined Ferenczi's informal group where the talk centered about what Freud was teaching and writing. A warm friendship sprang up between Ferenczi and Rado, the former generously sharing his correspondence with Freud. In the fall of 1913 Rado made a pilgrimage to Vienna to meet Freud. As an enthralled young student he listened to Freud's two-hour lecture on the "Interpretation of Dreams." In 1914 Rado gave his first paper, "The Contribution of Psychoanalysis to Medicine," to the Hungarian Psychoanalytic Society. His second paper ("The Paths of Natural Science in the Light of Psychoanalysis," 1922) also emphasized the relationships between science and psychoanalysis, and expressed his methodological interest.

In the fall of 1922 Rado went to Berlin for a personal analysis with Karl Abraham, Director of the Berlin Psychoanalytic Institute. Several months later, Sandor Rado was invited to join the faculty. In 1924, Freud invited Rado to become executive editor of the two official journals of psychoanalysis: Zeitschrift and Imago. Rado held these posts for many years.

In 1929 Rado visited Washington, D.C. for the first International Congress on Mental Hygiene, and the following year he was invited by the New York Psychoanalytic Society to come to America to help them set up their institute on the Berlin model. Rado's acceptance was partly based on his uneasy foreboding about the political climate in Germany.

The Psychoanalytic Institute in the United States was established in 1931 in New York under the leadership of Dr. A. A. Brill with the assistance of Dr. Monroe A. Meyer. The task of organizing it and making innovations was carried out over a period of years under Rado's directorship, in close collaboration with many other devoted members of the New York Psychoanalytic Institute.

Rado worked indefatigably as an editor, for which Freud was highly appreciative. But rifts occurred between them. According to Rado, the first of these was because of Rado's strong insistence that psychoanalysis remain exclusively part of medicine. In a Zeitschrift issue which discussed the question of the relationship of psychoanalysis to medicine, Rado, then the editor, published letters from every prominent analyst except himself, out of loyalty to Freud, since their positions were opposite. But by his silence, Rado emphasized his position favoring psychoanalysis being part of medicine.

Rado views the second misunderstanding between Freud and himself as arising from his political conviction that there would be a serious military invasion and that psychoanalysis in Berlin would be lost; on the basis of this, Rado planned not only to migrate to the United States but encouraged and later financed others to do so. He suggested that the files containing original manuscripts and such be moved to the United States. Freud, who was much less convinced of the impending doom or felt that his prominence would protect him and psychoanalysis, viewed this suggestion as an attempt to shift the editorial control of psychoanalysis from Europe to the United States. Later, part of the writings were moved but, as is now well known, much was destroyed and many psychoanalysts had to flee the country. It is of interest that some of Freud's writings and possessions were purchased by, and now reside in, the library of the New York Psychiatric Institute, the building in which the Columbia Psychoanalytic Clinic was founded.

The misunderstanding between Freud and Rado was patched up. But it is difficult to believe that Rado's empirical teachings, which he termed adaptational psychodynamics, and his criticism of certain basic tenets of psychoanalysis could have allowed the breech to be completely healed.

By the mid-thirties, Rado had severed most of his European ties and was licensed to practice in the United States, where he was preparing to become an American citizen.

By 1939, at the joint meeting of the American Psychoanalytic and American Psychiatric associations, Dr. Rado wrote, "My own therapeutic efforts gradually led me to realize that we had reached a stage of development when our understanding of the etiology and treatment of the neuroses was hindered rather than aided by the theory of instincts itself. This theory was repeatedly modified by Freud, each time becoming more speculative, more general and remote. Although captivated by the philosophical implications of this theory, Freud was aware of its scientific shortcomings. . . . Obviously this hypothesis, though of great heuristic value in the early development of psychoanalysis, has outlived its usefulness. In order for Freud's discoveries to bear new fruits by stimulating further scientific inquiry, it was necessary to segregate the factual findings of psychoanalysis from its metaphysical elements and to build some other frame of reference that would rest on our established biological knowledge of man and suit our medical needs.

"We attempted to meet this need by describing the actually observable dynamics of the mind in terms of integrative ego functioning or to introduce a convenient designation, in terms of any egology.* This egological concept has gradually evolved from a theoretical position first stated in 1927 and further elaborated in 1933. It has enabled

*A term introduced by Rado referring to the study of the ego.

us to go look upon the neuroses as disorders of integrative ego functioning and thus to study and describe them in terms of an ego pathology."

Soon after this address, the previously mild opposition to Rado's
teachings increased, precipitated in part by the arrival of many refugees
from Europe, among them some who had previously attacked his
writings in the *Zeitschrift*. In 1941, Dr. Rado gave up his teaching post
as director of the New York Psychoanalytic Institute. (He has continued
his membership in the New York Psychoanalytic Society.)

After 1941 Rado devoted his energies to the implementation of his
long-held dream—to bring psychoanalysis under medical auspices. He
was aided in this in June, 1944, when the Columbia University Board
of Trustees approved the proposition of the medical faculty that formal
psychoanalytic training be organized within its auspices. Dr. Rado was
appointed the first director of the program at a time when the initiative
in psychoanalytic training and research was shifting to the United
States, as a result of the unhealthy atmosphere in Europe during the
war. In some respects this unbroken progress in the field surpassed
Freud's own expectations regarding the founding of the first fully recognized psychoanalytic training faculty within the structure of a university
medical college.

This finally occurred in the autumn of 1944, when the university
established the Columbia Psychoanalytic Clinic for Training and Research within the department of psychiatry; a faculty was created that
was given the unique opportunity to put into operation a graduate
psychoanalytic curriculum. This has since been duplicated throughout
the United States.

In addition to Freud's deep impact on Rado throughout Rado's professional lifetime, another major psychoanalyst who influenced Rado's
development was Ferenczi, who introduced Rado to psychoanalysis in
1910. Between 1911 and 1922, excluding the war years, these two
lunched or dined together four or five times a week. The effect of one
on the other must have been significant. Rado incorporated Ferenczi's
concept of autoplastic and alloplastic adaptation, and his ideas paralleled
Ferenczi's concept of magical thought as being nuclear to obsessive behavior. In addition to the encouragement and moral support Rado
received from Abraham, he increasingly utilized Abraham's emphasis
on orality into his own concept of elation and depression, and incorporated Abraham's emphasis on the crucial importance of emotions
in psychoanalytic theory.

Among the other influences on Rado were William James and a

multitude of biologists, particularly Charles Sherrington and Walter Cannon. Works from others, such as Ralph Gerard and Theodosius Dobzhansky, Rado viewed as true scientific research models. His professor of physics, Baron Rollad Eoetvoes, originally had taught him scientific methodolgy, which was to dominate Rado's own primary interest throughout his lifetime.

Rado never tired of impressing upon his students that scientific methodology in investigative sciences contains principles that apply to any branch and that through the genius of Freud a method had been made available for investigating the mind. From the beginning, Rado considered that the physiology of the brain and the psychology of the brain were inseparable. In reminiscing he says that he approached psychoanalysis with this one idea and still held to this scientific principle sixty years later. It was the original methodological approach that interested him. This was the theme he emphasized in his years at the Berlin Institute, during his years of teaching at the New York Psychoanalytic Institute, and at the Columbia University, College of Physicians and Surgeons, Medical College, Psychoanalytic Clinic (Institute).

Some of Rado's ideas have been gradually absorbed into psychoanalytic and psychiatric thinking, sometimes without reference to their historical origins, or have been retranslated and expressed in other terms. But there is no doubt that his has been an imaginative and adventuresome contribution.

Dr. Rado gave this general introductory course in motivation and control to each incoming class, to which he expressed his personal point of view. The course coincided with the major ones being given simultaneously on Freud's writings. In 1966 we discussed with Dr. Rado the possibility of publishing the lecture series he had given since the 1930's to beginning students of psychoanalysis. He was first reluctant to have these lectures published because he had always revised them from year to year and did not view them as being in definitive form. Also, he himself hoped to prepare their final revision.

In Rado's concept of *Motivation and Control* in a context of adaptational psychodynamics, he uses the term "motivation," to include all inner promoting, drives, tensions, and desires; by "control," he means all the shaping, organizing, and restraining influences the individual uses to attain his purposes.

Unfortunately, between the time he agreed to their publication and had written the preface to this volume, his failing health made it impossible for him to edit the contents. We, therefore, have been completely dependent upon the yearly transcriptions of his lectures given (1945 to 1955) at the Columbia University Psychoanalytic Clinic for Training and Research. Considering that the content of these lectures goes back 40 years, these lectures seem of historical importance to educators, psychologists, psychiatrists, psychoanalysts, and indeed, all students of motivation.

The material has been slightly rearranged and edited but hopefully represents the voice of Sandor Rado.

J. Jameson, M.D.
H. Klein, M.D.

New York 1969

# Acknowledgements

We wish to express our sincere gratitude to Paul A. Bradlow, M.D., James P. Cattell, M.D., and Ruth Easser, M.D., former students of Dr. Rado, for their cooperation in the use of their personal Rado lecture series of various years. We also thank Lawrence C. Kolb, M.D., John A. P. Millet, M.D. and George Daniels, M.D. for their cooperation.

We are especially grateful to Arnold Cooper, M.D., George B. Goldman, M.D., A. Kardiner, M.D., Aaron Karush, M.D., and Lionel Ovesey, M.D. for reading parts of the manuscript and for their assistance in suggesting crucial changes. To Dr. Ruth Easser we owe special thanks for her invaluable help.

We wish to express our obligation to Miss Lena Maniero for her tireless editorial work; and to Miss Henrietta Gilden whose editorial guidance determined the final form of this volume.

We are indebted to Bluma Swerdlow, D.S.W., who made available the transcriptions of her oral history collection, on which we drew, and for her consultation.

For the financing of this project, we are indebted in part to the New York School of Psychiatry and the Medical Research Fund of Columbia University Medical School, College of Physicians and Surgeons.

We are indebted to Grune and Stratton, publishers of the collected papers of Sandor Rado (two volumes) for providing generous access to the published material.

# The Editors

Jean Jameson, M.D. was one of Dr. Rado's students in the early 1950's at the Columbia University Psychoanalytic Clinic for Training and Research. She is currently in private practice in New York City and is a Training Psychoanalyst at the Clinic.

Henriette R. Klein, M.D. received her training in psychoanalysis at the New York Psychoanalytic Institute. She has been on the staff of Columbia Medical College, College of Physicians & Surgeons, since the 1930's, where she has been Clinical Professor in the Department of Psychiatry. She has had a vigorous interest in education throughout her entire professional life, and has done a variety of studies associated with this interest, including one on the selection process for postgraduate training in psychoanalysis.

# ADAPTATIONAL PSYCHODYNAMICS:

## MOTIVATION
## AND CONTROL

# CHAPTER 1

# From Ancient Knowledge

# to Modern Insights

MAN, AS ARISTOTLE OBSERVED LONG AGO, IS A SOCIAL ANIMAL. LIVING in organized groups, members of the human species are interdependent. They may thrive by mutual aid or destroy each other and the whole species. Man has at all times grappled with the problem of his own nature, seeking to understand, predict, and control human behavior.

Archaeological findings indicate that prehistoric man had already evolved a craft of human relationships. Reflecting about behavior may have begun with the observation that men always wanted certain things and went after them. Our predecessors learned to view themselves as charged with wishes, desires, intentions, aims, and goals that prompted them to act in certain ways. Only in the light of men's motives could one understand their willed actions. The idea of motive forces was complemented by the ancient discovery of the regulatory function of pleasure and pain. Observation showed that man sought to repeat pleasurable experiences and avoid painful ones.

Mankind has at all times sought to control the natural phenomena upon which its welfare depended by intelligent action based upon experience and learning. Inherited from our subhuman ancestors, this captive use of intelligence proved to be sufficiently effective to support and advance our species in changing environments. Primitive tribes perpetuated and slowly enlarged their scant store of practical knowledge. But primitive man was often terrified and frustrated by phenomena that lay beyond his comprehension. In response to this frustration, the organism's hedonic self-regulation released men's primordial craving for controlling such phenomena by emotional intervention. This craving relied on the power of the wish to bring about the desired change.

To make the power of the wish effective, primitive man invented a variety of magical procedures that became ritualized by the tribal chieftains, priests, and medicine men. Though these procedures resulted only in an illusion of adaptive control, they engendered hope and ameliorated despair. In man's perennial struggle for a better life, the magical techniques of illusory control have continued to this day to supplement the rational ones.

Ancient man's practical knowledge was always blended with a varying portion of emotionally inspired, magical thought. But the Greeks succeeded in paving the way for a decisive change of outlook. Greek philosophy crystallized the insight that before we can hope to control natural phenomena effectively, we must learn to understand them, and it boldly advanced the proposition that the human intellect is fit to comprehend the display of nature. Modern science rests on these ideas.

Science is an organized body of knowledge dealing with established facts and generalized inferences derived from them. Since all science is basically composed of facts and ideas, I propose to examine the mutual relationship of these components at the common-sense level, avoiding the heavy conceptual apparatus of the technical epistemologist, but retaining a psychodynamic point of view of adaptation.

Science begins with the systematized description of presumably significant facts, and its next step is to correlate such facts. Every investigation starts with the idea that certain facts are related to one another in a definite way. Such an idea is called an assumption or working hypothesis. If verified within satisfactory limits by observation or experiment, it becomes an established empirical correlation.

The next aim of science is to correlate the correlations and build theories or conceptual schemes of increasingly broader compass. A theory generalizes a set of empirical correlations and brings them into a logical arrangement. It must show, by explicit or implied methodological instruction, how we may observe and, if possible, measure the facts that fall within its scope. The degree of consistency and economy of thought that a science may attain depends upon the logical system it uses. The mathematical sciences, for example, are at the stage of logical development known as postulational organization.

A scientific theory need not be true. Theories that later proved erroneous have more than once led to the discovery of facts. In the course of time, theories are supplanted by more serviceable ones, but the facts discovered through the earlier theories remain. We must not think that our knowledge of an established fact of observation is no longer subject to change. In an empirical science, both theoretical organization and factual knowledge are continuously undergoing reexamination and revision. The development of contemporary physics is a good example of this.

The field of medicine presents a different picture. The clinical sciences have hardly begun to free themselves from the grip of a traditional dogmatism that prefers to perpetuate the more or less arbitrary dicta of one authority or another. In the analysis of observational data, the clinician's foremost tool is basic knowledge in the underlying physiological sciences. As long as such basic knowledge is insufficient, the clinician is tempted to look for an authority or create one on whose intuition and judgment he may blindly rely. The clinician thus resorts to magic.

In the absence of postulational organization, a science tends to regress in the following ways: The authority is viewed as the fountainhead of knowledge. All observation and reasoning aim at corroborating the propositions of the authority which are considered infallible. Concepts are undefined or so inadequately defined that even if observational testing is attempted, it is reduced to a sham.

Compared with other branches of clinical medicine, psychiatry has so far derived the least benefit from recent advances in the physiological sciences. This is due to a combination of causes. The organizational complexity of the brain is staggering. Knowledge of its physiology lags far behind that of the other component systems of the organism. Also, the basic science closest to psychiatry is psychodynamics, the only branch of human biology that views the organism from within. Hence psychodynamics, the view from within, must be correlated with the physiological sciences, the view from without.

Here we run into a snag. Physiological thinking operates with the fundamental concepts of matter, space, and time, which were evolved for exploration of the physical world. But psychodynamic thinking operates with the concepts of motivation and control by self-regulatory arrangements, which were evolved for exploration of the world of inner awareness, of the organism from within.

Thus we can evolve two scientific pictures of the organism, one inspection, the other introspection. Should we succeed in making these two pictures truly complementary, then we could comprehend man more fully.

The importance of a unitary conceptual scheme in human biology is not generally recognized. When called upon to switch suddenly from the inspective to the introspective, the investigator may have the ground swept from under him, and the transition precipitates a relapse to emotional thought. With this retreat from reason to magic, he inescapably splits the human organism into a scientific body and a faith-laden mind, as Descartes did before him. Our immediate task is to lift the investigation of the inner aspect of the organism to the level of unemotional thought by an increasingly consistent application of the scientific method.

## Biological Aspects of the Organism

In adaptational psychodynamics we analyze behavior in the context of a biological organism interacting with its cultural environment. The human organism, like other living organisms, may be defined as a self-regulating biological system that perpetuates itself and its type by means of its environment, its surrounding system. From this it follows that life is a process of interaction of the organism and its environment. As a biological entity, the human organism shows a definite chemical composition, a definite organization, maintenance and growth through assimilation, reproduction and heredity, irritability and adaptation, and awareness of itself and its environment.

In the human organism the cortex with its receptors dominates the brain, the brain dominates the spinal cord, and the whole nervous system dominates and controls the entire body. Since the brain is in turn dominated by the mind, the latter almost completely controls the entire organism. Integration of parts into a whole is mediated by mechanisms of communication which may be transmissive, such as the nerve impulses, or transportive, such as the hormones. However, there are also gradient mechanisms.

In the theory of evolution, the crowning achievement of eighteenth- and nineteenth-century biologists, adaptive value is a statistical concept which epitomizes reproductive efficiency in a certain environment. This is strongly influenced by the type's ability to survive. Hence "more adaptive" means more able to survive and reproduce. The slow maturation of the human organism accounts for the strength of its aboriginal dependency needs. Progressive adaptation is the driving force of evolution. However, man's increasing control of nature has created evolutionary problems that can no longer be successfully met by a mere increase of reproductive efficiency. The human species now faces the inescapable task of limiting population increase on a global scale.

Moreover, man's most important environment has become man himself. The one who threatens the human species with extinction is man. The fight against other species is eclipsed by the fight between and within diverse organized population groups, states, nations. Survival and evolution of the human species now depend upon improved adaptation of the diverse population groups to one another.

Cultures, in general, advance in the following ways: from bigotry, dogmatism, and regimentation to freedom of conscience, thought, inquiry, expression, teaching, and learning; from violence to peaceful cooperation marked by equitable human relationships and readiness of the members to compose their differences; from government by coercion to government by consent of the governed; from rigidly centralized control with little local independence to a sound balance between centralized control and local independence; from a rigid hierarchical stratification of society (castes) to a complete vertical mobility, fostering individual initiative and productive effort and enterprise, and the creation of equal opportunity for all.

In seeking a comprehensive approach to the subject of human behavior, I have developed over the past few decades the body of theory I call adaptational psychodynamics. It places the analysis of behavior in the genetic, physiologic, and cultural contexts of the organism. I have tried to replace undefinable concepts with defined ones, and one of my goals was to evolve a close-to-the-fact scientific language that would convey the most information in the fewest words. I believe that the establishment of an accurate vocabulary is an indispensable step toward formulating theories that can be verified or refuted by observation.

To sum up, modern science, effecting a rapid transformation of man's world, began with the life of Galileo, about 300 years ago. The technological utilization of nuclear energy, holding the promise of welfare for all and the threat of extinction of all, is an achievement of our time. The impending perfection of a blueprint for some chain reaction of a solar order of magnitude may place us in a position to blow up our entire planet. Beyond a doubt, man is a unique upshot of the animal kingdom.

# CHAPTER 2

# *Orientation*

ADAPTATIONAL PSYCHODYNAMICS SHOULD BE LOOKED AT AS THE BASIC component of a comprehensive dynamics of human behavior based on the psychoanalytic method of investigation. Its emphasis is on the part played by motivation and control in the organism's interaction with its cultural environment. It deals with pleasure and pain, emotion and thought, desire and executive action, interpreting them in terms of organismic utility, in an adaptational framework. In the theory of evolution, the pivotal concept is adaptation. Adaptation is a point of view of the observer, not the organism. Its foremost objective is to discover the mechanisms whereby the psychodynamic cerebral system accomplishes its integrative task. The potential range of the organism's development and activities is circumscribed by its inherited constitution, the "norm of reaction" of its genotype. Behavior is then defined as the actual organism's (phenotype's) systemic interaction with its cultural environment.

Psychodynamics must be recognized as the basic component of this structure because it alone can discover the behavior problems which await their solution from physiology and genetics.

In the life cycle of the individual, the significance of the experience during the first period of his life, which is the alimentary period, lasts for a lifetime. The behavior patterns evolved in this period are indelible because they represent the first adaptation of the organism. They may be called into service at any future time, even though they no longer fit the environmental situation, because of a basic tendency of the organism to fall back on previous patterns that have been found successful when newly acquired patterns of behavior fail. Only new frustration can come of this effort. These two observations are as important as any of the discoveries of psychoanalysis. I shall repeat them. The early experiences of the human mind are indestructible. In times of failure the grown-up organism tends to resort to more primitive patterns. This is the essence of the story.

Since the organism's life cycle is but a phase of evolution, it is consistent to make the same concept basic to the study of behavior. Let us look at the term *adaptation*. In biology *adaptation* means change within the organism, calculated to equip it better for survival in given environmental conditions. Accordingly, in a good part of psychiatric literature, *adaptation* means change in human behavior that is calculated to fit the environment better. This is not the meaning in which I use the word *adaptation*. In talking about the human species it is necessary either to coin a new word or to extend the meaning of the word *adaptation* so that it includes all those ecologic reactions by which the individual influences the environment for its own purposes.

The human species, more than any other, builds its own environment. Ferenczi used the terms *autoplastic* and *alloplastic* to distinguish adaptation and environment-building activities. Autoplastic adaptations result from changes undergone by the organism itself. This is adaptation in the narrower sense. Alloplastic adaptations are changes wrought by the organism on its environment.

We can distinguish between autoplastic and alloplastic adaptation. Autoplastic adaptation is characteristic of the lower animals. It is also characteristic of the human, but in humans the autoplastic is overshadowed by the alloplastic in that we build houses and cities and production plants, and we fly into outer space to explore the moon. The previous generation creates the environment into which the new one is born. The new generation goes ahead and retransforms that environment, creating a new one for the next generation. The most important part of human environment is society, which is most certainly a man-made organization. You can see the tragic and far-reaching implications of the statement that man is builder of his environment.

In psychiatric literature there is a tendency to forget that fact which is most characteristic of the human being and to interpret adaptation as an adjusment to existing conditions, as if those existing were natural. They are not.

We define *ontogenetic adaptations* as improvements in the organism's pattern of interaction with its environment which increase its chance for survival, cultural self-realization, and perpetuation of its type. In ontogenetic adaptations, the master mechanisms are learning, creative imagination, and goal-directed activity.

Phylogenetic adaptations are based on genetic mechanisms, such as favorable mutation—the appearance of potentially valuable new equipment. The phylogenetic accumulation of unfavorable mutations may lead to adaptive degradation if not extinction of the organism and the species. Corollary to our adaptational framework is our adaptational principle of investigation. We examine behavior first from the point of view of means to an end, and then from the point of view of cause and effect. In end relating, the question is, "What is its purpose?" In cause searching, the question is, "How does it fulfill its purpose?" End relating is our preparatory reconnaissance; cause searching our ultimate task.

In contrast to old time teleology, the adaptational principle does not assume that all behavior of the organism is inherently purposive. Evaluation of the adaptive value of behavior is the job of the observer and must not be confused with the work done by the organism itself. In the class of "goal searching behavior" the organism is seen to do its own goal searching, goal finding, goal pursuing, and goal attaining. This class of behavior is distinguished by the fact that here the organism's own expectancies enter as components into the causal mechanism of its behavior. To appraise the adaptive efficiency of the organism's own goal mechanism is naturally a task for the observer. In other classes of behavior no goal-directing mechanism is demonstrable. Acting upon clues, the organism may repeat blindly an established pattern. It is then once again the task of the psychoanalyst to determine the adaptive value the pattern had when it was established and the adaptive value it has here and now.

The regulatory function of pleasure and pain has been known at least since Aristotle. The utility and pleasure aspects of all behavior modalities is fundamental. The pleasure aspect is the normal, natural emotional evaluation of a behavior modality. Does it under ordinary circumstances yield pleasure? Or does it yield pain? And which does it yield and under what conditions?

In pleasure and pain the animal organism possesses a dependable system for evaluating behavior. The activities described as "moving toward" and "moving away" depend on the pleasure or pain they bring the organism. Hedonic self-regulation extends over the organism's entire operating pattern. Pleasure is the reward for successful performance, and the memory of pleasure invites repetition of the beneficial activities. Pain is the punishment for failure, and the memory of pain deters the organism from repeating the self-harming activity. Nature has placed massive pleasure rewards on the operations that will supply the organism's needs. At the same time, pleasure-yielding yet socially undesirable activities must be vigorously combated by the threat of punishment. Any organism not regulated by pleasure and pain would soon be out of business.

Intellectual insight or thought may overrule the decisions of the emotions, and that which is pleasant according to the emotional tendency of behavior may prove harmful from the utility point of view, though in most instances this is not so. The pleasure aspect and the utility aspect represent the emotional level and the thought level respectively.

Never is man happier than when he succeeds in stealing the pleasure reward alone from the utility pursuit. Thumbsucking is an example of a pleasure-yielding activity which is pursued for itself alone. But for all practical purposes, the inverse is quite important. This is the fact that cultural life creates so many activities that are useful and necessary, but have no pleasure reward attached. The trick is to imitate nature and make the necessary activity pleasure yielding, because all activity accompanied by pleasure is carried out with much greater ease, for example, the stringencies of camping.

The problem is that isolated pleasure pursuit tends to spoil the organism and lessen the drive for useful activity. But, useful activity not accompanied by pleasure is very exhausting. Nature once solved this problem for the species. Every man in his own life has to solve it in his own individual way. Pleasure pursuits are also additive. For example, a child sitting on a pot defecating will also enjoy sucking his thumb or munching a cookie.

## Mind and Body

Because of the structure and function of his private and public worlds, man has found it difficult to explain man as an entity. Therefore the one human being has been divided into a body and soul, or mind. In the seventeenth century, Descartes set down the divisions and thought that these two entities influenced each other through the pineal gland. This theory continued to have enormous influence up to the present. In Germany, it led to the division of science into the natural sciences and the social sciences.

Spinoza, like Aristotle before him, had a different view. Aristotle had felt that the mind or soul wts inseparable from the body. He believed there was only one substance or one body, but two different ways of knowing it. In actual practice not much was gained by Spinoza's contribution, but it did establish a new frame of experience which would include mental sciences. It led the way in a new attempt to deal with the mind-body problem. At present there is no conceptual system that unifies the data derived from two kinds of investigation, the inspective and the introspective. But after the suggestions by Aristotle and Spinoza, each method of observation can be viewed as a different way of describing the same substance.

The importance of a unitary conceptual scheme in human biology is not generally recognized. Certain influential schools of thought, such as behaviorism, reject introspection as a method and reject consciousness as a subject of science. In their view, science deals only with the phenomena of matter, space, and time. Consciousness is viewed by them as an epiphenomenon—presumably installed by nature in the brain for decorative purposes. This view is untenable.

Living in social groups, man at all times is forced to grapple with the problem of his own nature, trying to understand, predict, and control the behavior of other men. Mankind's time-honored knowledge of man, a craft of human relationships, testifies to the unique practical value of introspective inquiry.


## Private and Public World

If I look around me, I find myself surrounded by events that can be observed by anyone else as well as myself. If I turn my attention inward, I become aware of events within myself that can be observed only by myself. This means that the material of direct experience is divided into two worlds, one public and one private. This has been the situation ever since man appeared on earth, and as far as we know will continue. This division of our experience into a public or outer world and a private or inner one has very far-reaching consequences. Nobody can read the events in my mind; nobody can know what I think, how I feel, what I intend to do.

How do we then find out about such events in another human

being? He will reveal some of his private life by his behavior, and he may choose to tell us what is going on in his internal world. People tried to watch and observe each other's actions. To the extent to which these actions are accessible to observation, the observers were successful.

The public phase of human behavior can be seen by others unless it is intentionally hidden. But the preparatory phase of behavior, feeling, and thought is hidden to begin with. So, although men can question each other about their own behavior, interrogation is a limited means of information.

The reasons for this were known in antiquity. The Latin saying "*Bellum omnium contra omnes*" is a description of social life in which men are motivated to make themselves appear in as favorable a light as possible, not to speak of intentions that would be harmful to them in competitive struggle. Thus knowledge about men remained a cherished and privileged possession of a few gifted intuitive men, notably philosophers, writers, poets, statesmen, and physicians.

Still another problem is that there are two languages in the introspective world. One is used to describe facts and events. The other is an emotional language describing the speaker's feelings and used to convey and arouse emotions. One is what the semanticists call referential language, the other emotive. The psychoanalyst must use both. Throughout history the knowledge and understanding of man was slow to advance because of the hesitancy of men to explain themselves to others or even to themselves. The private world described in psychological language referring to a nondemonstrable event can only be understood if the person has had similar experience. A German psychologist invented the word *Einfühlung*, and American psychologists attempted to translate it with the word *empathy*. The German word means feeling oneself into a situation; the English word means intellectual or imaginative apprehension of another's state of mind.

Words have a greater significance in psychological science than in physical science where you can point to the things that are described. In psychology the word has to re-create the experience in the internal world of the listener. We all communicate by means of what I term *emotional resonance*, which is the method of ascertaining another's emotions by the effect those emotions have on the observer's own emotions. The vocabulary of this private experience is limited. The English language probably has only a few hundred words with which to describe this inner world; of these only a few dozen are understood by everybody.

# CHAPTER 3

# The Reporting and

# Nonreporting Processes

THE ORGANISM INTEGRATES ITS BEHAVIOR CHIEFLY BY WHAT IS KNOWN as its mind. The old scientific gap between mind and brain has been widened rather than narrowed by the introduction of the ambiguous concept of the unconscious mind. In adaptational psychodynamics the mind is both the loudspeaker and audience of the brain. When we look at it this way, we can see that consciousness is our awareness of the running report produced (as its inward expression) by the underlying nervous activity of the brain. We shall call the nervous activity of the brain underlying the awareness process the reporting process, and consciousness, the awareness process. Almost three hundred years ago Spinoza said, "The order and connection of ideas is the same as the order and connection of things." Translated, this means that the awareness process is exactly synchronous and exactly congruent with the reporting process.

The cerebrum and the rest of the central nervous system buzz with activity at nonreporting levels. Such nonreporting nervous activity by itself has no effect upon consciousness, but this physiologic activity may be relayed to the reporting levels and thus eventuate in the awareness process. In reverse order, awareness and reporting may elicit activity at nonreporting purely physiologic levels.

Freud discovered that the psychodynamic meaning or the motivational significance of this nonreporting activity could be inferred from convergent contextual evidence gathered for this purpose by the psychoanalytic investigative technique. He also demonstrated that this inferred meaning can be stated in terms of unconscious tension, unconscious emotion, or unconscious thought. In the terminology I am suggesting, I am substituting *nonreporting* for *unconscious*, so that when I speak, for instance, of a nonreporting desire, I am talking about a missing causal agent which has been acted upon as if it were a desire, though in fact it is a purely physiologic event. The psychodynamic meaning of nonreporting nervous activity can be arrived at only by psychodynamic inference, and can be expressed only in an extrapolated language of psychodynamics.

To the emotionally inspired imagination, Freud's "unconscious mind" appears as a department of mind working "below" or "outside" awareness and seems to be another mysterious thing in itself. This metaphysical conception of the unconscious mind was based upon Kant's philosophy of *Ding an sich* [thing in itself], which lies outside the conditions of possible experience. Unfortunately, this Kantian construction tends to remove the unconscious mind from the province of investigation to the realm of metaphysical speculation. But there is nothing metaphysical or mysterious about the unconscious mind. It is a nonreporting organization of causative links existing between processes of which we are aware. These nonreporting causative links have to be psychodynamically inferred from, and may be verified by, examination of these conscious processes. These inferred causative links bridge the gaps and thus make motivational dynamics a workable scheme for the psychodynamic analysis of behavior. I think it is important for you to realize that the unconscious mind is an extrapolated concept rather than a thing in itself. Only through methodological clarification can we hope to avoid spurious problems and effectively advance Freud's own scientific objectives. For this reason, I substituted the term nonreporting process for the unconscious, and changed the other processes to fit.

The nervous equipment of the human being is flexibly attuned to the fluctuation of pressures and tensions in two ranges: nonreporting and reporting range, the latter including the awareness process. Between the nonreporting and self-reporting ranges is the pain barrier which selectively regulates the flow of nonreporting activity with the self-reporting range and upon which hedonic control rests. Fundamental to its action is repression.

By automatically excluding painful memories from recall, the mechanism of repression guards the awareness level against the onslaught of paralyzing, if not killing, pain. Repression is therefore an effective hedonic mechanism. However, by vetoing the recall of recorded information, repression interferes with the mechanism of rational thought.

Now let us look at some of the other forms of activity in which the nonreporting levels are involved. Some phases of the behavior mechanism may be lowered to the nonreporting levels through automatization, which saves conscious effort and increases the efficiency of performance. Memories are stored at the nonreporting levels. If they were not, they would clutter up the awareness level, which must be kept free for the arriving sensory messages. But like any kind of stored data, they are on recall. Again, storage and recall are efficiency mechanisms. Thoughts that have sunk in, such as the multiplication table, convictions, clichés, and more complex sequences, are on preferential recall. This mechanism may be used to rush old stereotyped solutions into service instead of thinking afresh. Preferential recall is another efficiency mechanism.

Unwanted tension, excluded from awareness by repression, may either subside or linger at nonreporting levels. In the latter event, it may contact repressed memories, gather momentum, and elicit activities of goal finding and illusory goal attainment at nonreporting levels. However, a relative overflow of such latent tension will force its way upward to the awareness level or downward to the lower physiologic levels or both. Emotional tension that has thus become manifest pushes for outward bodily expression and actual goal attainment. It is from the events of this reporting phase that one can infer the events of the preceding nonreporting phase. The discharge of latent emotional tension forced downward via the autonomic nervous system may be detected from the changes it precipitates in physiologic functions. The overflowing tension of a repressed desire may be discharged in a dream or daydream about desired action. However, the repression or, in other words, the fear of painful consequences may be strong enough to inhibit even this illusory expression. In this event, the overflowing tensions of the repressed desire may precipitate discharge through some imagined or real action involving the use of symbols that do not arouse this fear.

For instance, in a dream a man's fascination with a certain type of landscape may express and fulfill his strongly repressed desire for encountering a woman in the nude. Whether or not a certain thought or action of an individual has a symbolic meaning can be determined psychoanalytically through the associative exploration and disclosure of its hidden motivational context.

But this is still not the whole story. We have good reason to believe that while conscious thinking is proceeding on one of these higher levels, nonreporting activity is going on all the time on the lower levels—nonreporting activity which is not directly traceable by any method, though its existence is inferred by the method of extrapolation.

I suspect that the top levels are highly vulnerable and the lowest levels are most resistant. This is understandable because the top levels are recent acquisitions, and in accordance with the biological law the more recent an acquisition is the more vulnerable it is.

Now let me be bold and venture to speculate further on what is going on in these lower levels, which I view as the residuals of an ontogenetic development. If this is true, these lower levels must be the storehouses of the various infantile patterns of thought and motor behavior. It is possible that the individual habitually starts off a thought activity with the infantile patterns of mastery, which have to be corrected by thinking on a higher level to be adaptive behavior. Whenever these more primitive behavior patterns intrude on thinking on a higher level, we are confronted with behavior that tends to be more emotional and more egocentric than rational and has all the earmarks of the childish ways of thought and motor behavior.

But there is another interesting aspect of nonreporting thinking. People who have studied inventive and creative thinking invariably come up with the same story. It seems that when an idea comes up in an almost ready-made fashion, it is never the result of conscious thinking. Conscious thinking receives an idea that pops into your head. But, where does it come from? It comes from the lower levels, and the relationship between these levels is a very ticklish matter. It looks as if a good deal of childish thinking goes on in everyone. Even in the highest kind of scientific thinking these nonadjusted, nonadaptive, childish patterns of thought are in some way involved in and related to the creative activity of the top levels of the mind.

# CHAPTER 4

# *Motivation*

WHAT IS MOTIVATION? FROM WHAT DOES IT DERIVE? HOW DOES IT work? Actually, we do not know very much about it. We have theories but I have not been able to satisfy myself that they fit all our facts about man. Before Freud developed the libido theory, he used the everyday, well-known motives to explain behavior. That is what I fall back on. The study of motivation is the study of man.

## *Needs and Behavior*

Let us start with the fundamental assumption that the behavior of a human being, like that of the protozoan, is organized by subjective phenomena. Now, what happens in the protozoan? We do not know what "pushes" the animal, but we do know that the animal has "needs." These subjective phenomena are tensions that arise in the organism in consequence of stimulation from the external world or within the organism. These are what have been called instinctual tensions or bio-genic tensions. I suggest we think of them as physiogenic tensions or physiologic requirements of the organism which exist according to the design of that organism.

These tensions, characterized by the direction toward which they point, can be specified as requirements for food, for moisture, for oxygen, for certain temperature range, for sunshine, for copulation, and for other needs. We are assuming that, by perceiving these physiogenic tensions and the stimuli received from the outside world, the organism experiences subjective states that are either pleasure-like or pain-like sensations. As a result of systemic requirements, the organism brings the neuromuscular system into play and transforms stored potentials into motor activity aimed at controlling the environment. This is true, of course, only for the need-to-*do* tensions. The organism also has the need-to-*rest* tensions.

We can safely assume that the psychological organization of the human being, at the most primitive and lowest level, duplicates this functional design of the most primitive animal. A human being's psychological needs are probably perceived and acted upon by man in much the same way as the physiogenic tensions are experienced by the protozoan.

Now what does the word *need* mean? It is an explanatory concept rather than an investigative tool. Let us say that the individual's systemic requirements are his needs. Like his other traits, they are an outcome of the interaction between his inherited predisposition or genotype and his environment. We speak of aboriginal needs, which show predominantly the influence of the inherited predisposition, and of acculturated needs, which reflect predominantly the forming influence of the culture in which the organism lives.

Due to his slow maturation, the individual has aboriginal dependency needs. He also has aboriginal needs for safety, maintenance, growth, repair, reproduction, and sexual activity. In addition, he has acculturated needs for security, cultural development, and self-realization, for feeling important and gaining recognition as an adult in an organized society. The needs demonstrable in all known societies, which anthropologists call universals, are the common denominators of human existence.

To think in these terms, we must avoid the pitfalls of examining pleasure and pain as isolated psychological experiences and studying motor behavior as something independent and isolated. In a general way, we can say that the cycle of behavior runs from desire to fulfillment and back because successful control elicits a sense of satisfaction that usually stops the motor activity. Or, more specifically, we can say that the end result of each motor behavior pattern is relief from tension and the restoration of a new state of equilibrium, so that the full cycle goes from equilibrium to equilibrium.

Let us clearly understand that the regained equilibrium is not the same as the original equilibrium. The new equilibrium can never be the same as the old because time has elapsed and this time has permitted changes in the organism. Characteristic of the organism is that it is subject to a good many irreversible processes. Also, the relationship of the animal to the environment has changed in the meantime. The only characteristic that is the same is that the organism is in a state of equilibrium at both points of the cycle.

I have found it relatively fruitful to describe the motive forces of behavior in terms of feelings, thoughts, and impulses to act, and to think about the mechanisms of behavior as organized sequences of feelings, thoughts, and actions. The organism's interaction with its cultural environment may then be analyzed in such terms as *behavior areas, mechanisms, patterns, functions,* and *social institutions.*

There is one other working assumption about man's needs that I have come to accept: the organism seems to have a certain pleasure need, like a need for food, that has to be satisfied in order to keep going. It looks is if it were possible, within limits, for the individual to adjust the menu from time to time so that he gets a little bit more pleasure from one area and settles for a little bit less pleasure from another area. This is too strong an assumption, mind you, but it seems more reasonable to me to use it as a working theory than to predicate that all the pleasure modalities are expressions of one underlying drive (the libido) as did Freud.

## The Nature of the Central Motive State

Let us now look at what I call the central motive state. Generally, this may be defined as a state in which at a given time the behavior of the individual is organized and integrated by one outstanding and dominating interest. Later I shall talk about the central sexual motive state and the central alimentary motive state, which are the counterparts of the central motive state and are characterized by the same elements. To the last detail, the same phenomenon occurs in every central motive state. The alimentary and sexual motive states are the clearest examples of such integration of behavior.

What, then, are the characteristics that appear in every central motive state? The first element that must be present is motivation of one kind or another. Man is constantly being moved by his inner promptings, drives, tensions, desires, or sensory needs to get something for himself or to do something or to act in some way so that he can fulfill the wish that has upset his equilibrium.

The second characteristic is that the desire to fulfill this one need becomes dominant. It takes precedence over other behavior and motivation. The only phenomenon that invariably overrides a central motive state of any kind and intensity is the eruption of the emergency emotions that warn man he must look to his safety and interrupt his pursuit of pleasure, sex, food, or whatever it may be.

The third characteristic is that man is motivated by the nature of the central motive state to look for a certain type of stimulus pattern or stimulus constellation in the environment. By developing his ability to perceive selectively, the need enables him to find what he wants. This process can go beyond the fact of selective perception because man can mistake an object for the item he needs. This process of symbolization, by means of which man sees items in the environment in terms of his own central motive state, plays a tremendous part in some emotional states.

The fourth characteristic is that the central motive state arouses special motor activity that operates to satisfy its needs. Because the central motive state renders available the necessary motor patterns, the individual is primed and ready to act at a moment's notice when he receives the stimuli he is seeking.

All these behavior forms are constantly integrated with one another. Just figure out how much postural, locomotor, and manipulative behavior is being enacted by a salesman when he is selling neckties in a department store. In actual performance, all these behavior modalities pertaining to various behavior areas are molded together into one kind of behavior.

The psychological organization that can be observed when a human being is concentrating on any activity is always of the same kind. When you concentrate on your work, when you have a single-mindedness of purpose, you have actually set up in yourself a central motive state. When you are reading a book, when you are using tools to build yourself a desk, when you are working in your garden, or when you are examining a patient, your state of mind can be described as a central motive state of a certain kind.

You all know what it is like to be unable to concentrate. Everybody has had the experience of being unable to keep his mind on the textbook or listen to the dialogue in the theater. When an individual says he cannot concentrate, he means he is unable to develop a central motive state of a required variety. He cannot organize himself as he is customarily able to do, so that the dominating motive becomes powerful enough to subordinate all other mental and emotional activities. Failure of concentration is important in many neuroses. I must emphasize sharply that the central motive state is the psychological condition in which every concentrated activity is carried out.

The amount of involvement and mobilizing of the attitude required by this central motive state will depend on what you are doing. When you are listening to a concert, you concentrate on your hearing and repress most of your other functions; when you are playing football, you involve and coordinate practically every function of your body and mind. But, either act requires organizing yourself into a central motive state that is essentially the same.

If you will permit an aside here, I would like to say that death is not the result of an instinctual operation. It is a failure of adaptation. The organism has been vanquished in its effort to survive. In environments that do not tax their adaptive powers, primitive organisms can be kept alive indefinitely. The germ cells of the extant metazoa have been alive for about a billion years. Freud's interpretation of life as a titanic struggle between the two forces, Eros and the Death instinct, seems to me to perpetuate the eternal wars between the forces of light and the powers of darkness that exist in all ancient mythologies. It is the business of the scientifically minded psychoanalyst to reduce this Olympian drama to the observation that pleasure is the source and fulfillment of life, and death is its problem.

# CHAPTER 5

# The Emotions

WHAT IS AN EMOTION? THERE IS ALMOST NO WAY TO ANSWER THIS question with one answer. I can say that it is an organismic event; that it is necessary to combine both psychological and physiological data to understand the emotion; that emotion is a gestalt phenomenon; that almost every facet of it can be changed yet the whole thing remains the emotion from which it started. I can say emotion is a component in a behavior pattern because it is a regulatory signal in the chain of the behavior pattern. And still I am a long way from telling you what an emotion is. This is one of the most important questions of psychodynamics and the basis of the study of man.

Emotions are central mechanisms for both the arousal of the peripheral organism and the peripheral disposal of superabundant central excitation. There are the emergency emotions, based on present pain or the expectation of pain (such as fear, rage, retroflexed rage, guilty fear, and guilty rage) and the welfare emotions, based on present pleasure or the expectation of pleasure (such as pleasurable desire, affection, love, joy, self-respect, and pride).

You cannot discuss the emotions unless you keep the resulting behavior pattern in mind. The behavior pattern is a cycle of operation that starts with a disequilibrium and ends with the restoration of equilibrium. Sensations are the lowest and most primitive forms of feeling, according to adaptational psychodynamics, and emotional behavior is a complicated and elastic phenomenon.

## The Nature of the Emotions

The first characterization of emotion, being a component part of behavior, belongs in the interaction between the individual and the environment. Whatever goes on in the organism has to be considered in relation to the situation. One must never lose sight of the nature of emotion as a relationship between the individual and the stimulus pattern in the environment that evoked the emotion. But it is difficult to explain just how and why the same environmental situation will arouse fear in one instance and rage in another. One part of the answer is obvious: the nature of the response will depend on the previous history of the individual. We talk about learning or conditioning to describe some experience in the previous history of the individual, which indicates a certain set tendency of the organism to respond in a certain way in certain environmental situations.

The second group of elements are those we call psychological data. Psychologically, every emotion has a specific feeling tone which is pleasant or unpleasant. The specific feeling tone makes it fear or love or rage or whatever it is. We cannot describe the feeling: everybody has to identify it from his own subjective experience. We could put together forty descriptions and they would not help. How can we describe the specificity of the feeling of fear as distinguished from rage? We can talk all we want about a systolic murmur, but the medical student will only know what it is when he puts the stethoscope against the patient's chest and is told, "Now this is a systolic murmur."

Apropos of this, I would like to point out that one misleading aspect in the study of psychology is the use of such words as *fear* and *rage*. We tend to forget that when we do this we are guilty of both schematization and abstraction. In pharmacodynamics we are much happier. If somebody asks whether digitalis is bad or good, you can explain that "a few grains are a blessing and a few pounds are poisonous." All you have to do is give the figures and it is obvious that the therapeutic dose of digitalis is one thing and the lethal dose another.

The phenomenon of fear goes from one end of the scale to the other. We cannot measure it, yet we talk about it in quantitative terms, and we know the action of fear changes as its amount increases or decreases. In the bowels, for instance, the action of a small amount of fear may be quieting and the action of overpowering fear may be the opposite. So each emotion has a quality, a characteristic of pleasantness or unpleasantness, a quantity of "felt" tension or intensity that it is infused by, and a specific ideational content. You know that sexual orgasm is pleasant and that fear and rage are unpleasant.

The cluster of ideas associated with these emotions varies considerably, ranging from rudimentary to very elaborate ones. It is probably correct to say that the greater the intellectual content in the emotions, the greater the differentiation and refinement in new shapes and grades and varieties of emotion. Most of what we are saying has to do with the four basic emotions: love, fear, rage, and grief. But we could probably distinguish fifteen to twenty emotions without difficulty.

Of great importance in the psychological data is the question of what to do about the emotion. "Shall I run away? Shall I hide? Shall I stand up and fight?" The nature of the organism demands that it do something if pain and injury are involved. Here emotion functions as an organizing and integrating part of the pattern.

The third characteristic of an emotion is the somatic aspect, the voluntary motor aspect. These are the so-called centrally somatic-originated aspects of emotions, mediated by the central nervous system. Related to the expression of emotions, this aspect involves changes in the muscles of the face as well as in the skeletal muscles. The outward expression of emotion has social significance because it is a means of communication.

The fourth characteristic of an emotion is the autonomic aspect, commonly referred to as the visceral expression of emotion, which is to be subdivided into items of smooth muscle intestinal motility and vascularity and glandular secretion.

The visceral scheme, though very extensive, is less specific than the responses of the somatic system. Walter Cannon found that the same visceral changes occurred in both rage and fear. The great differences between rage and fear seen in the behavior elicited by these emotions is not present in the inward phenomena. This is not difficult to understand: the inward phenomena of fear and rage are organized according to the common feature of the two. They are both emergencies and both require action. Accordingly, the organism is energized and its resources mobilized in both instances for the purpose of survival.

The concept of emotion as a gestalt applies particularly to the autonomic components of emotion. Widespread involvement of the viscera, which characterizes fear and rage, is subject to very peculiar modifications. In some cases one component or the other stands out and dominates the picture, while other components recede. In one case you will be impressed by the profuse perspiration, by the pallor; in another case by the diarrhea, by the pounding of the heart. These are all part of the whole fear and rage complex, but emphasis can shift to any one particular component and eclipse others.

If the visceral emotions are indeed as alike in fear and rage as we now think they may be, then on the basis of the visceral changes alone we cannot tell whether the emotion is fear or rage. It is the psychological part of the total event that permits the individual who is experiencing the emotion and those who are observing him to identify it as fear or rage.

The subjective experience then is the essence of emotion. We can, however, be misled into reading emotion into an expression; for example, the rage reaction in a cat without cortex does not have the subjective experience of rage. This, then, is not emotion. This is what we call a sham rage. It is the outward manifestation of rage, perhaps even the whole motor pattern, without the meaningful situation and the emotional awareness.

Let us take the individual in insulin shock as another illustration. As successive functional decortication is going on and as the higher levels are being knocked out, the individual exhibits behavior that appears to be expressing fear in the most impressive manner. But there is no fear present because the cortex is already knocked out, and without the cortex there is no emotion as we know it.

All the world's great literature is about pleasure and pain, a subject that has been dealt with eloquently and superbly. I would, however, like to point out that the great difficulty is that all processes of pleasure are a dark unexplored continent. Take the most spectacular forms of bodily pleasure, such as the pleasure of orgasm or the pleasure of satiation. What do we know about the underlying physiology? How does that pleasure come about?

Training transforms the innate forms of emotional expression into culturally conditioned patterns of response. My analysis of emotional behavior stresses the distinction on hedonic grounds between emergency emotions and welfare emotions, and hedonic self-regulation as the basis of the integrative apparatus.

A deficiency of the welfare emotions (joy, pleasure, happiness, love, affection, etc.), on the other hand, alters every operation of the integrative apparatus. No phase of life, no area of behavior remains unaffected. The welfare emotions under such circumstances contract. Pleasure deficiency vitiates welfare emotion in quality, as well as in intensity, thus causing a deficiency in the entire gamut of feelings. Ordinarily, these pleasurable feelings help to subdue the emergency emotions; here this counterbalancing effect is enfeebled or gone.

Pleasurable desire, like the greasing of an engine, facilitates performance; lack of pleasurable desire makes performance more difficult and reduces the person's zest for life. The absence of adequate pleasure and love impoverishes human relationships and makes healthy development of the sexual function impossible. Pleasure is the tie that binds. We see in schizophrenia what happens in its absence.

The welfare emotions also may discharge surplus tension. This is a theory of Ferenczi's which awaits confirmation. But this is just the beginning of what we do not know. What are the mechanisms by which the organism generates pleasure? What does the sensation or experience of pleasure rest upon? How are the various pleasure-generating modalities of the organism organized; how are they brought into play?

The best we have learned in physiology is by animal experiment, and unfortunately you cannot ask the animal when he is or is not having fun. Animal experimentation does not answer this kind of question. We are still in a state of shameful ignorance with regard to the details of the whole pleasure economy of the organism. And this pleasure economy is of outstanding importance in regulating the behavior of the whole organ, which is constantly attracted by the pursuit of pleasure and constantly deterred from pain-causing activities. We know little enough about pain and about the psychophysiology of pain. But we know close to nothing about the psychophysiology of pleasure.

The evaluation that the organism puts on this pain, which determines how it will react, depends on the interpretation the organism puts on it. If the organism overrates the pain, a spectacular emergency behavior may ensue; if the organism underrates the pain, nothing may happen. What does happen, however, is that the hypersensitive type individual, for example, the hysterotype, responding at the same threshold with the same sensitivity to pain, has an intense fear reaction to the pain experience, and his evaluation and interpretation of the situation change. The result is that the ensuing behavior will be exaggerated as compared with that of another individual. The phenomenon of the superimposition of fear on pain plays a tremendous role, as seen in hysterical behavior.

## The Emergency Function

Let us examine at length the emergency emotions, which are based on present pain or the expectation of pain, in contrast to the welfare emotions, which are based on present pleasure or the expectation of pleasure. The first important consideration is that we do not know what fear and rage are nor why these emotions exist in all men. We shall limit ourselves to the formidable task of sketching out how we think they work. In common English usage *anxiety* means distress of mind caused by the apprehension of danger but softened by hope that the danger will pass. Fear, on the other hand, is the perfect English rendering of the German *Angst*. However, Freud's early translators suggested that in technical usage *anxiety* be adopted as the English equivalent of the German *Angst*, both words being derived from the same Latin root, *angustia*. Also, the English translation *fear* was reserved for the German *Furcht*. Freud himself ignored the German idiomatic distinction between *Furcht* (which was said to have an object) and *Angst* (which was supposed to have none). Indeed, he showed that *Angst* may have and as a rule does have a repressed, unconscious object. Dynamically, such *Angst* is *Furcht*. The strength of *Furcht* may be due and often is due not to its avowed object but to its repressed unconscious object. Dynamically, such *Furcht* is *Angst*.

In current psychiatric usage *anxiety* denotes fear with some qualifications which, however, differs from school to school, if not from writer to writer. Unless used in its nontechnical sense, there is no basis upon which to differentiate it from fear. In order to aid clear thinking I have discarded this unhappy word from technical language and have reverted to the exclusive use of fear.

Everyday observation shows that fear is a response to danger in the environment usually. Pain from both external and internal causes and rage are responses of the same kind. Obviously, these responses are alerting events in the perpetual interaction of organism and environment, because they in turn prompt the organism to engage in further activities designed for the prevention and repair of damage.

I do not always find it easy to know what to call these emergency emotions. I sometimes view them as preparatory signals which prepare the organism for action. Sometimes I see them as regulatory signals because they regulate behavior and motor activity. Most often, perhaps, I think of the cycle rather than the emotion, and the emergency emotions should perhaps, then, be talked about as the emergency function.

The emergency function is all of the emotion and behavior and activity that is concerned with danger to the integrity and welfare of the organism. The conception of the emergency function, so central to adaptational psychodynamics, originated with Walter Cannon and was described in his book *Bodily Changes*. His description of the organism's physiological arrangements appeared in his later book, *The Wisdom of the Body*. In this, he gives in detail the bodily changes that occur in rage, fear, and pain to prepare the animal for danger. These are adaptive devices, such as increase in blood sugar, increase in adrenaline, increased heart rate, and the like. In civilization the emergency no longer requires these bodily changes, but they date from a time when they were adaptive.

There is then a specific emergency behavior pattern that is organized or selected under the pressure of the emotions. The emotion is the preparatory signal that prepares the organism for emergency behavior. And, finally, we have the terminal environmental situation brought about by this motor behavior. The goal of this behavior is to restore the organism to safety. Briefly, the cycle is (1) that from a steady state the organism is moved out through a stimulus pattern which arouses a preparatory signal; (2) this brings about emergency behavior; (3) which restores the organism to the steady state.

What is the stimulus pattern that elicits fear and rage? This question leads us to a controversial subject. Some authors assume that the infant is capable of only a general response and has no specific emotional responses. I disagree with them: just look at animal experiments to the contrary. The fact remains, however, that we do not know the stimulus pattern to which the human infant responds automatically with fear or rage. Nor do we know the stimulus pattern to which he responds with love. What we do know is that there are stimulus patterns that elicit these inborn emotional responses.

Are those stimulus patterns indicative of the presence of danger or do they characteristically represent what can be called an emergency? Obviously they do neither. Possibly, and this is largely speculative, they represent something that may have been an emergency in the evolutionary history of man.

The human infant, starting life with these inborn, automatic responses, has a long process of conditioning or learning before him. The goal becomes that of selecting those stimulus patterns that are truly indicative of the presence of emergency so that he experiences fear or rage when he has cause. You can immediately see that there is an opportunity for the development of fear responses to stimulus patterns that are not indicative of emergency. Fear that arises in the absence of any real threat is the so-called unrealistic fear.

It would be wonderful if I could show the development of unrealistic fear, but tracing the causal developmental history of such fear is a difficult problem and I must limit myself to a general outline. Unrealistic fear, fear not objectively justified, will incite the organism to the same kind of emergency behavior as is evoked by realistic fear. What happens is a sequence of wholly unnecessary and faulty measures of emergency function. Psychopathology, to a very large extent, consists of such fears and faulty emergency behavior. It is pathological because it was aroused by fear not representative of true emergency. Rage is intensified or precipitated by fear; it may not be primary. Often an individual becomes enraged to defend himself against danger from within. In paranoia, fear of fear leads to rage or aggression. The individual reactions in rage vary more from individual to individual than those in fear. It seems as if many individuals tolerate rage better than fear. Usually pride increases with rage and diminishes with fear, as does the action self (to be described).

An attack of severe panic is not a preparatory emergency signal: rather, it is a knockout blow to the organism, paralyzing the organism to the point of complete incapacitation. Instead of being a tiny sample that stirs the organism into defense, it is a full disease in itself. All excessive emotions tend to be paralyzing and incapacitating.

The goal of rage is to forestall pain from injury or damage, and it is best achieved by elimination of the opponent. The original animal goal of rage is killing, which is eventually followed by ingestion. Excessive rage is ready to become blind rage, which loses its target. The excess distorts what is supposed to be a directed effort into a diffuse discharge. Impotent rage can be discharged by being turned against the individual himself; such as when a child in an impotent rage hits himself.

I had already made a groping attempt at interpreting the emotions in this way in 1933, before I knew anything of Cannon's work. I was pleased and admiring that physiology has given us the concept of emergency emotions so that we could more closely think about the psychological aspects of emotions.

I had difficulty introducing this orientation into psychoanalysis because classical theory was centered on the concept of *libido* which had a predetermined development quite apart from the environment. Another handicap of the libido theory was that it shifted the emphasis from clinical reality of the emotions to the hypothetical construct of the instinct in which the emotions appeared merely as charges called "affective cathexes." Attached to the ideas that represented the instincts, the next step in this process was the substitution of ideational content for feeling. Freud put it this way, "It is not easy to deal scientifically with feelings. One may attempt to describe their physiological signs. Where that is impossible . . . nothing remains, but I turn to the ideational content which is most readily associated itself with the feeling." However, the most important consequence of emotion is not ideation but action; hence, the auspicious approach is to look for the total pattern of emotional behavior.

Under the libido theory, fear, one of the most important emotions in psychopathology, was interpreted as a consequence of pathogenic repression of libido rather than its cause. It was supposed to be generated by a sort of "fermentation process" from repressed libido. This explains the fact that in Freud's 1918 theory of the neurosis, fear was not even listed as a pathogenic factor. But in 1926, Freud explicitly repudiated this construction. He arrived at the common-sense view that fear was a reaction to danger. Accordingly, repression was now correctly viewed as a consequence of fear. In 1926 Freud stated with utmost emphasis that no emotion other than fear was to be held responsible for the production of neurotic disturbances.

The next logical step would have been to realize that pain and rage, too, may play a part in the causation of neurotic disturbances. But the libido theory directed the investigator's attention to "masochism" and "sadism," not to pain and rage.

Freud made another revision of his theory in 1930. In the libido theory, phenomena such as rage, hate, and hostility were viewed as manifestations of the sexual instinct and therefore interpreted exclusively in terms of sadism. However, in 1930 Freud realized that there was such a thing as "nonerotic aggression." He came very close to realizing, I believe, that rage like fear must first be understood in terms of the organism's relationship to the environment. This latter view, I believe, is correct.

To summarize briefly my relationship to Freud in regard to the emotions: I agree with the change of his early theory about anxiety, but I differ with his view of conscience; and I believe that rage, like fear, is a reaction to the environment.

In the original psychoanalytic theory, the emergency emotions of fear and rage were swallowed up by the concept of the instincts. The essential thing about the emergency function is that emergency behavior takes precedence over all other behavior. This is the basis of all neuroses. You are a peaceful citizen living in a little village: you eat your breakfast, play with your children, do your job. Suddenly the church bell rings; there is a fire. Everything stops, whatever it is, and you attend to the emergency. Now, the same thing happens in the human organism. The moment emergency signals come up, they take precedence over every other occupation, interest, or direction of the organism. The presence of emergency, especially the emotional signals of emergency, is incompatible with peaceful pursuits. Those which suffer first are the pleasure pursuits. Departure from this is punished by death.

When we talk about the expression of the emotions we have taken a methodological and philosophical step of great consequence because the presumption then is that the psychological event is the emotion, which is expressed in the peripheral system. Are we justified in saying this? Is the pounding of the heart an expression of something that exists without it? Or are all these peripheral phenomena part and parcel of what we call emotion? I do not know the answer.

Darwin talks about the expression of the emotions. Why is it that there is such a thing as the somatic "expression of emotion"? If the emotions energize the organism and throw it into a state of preparedness for action, we can grasp the utility of this arrangement for the survival of the animal. But what has this somatic expression of emotion to do with utility? Now Darwin came up with an explanation that I would like to translate into our frame of reference. I suggest it is very probable that the outward, bodily, somatic expression of emotions cannot be understood on the organismic level, and must be understood on the social level. If there were only one animal, outward expression of an emotion would surely be meaningless. Like each and every other means of communication, the outer expression of emotion may be an important means of intercommunication between members of the group.

Fear and rage function to integrate behavior only so long as both emotions remain within a moderate range of intensity. When the individual is functioning at top level, the emotion is confined to a flash of fear or a flash of rage. Intense emotion may be so crippling and incapacitating that the motor activity cannot be triggered.

# CHAPTER 6

# The Psychodynamic

# Cerebral System

WHAT IS MEANT BY THE PSYCHOLOGICAL ORGANIZATION OF THE INDI-
vidual? What is the meaning of personality or the mind or the mental
apparatus of psychoanalytic theory? Let us start our definition of the
mind by saying that this phenomenon is the structure of the top levels
of neurointegration in the organism that are accessible to psychological
methods of investigation. When we talk about psychological organization, we are always referring to the cortex in action as viewed by
psychological methods. I personally prefer words such as *psychic apparatus* or *psychic anatomy* to the word *personality*, which has a static
connotation. But they are all metaphors. The best we can hope for
is to try to keep our language dynamic and functional so that we can
speak simply of the functional organization of the individual so far
as it can be ascertained by psychological methods.

In adaptational psychodynamics, we call the mind and the nonreporting levels the psychodynamic cerebral system. This proposed concept
embraces (1) the entire self-reporting range of the brain's nervous
activity in both its psychodynamic and physiologic aspects and (2) that
range of nonreporting activity which is nonetheless accessible to extra-
polative investigation by psychodynamic methods as well as ordinary
investigation by physiologic methods. It should be clear that the "integrating apparatus" is not observable by introspection; its existence is
inferred from its function which is observable by introspection. Eventually, its existence will have to be proved by the physiologist.

In a general sense, we say that the integrative activity of the psychodynamic cerebral system is dominated by the action of pleasure, pain, emotion, and reason. These are the observable items on which we can focus instead of theoretical concepts such as the libido.

Theoretically, there are four psychological levels of integration: hedonic, brute emotional, emotional thought, and unemotional thought, which are unified by the action self or doer. All these will be working simultaneously in the intact organism, and the behavior of the individual may be integrated at any of these levels or at any combination of them. Each has its own organization and can exist in awareness and nonreporting process. Below these psychological levels are neural levels. (In this formulation, I am indebted to the physiological work of Hughlings Jackson, Charles Sherrington, J. H. Woodger, and others.)

This hierarchical arrangement of levels that go toward intellectual control and away from hedonic control is the evolutionary process that neurologists call increasing encephalization or corticalization. Functions that in lower forms were organized on lower levels have come in the human being under cortical control and have become a responsibility of voluntary action. I am fond of the saying that nature could not leave certain things to the will of the stupid individual. But I fear just the opposite happened. Too many things that were automatically enacted by reflexes in the lower forms of animal life are left to the will of the "stupid individual" in the human species. One of these is the sexual act.

These four superimposed levels of integration correspond roughly to the phylogeny of the human species. Each of these levels has its own distinctive organization. Emotions are handled differently at each level. Each level has advantages of its own, and this ascending order does not necessarily rank them in terms of their value to the organism.

In the human being all levels function at the same time. I shall give you one example. The hedonic level is by no means eliminated by the brute-emotional level or the emotional-thought level or the unemotional-thought level. Taking the Empire State Building as an example of the four integrative levels, any four floors may be lit up at one time or in one combination, depending on the activity. In man one of the consequences of pain will be fear of pain and of subsequent damage. Let me remind you that the human being has a cortex. Because of this, the human being responds to pain also with fear. And it is precisely the intensity of the fear reaction that determines what appears to be pain-born behavior in the human being.

Before we examine the characteristics of these four levels, we should

**TABLE 1  Emergency Behavior, Basic Mechanisms at the Hedonic, Emotional, and Emotional Thought Levels**

| Level | Alerting Signal | Emergency Move | Evolutionary Aspects | |
|---|---|---|---|---|
| | | | Expanding Range of Anticipation | |
| Emotional thought | Angry thought | Combat, defiance | Long-range anticipation of pain from damage | Improved performance due to more and better equipment |
| | Apprehensive thought | Escape, submission, cry for help | | Intellectual exploration of past and future, from near to far: cortical system |
| Emotional | Brute rage | Combat defiance | Anticipation of pain from impending damage | Sensory exploration of "shell of immediate future surrounding the animal's head": distance receptor |
| | Brute fear | Escape, submission, cry for help | | |
| Hedonic | Pain | Riddance (prevention of further pain) | Anticipation of further pain | Sampling of pain from damage incurred: contact receptors |

think about the organism as a whole. You cannot understand the organism, to be sure, without a searching analysis of its component cells, but you will never understand the organism from the study of the component cells. The whole is something *other* than the sum of its parts. Now let us take an example to illustrate the method of interpreting relationships as distinguished from analysis into the component parts. Let us take a soccer game. Here is a young man. Is he the team? No. The eleven young men plus the relationships between these young men are the team. Then you have the opponent's team. Here are another eleven young men and the relationships between them. Then you have a game between these two teams, which is the relationship between the relationships. You can go on endlessly building a pyramid of relationships.

To understand the organism as it is, the relationships between the component parts must be investigated. I suggest that this idea of elements being constructed into hierarchic, superimposed levels is a scientific approach that can be extended to encompass the entire universe. You can consider the atom as the lowest level of organization and the molecule as a higher level of organization. On the biological level you can, in ascending order, think of the cellular level, the tissue level, the organ level, the organ-system level, the organism level, and the population level. And so it goes. The whole idea of superimposed levels of organizations is an idea that has transformed all biology.

## The Hedonic Level

Pleasure and pain are always to be looked at as elements in a cycle of behavior that is a response of the organism to stimulation. The significance of an experience of pleasure or pain lies *beyond* the experience; the significance is that it moves, incites, and induces the organism to respond to it. As I see it, pleasure and pain are *integrating* factors. They regulate the organism by integrating, organizing, and selecting forms of behavior. The most primitive form of behavior is effected under the guidance of these primitive feelings.

This basic principle then of hedonic self-regulation can be stated quite simply. The organism moves *toward* the source of pleasure and *away* from the cause of pain. Let us look at how the organism reacts to pleasure. When the experience is in the nature of pleasure, the tendency of behavior is to absorb that pleasure. The most primitive manifestation of this tendency of the organism is to absorb literally the cause or source of pleasure by incorporation. Think of the one-celled animal engulfing food and of the baby trying to put everything it can into its mouth. In the human being, this expression of the tendency to absorb pleasure changes into a tendency to absorb pleasure by holding onto the source of pleasure. Yet another aspect of the pleasure-absorption principle is the reaction of the organism when the pleasure is lost or taken away from him. The deprivation elicits a readily discernible behavior tendency, the need to recapture the lost source.

Pleasure is the reaction to gaining something for the organism. It is enrichment and engorgement and it goes with swelling of the organism. It is an attraction that makes the organism want to decrease the distance between itself and the stimulus.

As for pain, the general tendency of behavior displayed by the organism toward the stimulus that causes the pain is to rid itself of the cause of the pain by any means. The painlike sensation is, generally speaking, a reaction to an experience of injury, and the word *injury* is to be interpreted in the broadest sense. Pain brings about a shrinking of the organism, a desire to make itself small, to increase the distance between itself and the pain-producing stimulus.

Pain is a very primitive signal of emergency because it occurs after the injury to the organism has already occurred. On this level, all emergency behavior is hindsight because it is an attempt to prevent further and greater damage after some measure of damage has already occurred. The organism, not yet equipped with sense receptors, has to sample damage to find out what it is all about. Just the same way that the organism has to sample food in order to find out whether it is bad or good. Everything was first based on the idea of taking a sample!

It is true that damage to the organism does not always cause pain, nor is pain always attributable to damage. Nevertheless, their linkage is so frequent and dependable that the organism can use pain effectively as a warning signal of damage. This signaling arrangement, developed at an early stage of evolutionary history, is the very basis upon which the entire organization of emergency behavior has evolved.

Regulation on the hedonic level is complicated and intertwined with phenomena occurring on the higher levels. Pain elicits not only a riddance behavior but also a fear or apprehensive thought. The moment something begins to ache or itch, fear arises. The organism makes its evaluation of pain in the climate of fear of further developments. In the hysteric, this fear multiplies the significance of the pain and leads to an alarmed type of behavior. This overevaluation of pain is due to the anxiety aroused by pain, while the underevaluation of pain as an emergency function is due to a diverting of attention. In so-called hypersensitivity to pain, it is necessary to deal with an attempt not so much to raise the pain threshold as to influence the anxiety. Most of the narcotic drugs do just that: the pain is still there but it hurts less because the anxiety of the person is knocked out; he is no longer preoccupied with the painful consequences of what is going to happen to him, and his agitated, fear-ridden behavior is silenced.

How much the hedonic level has things its own way depends on the individual. But for everybody the thought level intrudes. Here is one example. When pain persists and becomes unsupportable, the riddance mechanism will be activated. But, as a rule, riddance behavior is impossible and would do more harm than good. So the thought level intrudes and inhibits this activation of the more primitive riddance response to pain. The individual does not jump out of the dentist's chair, but sits there and suffers because he wants his teeth cared for.

The outstanding significance of the phenomena of pleasure and pain in regulating mental life is brilliantly described by Freud in the paper "Formulations Regarding the Two Principles of Mental Functioning," in which he describes the pleasure-pain principle and the so-called reality principle. Freud's description is chiefly concerned with the hypothetical construction of the infant's ways of behavior and with sense perception. Freud advances the thesis that in the beginning the organism perceives only the pleasant things and represses all the unpleasant things. He also suggests that this stage is pretty much superseded by the so-called reality principle, under which the individual is forced to take cognizance of what is actually happening. The regulatory significance of pleasure and pain is a fundamental proposition in psychoanalysis.

In the eighteenth century the British philosopher Jeremy Bentham described the pleasure and pain aspect of mental life in An Introduction to the Principles of Morals and Legislation. "Nature has placed mankind under the government of two sovereign masters: pain and pleasure. It is for them alone to point out what we ought to do, as well as to determine what we shall do." This is the thesis of his whole work, and he applied it as the key to the understanding of human behavior in the political arena.

The hedonic level is one of organization that precedes the appearance of distance receptors (the sense organs). This is the level of the unicellular organism which lacks eyes and other receptors that could tell it of events in the distance. At this level the organism experiences everything as immediate bodily contact, and the reaction immediately follows the experience. You will become aware of the extreme importance of this time element as we examine the three other hierarchic levels.

To recapitulate, hedonic self-regulation, which may have appeared already in the organization of the protozoan, has remained basic to the life process at all subsequent stages of evolutionary history, including man. Despite the complications introduced through the emergence and development of higher levels of integration, the human organism, like all other animal organisms, is a biologic system that operates under hedonic regulation. This assumption is a cornerstone of my theory of adaptational psychodynamics.

The hedonic self-regulation principle contains an interesting implication. It is possible that the organism is so organized that whatsoever is pleasant to it is, on the whole, favorable to its survival, and whatsoever is painful to it is, on the whole, detrimental to it. If this were not so, all animals would have disappeared from this earth a long time ago.

Little intellectual thought activity can be present in the lower animal forms. All behavior is probably guided by the sensations or feelings of pleasure and pain. Certain activities are rewarded by high pleasure. It is likely that the organism undertakes that activity in order to get the pleasure. This may be the method nature uses of making the organism seek that activity. My contention is that the man who loses sight of this pleasure-pain principle is like a sailor who is deprived of the instruments of navigation. He will never know where he is. This, I believe, is the problem of schizophrenia.

### RIDDANCE BEHAVIOR

Riddance behavior is fundamental, no matter on which level it is functioning. The organism in pain or fear makes every effort to rid itself of the source of suffering, as if expecting that otherwise the pain would continue. This elementary characteristic of all animal existence was noted by Charles Darwin, who wrote in *The Expression of Emotions in Men and Animals:* "Great pain has urged all animals during endless generations to make the most violent and diversified efforts to escape from the cause of suffering. If a limb or another separate part of the body is hurt, we often shake it as if to shake off the cause."

The riddance response is ingrained in our organization. In the gastrointestinal system all pain-causing agents elicit riddance behavior, consisting of reflexes, spitting, vomiting, or diarrhea. These are calculated to eliminate foreign bodies from the gastrointestinal system. The riddance system is not limited to the gastrointestinal system. The same thing exists in the respiratory setup. Sneezing and coughing are reflexes designed to eliminate pain-causing agents from the upper respiratory tract. Similarly, tearing is a reflex obviously calculated to remove pain-causing agents from the eye.

My assumption is that "mental pain" may precipitate riddance behavior just as readily as does "bodily pain." True, the attempts of the organism to rid itself of thoughts and emotions are less effective than are the riddance mechanisms designed to rid the organism of foreign bodies within or things without, but the principle is the same.

Let us look at a few examples. When the anticipation of pain or the tension of suspense becomes unbearable, it drives the individual to submit voluntarily to the threatening and dreaded evil and even to bring it about by one's own behavior to get it over with. This is one method of ridding oneself of tension, and the riddance from tension is the organism's more immediate and more urgent need.

Mark Twain gives a fine description of riddance behavior. He writes, "When I was twelve and a half years old . . . the summer came and brought with it an epidemic of measles. For a time a child died almost every day. The village was paralyzed with fright, distress, despair . . . every day and every night a sudden shiver shook me to the marrow, and I said to myself, 'There, I've got it! and I shall die.' Life on these miserable terms was not worth living, and I made up my mind to get the disease. . . . A playmate of mine was very ill with the malady. When the chance offered I crept into his room and got into bed with him. I was discovered by his mother. . . . But I had the disease."

Here I should like to add a war observation on "combat fatigue" pilots in World War II. Overwhelmed by the almost uncontrollable dread of being shot down, many a pilot was tormented by the overwhelming temptation to crash his airplane into the ground.

Riddance behavior plays a big role in neurotic behavior. One example is that of the neurotic girl who is morbidly afraid of defloration. Clinical data tell us that she will experience defloration not on the occasion when her desire is at a maximum but on the occasion when her panic is at a maximum, under particularly humiliating circumstances.

We are familiar with the impulse to tear away a severely aching part of the body. This impulse becomes a mechanism of grave importance in hypochondriasis and other forms of disordered behavior. In a delusional state the patient may suddenly remove one of his vital organs (e.g., eye or genital organ) and perceive this act of riddance as a triumph. The sexually incapacitated schizophrenic who experiences the genital urge as a threat rather than an opportunity responds with the "remedial" impulse to amputate his own genital organs.

Repression is another riddance mechanism, a fundamental mechanism that tends to exclude painful thoughts and emotions from the range of awareness. The existence of this mechanism alone seems to me to be conclusive proof that the activities of the human organism are subject to hedonic self-regulation.

A surprising number of activities can be classified as riddance mechanisms. Inhibition in the psychodynamic sense is actually automatized riddance. Pain dependence, as it is seen in intentional suppression and in dreams, is often a mechanism of preliminary riddance. Man tries to eliminate what is hurting him.

Riddance behavior, then, is an emergency measure against pain and fear. I prefer not to use the term "ego defense," for this term unfortunately implies some automatic reaction on the part of the individual that goes into effect when certain stimuli are felt, whereas the whole action self probably responds to an emergency situation, depending on the situation. In order to keep in mind the variability and flexibility of the action self in handling an emergency, I would rather speak of emergency measures undertaken by the action self in times of pain or fear as means of repair used by the action self in stressful periods.

In intense pain the organism will be incapacitated, and there will be a tendency to spare the aching part or to immobilize it. The riddance mechanism is no longer working then. Rather, there comes a second set of reactions, as a result of the paralyzing effect of intense pain.

## The Brute-Emotional Level

Now what goes on at the second level—the brute-emotional level? We shall consider here only the four basic emotions of fear, rage, love, and grief, all of which emerge at this brute-emotional level and can at a certain point in the evolutionary scale exist in animals that demonstrate visible emotional life. This level on the evolutionary scale corresponds to the metazoan.

It is significant that the emotional signals that prepare the organism to react to unpleasantness are unpleasant in themselves. They are warnings of more severe pain to come. The organism anticipates pain by giving itself a tiny dose of it, the same way as on the hedonic level. Very characteristic is the fact that when the danger is far away, the *tension* of anticipation, which may last for hours, itself becomes painful.

Emotional experiences on this level perform the same kind of service that is performed on the hedonic level by elementary feelings of pleasure and pain—the brute emotions organize, integrate, and select patterns of motor behavior. They do so in complete harmony with the basic pleasure-pain tendencies that were established on the hedonic level. The patterns of behavior integrated under the direction of fear will be patterns of escape and avoidance; the patterns of behavior integrated by rage will be those of combat or attack. Escape and combat serve the same purpose of riddance. The welfare emotions appear to mobilize the organism to action. The emotion of grief is a very complex matter. Its most decisive component is perhaps the desire to recapture and to retrieve the pleasure that has been lost.

Distance receptors and increasing specialization of the central nervous system must have preceded the appearance of the emotions of fear and rage. There is an increased delay of motor reaction to stimuli as the brain develops and, as a result, greater effectiveness and discrimination of action. The emotions serve for communication on a group level and have feeling tone and voluntary expression. The emotions are strong and primitive when threat or desire is immediate. This level warns the organism that a threat of damage exists and prompts preventive measures.

Now what is the difference between an animal that is able to organize on the emotional level and one that has not yet developed any level beyond the hedonic level? Why are there such things as emotions, since the fundamental tendencies of the hedonic level are consistently continued?

To answer these questions, we must look at physiology from an evolutionary point of view. The great innovation of this level of evolution was the appearance of distance receptors—the organs of seeing, hearing, and smelling. The eye of the animal sees the danger approaching or his nose sniffs the scent of the enemy. With the help of these distance receptors, the animal gets information about things to come.

I suspect that the emergence of the distance receptors in the evolutionary scale was accompanied by the corresponding emergence of the emotions. It seems safe to say that fear and rage cannot exist in an organism that lacks the distance receptors. And we have not yet ascertained the existence of distance receptors in any animal that seems to lack emotions. Darwin points out the remarkable continuity of the emotions. The same phenomena that appear way down in the evolutionary scale remain the same up through man. You are on dangerous ground, however, when you talk about "emotions" in animals, so let me caution you that I am talking very generally.

Foresight, the anticipation of things to come, is now possible for the organism. Now that it can anticipate future events, it develops behavior that is based on the anticipation of oncoming events. When the animal sees danger coming, it can behave in a preventive fashion to avoid the danger. It can be enraged or fearful before the dangerous thing gets to it. It works the same way in positive emotions. Anticipation of a sustained need is also actually the basis of love. Only if I know that my need will go on do I have an interest in preserving something and holding on to it. None of this anticipatory activity is possible to the animal that is functioning on the hedonic level.

In *The Brain and Its Mechanism*, Sir Charles Sherrington talks about the significance of distance receptors and their relationship to the future. Speaking of the animal, he writes: "The leading end, the head, has receiving stations signalling from things at a distance—things which the animal's forward movement will make near. . . . The nerve nets in the head are therefore busy with signals from a shell of the outside world which the animal is about to enter and experience. . . . No wonder then that the brain plays a great role in the management of muscles."

The animal that has developed to the brute-emotional level has something which not only integrates behavior patterns but also throws the whole organism into a state of preparedness for action. Flight and combat both require muscular activity, and by means of the emergency function the organism is prepared in the best possible way for motor activity of various types.

In the physiologic picture, we can distinguish between the autonomic manifestations and the so-called somatic manifestations. (*Somatic* is used here in the way that a neurologist uses this term, meaning the skeleton, muscles, and bones that are in the system.) An emotion includes autonomic changes and somatic changes, both of which are called the "expression of the emotion."

In man, the functioning of this brute-emotional level as compared with the unemotional-thought level is an inferior instrument for interpreting the things to which the organism is actually exposed. It is selective rather than objective. It tends to justify and thus to feed the emotions from which it springs and by which it is controlled.

Integration of the brute-emotional level, then, continues the biologic, autocentric, self-centered evaluation of hedonic self-regulation. As soon as you experience events, you immediately have guidance as to what to pursue, what to retain, what to absorb, and what to rid yourself of. In other words, your behavior is integrated by organismic events that carry the instrument of navigation with them. We know that this is what I want and this is what I want to avoid. The course of action is automatic when the behavior is organized at the brute-emotional level.

### The Emotional-Thought Level

Encephalization or corticalization produces a tremendous change in man. A remarkable change takes place in the emotions at this level compared with those on the brute-emotional level. They become more and more subdued and restrained, less and less intense. Sometimes the character of the emotion can be so reduced that it is hardly more than a thought with a certain qualitative emotional coloring. We do not even have the language to describe the phenomena of what is experienced at this level, so we will talk about apprehensive thought, which is the subdued derivative of fear, and about angry thought, which is the derivative of rage. Fear and rage, like the other basic emotions, become here the points of departure for the differentiation of new arrays of derivative emotions specialized for the mastery of diverse environmental situations.

By allowing intellectual preparation to grow as the emotional correspondingly diminishes, the phenomenon of the preparation of the body for action weakens. But man is rarely confronted with the necessity of jumping at the opponent's throat. This emotional preparation of the whole body for action is a nuisance, and modern man has to effect control to insure that he will not overrespond.

If you are a scientist, you can sit down fairly calmly and figure out what sort of collision of the earth is possible in one and a half billion years. Such long-range foresight is possible only for the organism that has reached the level on which he can contemplate emotionally charged future events without being thrown into that heavy state of physiologic preparedness. No known individual yet, however, has ever reached the level when he no longer deludes himself.

How then is integration of behavior effected on this emotional-thought level? What motivates behavior on this level as pleasure and pain do on the hedonic and the emotions do on the brute-emotional level? I suggest that the integrating force is performed by the emotional thinking. Angry thought leads to a kind of combat behavior, but not an explosive temper tantrum as does brute-emotion.

There is, naturally, a modification of technique. The goal of killing is abandoned and gradually replaced by the new goal of conquering and ruling and exploiting. Combat may be represented by an angry remark, by an ironic remark, by an aggressive joke. The complexity, the manifoldness and variety of behavior patterns that can be worked out, is almost infinite as compared to the primitive behavior patterns of the brute-emotional level.

The individual's subjective awareness of his degree of emotional involvement is not a true yardstick of the intensity of emotional stirring within him, and some of the emotional stirring may be unattended by the individual. If this is so, we call it nonreporting emotion. And this subduing is accompanied by a curbing and subduing of the autonomic expression of emotion. This latter job is carried out in a less satisfactory manner. Many individuals who remain outwardly calm, showing no signs of emotional expression, are nonetheless emotionally stirred and in a high state of inner tension. This inner tension may then be discharged through autonomic channels. This fact is the foundation of so-called psychosomatic medicine.

Where the individual's subjective awareness of his emotional involvement is negligible or absent, corresponding tension is present in a way that is difficult to describe in psychological terms. This tension state probably involves the whole autonomic range, and this emotional tension without subjective experience has a driving force and represents a pressure toward the respective behavior pattern. This pressure may break into the area of awareness, and the individual may find himself carrying out the corresponding behavior patterns of escape or combat without having even a remote inkling of what he is doing or why.

That is the significance of the nonreporting emotion. It is a tension state, without subjective awareness, that puts a pressure on the action self and has a driving, impelling tendency toward discharge in the corresponding form of emergency behavior. If the unconscious emotion is fear, there is a tendency to run away; if it is rage, a tendency to attack. This remarkable cortical development also has the consequence that these basic emotions, fear and rage, split up into a variety of emotions.

## The Unemotional-Thought Level

The highest level of our hierarchy is the unemotional-thought level, the possibility that the situation can be mastered by intellectual means alone. When this can be done without the accompanying bodily preparation that the lower levels have to mobilize, it vastly increases the potentiality and the range of preparatory behavior.

Just imagine the condition of a statesman contemplating the possibility of atomic warfare if he were thrown into a state of fear or rage by his speculations. He could not do very much constructive thinking, if he had to exist in this excitement. Reasoning and long-range preparation in some situations are impossible when the individual cannot get above the emotional levels.

Another gain achieved by the development of the unemotional-thought level is that deferment of response is permitted. Such deferment, of course, is also possible at the hedonic level. Why is it so difficult to defer response when behavior is being integrated on the brute emotional and the emotional-thought levels? Because the tremendous preparation for action is half the reaction. It is difficult for the individual to stop himself when he has already responded with fear or anger. But if you only think about something and you do not get up a big emotional response about it, you are free to postpone the idea. "Today is Sunday, let's have a golf game. Tomorrow we'll worry about what to do about the atom bomb."

These two principles—foresight plus the possibility of postponement of reaction—brought about greater adaptivity of behavior. The deferment of reaction makes it possible to emancipate ourselves fully from the pleasure-pain regulation of behavior, because it permits us to contemplate and engage in painful means toward pleasurable ends. Reason can overrule the evaluation dictated by the immediate pleasure-pain feeling and can contemplate such things as endurance of pain for an ultimately pleasurable end.

This is what Freud called the reality principle. Scientific research (which itself is made possible by the existence of this level) says, "This is sweet-tasting, but it is poison." Or, it says, "This is bitter-tasting, but it is the only way of bringing about desirable ends." Reason over-rules the wisdom of the body, to use Cannon's phrase. By reason, man can evaluate the survival value of events by a method superior to the hedonic regulation of pleasure and pain. And that again increases vastly the possibilities for a better adaptive behavior. That is the essential point for the understanding of the various strata of the human mind.

Because the unemotional-thought level is characterized by the absence of this stirring up of the body by emotions, its activity can be carried out at a much lesser cost of energy. The processes that we call thinking have been characterized by psychologists, first of all by Freud himself, as trial action, which is carried out not by the muscles on objects of the outside world but by the mind on symbolic representations of those objects.

Conceptual thinking is trial action on a higher level that requires the minimum of actual energy. If you think out in your mind what would happen if you turned a table upside down, you would not have to push with your muscle energy. You do all the pushing within your mind, and what you push around are the concepts in your mind. Conceptual thinking saves an enormous amount of motor effort which is the essence of realistic thinking.

On the unemotional-thought level the same principle of anticipation that occurs on both the brute-emotional and the emotional-thought levels is continued and vastly extended. Foresight, because of the services of distance receptors, still deals with the immediate future, but thought can foresee things far beyond the present range of our receptors. We can foresee what may happen in a month or a year or ten years, beyond the range of the eyes, ears, and nose in a physiological sense. Anticipation is vastly increased and extended on the thought level, but it is still the same principle.

The primacy of the unemotional-thought level over the preceding levels is not completely established. Since this is not a completely independent and self-sufficient level of integration, there is a constant struggle between this level and the other three levels. When I talk about an unemotional-thought level, I am expressing a generalization. We probably have an ascending scale of superimposed thought levels because there are very different types of thinking on different strata.

On the unemotional-thought level, we forge the tools of reason, common sense, and science that prepare the ground for intelligent action and self-restraint. When we function on this level, we can evaluate advantage and disadvantage, positive and negative survival value, by the entirely different methods of analysis and insight. This ability to go far beyond the pleasure-pain appraisal of experience, this capacity to overrule the pleasure-pain principle, has occurred in the evolution of man. It is on this level that man has learned to appreciate painful means to pleasurable ends and pleasurable means to painful ends.

I shall make just a few comments on the very important interaction between the unemotional-thought and the brute-emotional level, one that is of fundamental significance in neurotic behavior. This is the utilization of the resources of the thought level to cope with phenomena coming from the emotional level. The full-blown anxiety attack is no longer a preparatory signal, it is itself a damage to the organism. The emergency now is to get rid of this paralyzing attack and to forestall its return. The result is apprehensive thought that concerns itself with the anxiety attack, the fear of fear. "I am afraid that I'm going to have an anxiety attack. What can I do about it?"

The individual experiences an anxiety attack on the street, hence, to prevent the recurrence of the attack, he will not go on the street. He will avoid or escape from the situation in which he experienced the first attack. The same intensities apply to rage when blind rage loses its target and becomes harmful.

So the next faulty emergency behavior, which is prompted by the fear of fear, is avoidance of the situation in which the anxiety attacks occur or avoidance of the activity in the course of which they occur. Or, the behavior may be a retreat from functioning itself, which ultimately is a retreat from life. The larger the number of activities that are charged with anxiety attacks, the more the individual has to retreat to save himself from anxiety. And other similarly faulty mechanisms are brought into play, all of which represent faulty emergency behavior and populate the chapter of psychoneuroses.

But when you are trying to function completely on the thought level without emotional involvement, a strange situation arises. You are then capable of objectivity and of abstraction because you can concentrate on the world about you independently from yourself. You are capable of so-called scientific thinking. You are, for the first time in evolution, free from the necessity of always evaluating everything from the point of view of what is immediately good or bad for your own organism. You can be a philosopher, a scientist. But the price is high: you no longer know how to act. For when your thinking develops to this level of abstraction and you are no longer guided by any kind of feeling (a state that is the prerequisite for any objective type of thinking and exploration and understanding of the world about us), you will have a very poor instrument to guide you in action because you will not know what is unpleasant and what is pleasant. If you could conceive of a human being who functioned only on the unemotional-thought level, you would have to visualize an individual who was incapable of action. He would always have to carry along books and charts and graphs to find out what is good and what is bad. He would be some kind of monster who had to find out in his books that it was nice to kiss a girl and that it was bad to be stabbed in the back. His natural feelings would not tell him that. He would be a robot with no zest for living. Compensated schizophrenics sometimes approximate this: in other words, they lack the welfare emotions.

Many psychiatry books state that the goal of the psychiatrist is to enable human beings to be reasonable individuals and emancipate the patient from his emotions. These statements are dangerous kinds of sweeping generalizations. Naturally this is absurd. An unemotional human being has never existed and cannot exist. Control of emotions is another matter. The unemotional thought level is incapable of independent existence and independent government of the body.

Man is not a computing machine. His emotional needs must be met if he is to function in a state of health and prosper. The gradual subordination of the organism's hedonic self-regulation to the dictates of reason in turn increases the adaptive value of intellectual activity. Consequently, man's knowledge and control of both himself and his environment become increasingly scientific. But the organism's hedonic self-regulation established limits for scientific knowledge as man needs the emotions of love, affection, trust, and all the others to live by.

# CHAPTER 7

# The Action Self

BEFORE I TALK ABOUT THE ACTION SELF, LET ME GIVE YOU A HISTORICAL background of the terms used to represent the mind. The German language has no word for "mind." "Seele" means soul, while the use of "Psyche" is scientific only in such compounds as psychiatry. Theodor Meynert, Freud's teacher, sought to fill the void with the term "das Ich"—the ego—which he redefined as "the contents of consciousness" that is, as the mind. With the same intent Freud substituted "das See-lische" for "Seele" and "das Psychische" for "Psyche" in all his writings.

In 1900 Freud introduced the concept of "mental apparatus." Based on neurological foundations, this apparatus included an "unconscious system" separated by repression from a "conscious system." Freud later labeled the conscious system the ego. Derived from the pronoun "I" which denotes a person, "the ego" is a personification, a product of artistic thought. The concept of mental apparatus, on the other hand, is a product of mechanistic thought.

In 1923, Freud redesigned the mental apparatus on metapsychological principles; he named the unconscious system "the id" and added a moral system, "the super ego."

Let me give you my interpretation of this. The standards of conduct that society imposes upon its members come traditionally from divine commandments. To ensure compliance with these standards, the conscious mind must control the organism's intrinsic needs and primitive desires by modifying or repressing them. But the imperfections of such means of control subject the conscious mind to traditional "satanic temptations." Like the Earth between Heaven and Hell, the conscious mind is sandwiched between divine commandments and satanic temptations.

In this light, all three systems of the mental apparatus are personifica-

tions: the superego—conscience representing the divine commandments; the id—the organism's repressed desires and satanic temptings;
the ego—adaptive common sense. The entire conception depicts mental life as the dramatic interplay of these three homunculi, of whom
the ego is supposedly the leader because it knows what is going on
in the outside world. Meynert invented the ego; Freud, the mental
apparatus.

In 1927, then again in 1931 and 1933, I attempted to place the
reality function of the ego into the center of theoretical construction.
In 1939, I suggested that actual observance dynamics be described "in
terms of integrative ego functioning, that is, in terms of egology and
correspondingly, that the neuroses be interpreted "as disorders of integrative ego functioning" and described in terms of an "ego pathology."
Finally, I decided that psychodynamic structure called for a different
approach.

Now I should like to examine the common stem that connects
the four levels of the psychodynamic cerebral system—the action self.
According to my hypothesis, the action self is the organism's systemic
picture of itself, derived from the information it receives about its own
activities by means of its sensory equipment. How does this action
self develop? I should like to start out by reminding you of the basic
fact that the organism is aware of itself as a unitary entity. The organism's awareness of itself is the central phenomenon of human
existence.

The conscious organism is integrated into a self-aware and intentionally acting whole by the action self. Located axially to the four
levels of the psychodynamic integrative apparatus, the action self is
obviously the controlling unit of the entire apparatus and of the entire
organism. The action self ascertains the boundaries of the organism
and distinguishes between "within" and "without" and between the
doings of the organism and the events in its environment. This distinction is then further elaborated by other sense data that arrive through
olfactory, acoustic, optic, and other sensory channels, including the
comments on its performance that the organism receives in its communicative exchange with its human environment. Through its action
self, the organism thus evolves the two fundamental and contrasting
integrations—total organism and total environment—upon which its
selfhood rests.

The action self of adaptational psychodynamics is similar, but I
prefer it to the ego for the reasons given. I also have objected to the

term *ego defense*, because it suggests an armed wall encircling the ego. It seems more tenable to think of a fluctuating action self that is always alert to handle tension and stress, in particular, to act in terms of the emergency emotions.

Instead of using the term *ego strength*, I prefer to view the individual as born dependent and helpless, and having to grow, develop, and learn how to be self-reliant or self-confident. If only one general over-all term is to be used to evaluate the individual, I prefer *self-reliant* which is the opposite of dependent and is more easily observable. Self-reliance is usually accompanied by high self-esteem and confident functioning. The individual subjectively evaluates himself in terms of self-reliance and self-confidence.

It might be reasonable to expect that self-reliance develops rationally on the basis of successful activity. But the psychoanalyst treating the adult who is suffering from a weak action self (from morbid need for dependency), may discover that the life of his patient is full of successful activity. The result of a rational presentation of the facts to the patient is precisely zero. He will answer, "Yes, I know all that, and I feel insecure just the same."

From such experiences I have come to conclude that a strong action self characterized by high self-reliance cannot be acquired in an intellectual way by rational analysis of one's successful activity. How then does the strong action self come into being? It is an emotional phenomenon that rests upon emotional processes. It is the result of the pleasure derived from successful activity. If a man cannot derive a kick out of what he does, if he cannot feel happy and satisfied through his successful actions, he has nothing to feed his action self with because the action self is nourished upon the pleasure experiences derived from successful activity. Factors that go into developing this certainly include genetics and past experience.

The action self expands and contracts in direct proportion to the amount of pleasure the action self consumes, just as the bodily weight of the organism rises and falls with its intake of food. It is necessary to keep this in mind in every single psychotherapeutic procedure that confronts you with the problem of building up the action self and fighting against the patient's inactivity. Here lies a pitfall of psychoanalytic therapy. Intellectual understanding of inhibitions thwarting successful activity, as well as intellectual appreciation of successful activity, has little benefit. The physician must help the patient convert intellectual understanding to emotional understanding.

The emotional appreciation mediated by the action self based, I believe, on self-reliance, is known as pride. The action self absorbs the pleasure of all activity and success, above all the pleasures of loving, of being loved and respected, of loving and respecting oneself. As the action self expands and contracts, the pride of the organism rises and falls, in direct ratio to the amount of pleasure the action self consumes. Pride, the emotional stature of the organism, is thus determined by the size of the action self.

Language abounds with idioms that bear out our construction of the fluctuating nature of the action self. We say of a person that he is swelling with rage and shrinking with fear. This reflects the swelling and shrinking of the individual's pride, and, in turn, of its action self. Presumably, fear becomes paralyzing when it paralyzes the action self.

The organism has its established sources of pride, but it may shift these sources and manipulate its pride. Its management of pride is a highly significant determinant of its behavior in emotional health and disease. In addition to pride, the organism experiences through the expansion of its action self a whole series of more exalted emotions, such as triumph, ecstasy, elation, and narcotic intoxication. Their common root is the intoxicating pleasure of satiation at the mother's breast.

If your pleasure has a spurious base, you run the risk of overinflating your action self, as when you drink alcohol, for instance. The pleasure derived from this activity is out of proportion to the activity and you become intoxicated. When intoxicated, you are undergoing a temporary inflation of your action self, and the stronger the action self, the less afraid it is. When the action self is really overinflated and expansive, the anxiety threshold is so high that even really dangerous things no longer can make an impression. At this point the individual is suffering from the kind of overconfidence that is pathological.

If the action self is underfed and weak, if it is in a contracted and shrunken state, the proneness to fear is great and the anxiety threshold is low. In the state of alcoholic hangover, the ego shrinks and the anxiety threshold is lowered with the size of the action self. At this time very trivial things loom as threats and elicit anxiety responses that are not rational. The individual can be in the state of morbid underconfidence, indicating the deflated action self. In the intoxication state, however, the individual is highly overconfident.

Parental reward and punishment force the young organism to seek security through obedience. Anticipating parental criticisms and demands, the psychodynamic cerebral system develops a semi-automatic organization of self-restraining and self-prodding responses known as our conscience. The action self, though restricted in its freedom of action by conscience, is forced to make it a more or less autonomous part of its own organization. By means of the conscience, the organism becomes better fit for peaceful cooperation with other members of the group. Now it must and can accept full responsibility not only for its action but often for its thoughts and intended actions as well.

Variations in the extension of the action self directly influence the self-restraining and self-prodding responses of conscience. By expanding, the action self increases the sense of self-reliance; by contracting, it increases the sense of dependence. Accordingly, the expansion of the action self weakens the restraining action of conscience; contraction of the action self strengthens it.

Awareness of "willed" action may be stripped of the self-attributive effect of the action self. This is seen in thoughts and feelings elicited under experimental conditions by direct electric stimulation of the brain. Obviously, such stimulation bypasses the action self and its established channels for willed activity. In dreams, presumably for similar reasons, the whereabouts of the dreamer is often uncertain, and his identity confused or completely lost. Moreover, even the fully awake and conscious organism may under certain circumstances lose its awareness of self, its action self. During sleep or in the presence of serious disorders, the action self may treat certain thoughts as if they were forced upon the organism by the environment. Hallucinations are such thoughts, which are disowned and transformed by the action self into what appear to the organism as sense data of external origin.

On the basis of recent physiological findings, I suspect that the action self depends for its alertness on activation by neural activating systems and that it may be aroused by these systems to varying degrees of alertness. The fact that the action self works under hedonic control has far-reaching consequences. "The mind," observed Spinoza, "shrinks from conceiving those things which diminish or constrain the power of itself and of the body."

It is, of course, the action self that rids consciousness of certain thoughts and feelings thrust upon it from within or without. Man is the only animal that does not learn from experience; he rationalizes away his mistakes. Moreover, to satisfy its pride, the action self continuously edits and re-edits the entire remembered history of the organism. This was sensed by Nietzsche: " 'I did this,' says my memory.

'I cannot have done this,' says my pride, and remains inexorable. In the end—memory yields." The material thus excluded may become lastingly repressed through the pleasure-connected counteraction of auxiliary mechanisms. However, if the material increases in strength, it may enable repressed motivation to influence behavior in round-about ways.

I hope you will keep in mind this picture of the completely fluid, constantly fluctuating action self as we analyze the various aspects of man. Let me now give a summary of the action self.

Of proprioceptive origin, the action self is the pivotal integrative system of the whole organism. Guided by willed action, it separates the organism's awareness of itself from its awareness of the world about it, and completes this fundamental separation by building up the unitary entity of total organism in contrast to the total environment. It is upon these contrasting integrations that the selfhood of the organism depends, as well as upon its awareness of its unbroken historical continuity. In accord with these functions, the action self plays the significant part in the integrative action of the awareness process. This part is enhanced by its automatized organization of conscience, which increases the fitness of the organism for peaceful cooperation with the group. By its expansion and contraction, the action self serves as the gauge of the emotional stature of the organism, of the ups and downs of its successes and failures. In its hunger for pride, it continuously edits for the organism the thought picture of its present, past, and future.

# CHAPTER 8

# Alimentary Behavior

ALIMENTARY BEHAVIOR, ONE OF THE MOST IMPORTANT CHAPTERS IN psychodynamics, is concerned with the finding and ingestion of food and water. The psychological need prompting such behavior is labeled hunger, appetite, and thirst. The underlying physiological realities are the food requirements of the organism. Of this complex matter I shall say only that the adult organism, an organism which no longer grows (except to grow fat), utilizes food for the continual replacement of the structural unit and for liberation of energy.

## The Dynamic State of Body Constituents

The new baby is completely dominated by the mouth. Because of its dominant characteristic, this period is called the oral phase of development by classical psychoanalysts. In the almost blank mind of the baby there is nothing so important as his experience of the alternating stages of hunger, ingestion, and satiation, and almost nothing else matters.

Here, then, is the baby—the crude egotist who wants to have fun and pleasure and to guarantee his own survival. He depends for his survival on being fed by his mother. Each of us has a basic tendency to continue and repeat pleasure-yielding activities, and we begin to love the things that give us pleasure. The first thing to be loved is the mother's breast. The next thing to be loved is the mother to whom this breast belongs. The child is attached to the mother with the strongest type of love, which is so binding that it insures that the mother will always be there.

The newborn baby is in a process of rapid growth. His most important physiological need is the need for food. The cycle of hunger and ingestion fills by far the greatest part of the baby's waking life. The rest of his existence is filled out with sleep.

The flow of food into the mouth of the newborn baby is secured by the mother. This is an exception to the fact that putting food in one's mouth is voluntary activity that one does for himself. Sucking and swallowing are reflexes. They are apparently ready early in pregnancy because they can be elicited in prematurely born babies. These reflexes may be the first mature motor skills that the baby possesses. In the first few weeks, the sucking reflex is chiefly an affair of the lips and mouth. After the fifth week, the baby gains control of his eye muscles and brings his eyes into play. After six months, the manipulative skills develop, and the baby is able to play with his mother's breast. Chewing, like the manipulative behavior needed to get food into the mouth, is voluntary and learned behavior.

Throughout our lives, these primitive mechanisms of sucking and biting and chewing remain a most simple mechanism for the discharge of tension—a prime instrumentality of the individual. The manufacturers of chewing gum have made millions of dollars from this elementary truth. Nail-biting is another manifestation of this fact. (There are, of course, always other factors involved in an activity.) By these means, unpleasant tension is dissipated and pleasure gained.

Culture influences alimentary behavior in instances such as the following: habit training of the baby and the child; restrictions placed on the selection and ingestion of food by religious law and social custom; situations in which eating is a component of other arrangements—public festivals, celebrations, ceremonials, and the like. For punitive purposes, the extreme form of restriction—the withdrawal of food—is invoked. The changes in cultural traditions of eating have been vast. According to some tribes, the man who gets his hands on something to eat goes into hiding to eat it. Our custom is to congregate for meals because we like to eat in company.

The alimentary adaptations of the organism are the foundations upon which all later developments occur. The tendency of the organism is to generalize. Once this apparatus of the mouth has proved so serviceable for the solution of one type of problem, namely, getting food and having fun, the organism believes it is good for the solution of all sorts of problems, and it tends to employ this behavior pattern elsewhere. In other words, other patterns of behavior that later develop or are learned tend to be influenced, perhaps even shaped, by this early oral pattern of intake and ingestion. A simple illustration of this is the way the growing child puts everything that attracts his attention into his mouth. He acts as if this were his chief means of getting information about objects.

Here is another illustration. If I have to evaluate a stranger, the underlying idea is that I put him into my mouth and taste him. If he tastes good, he is a fine man. If he doesn't, I'll just spit him out. Now this is all part of an even larger principle—the one of extension of successful adaptive patterns. Once a task is successfully solved, the individual applies the mechanism to the solution of new tasks in the hope that the new tasks, too, can be mastered by this mechanism.

The indelible nature of the alimentary patterns has some unfortunate consequences for the human being. The tendency to regress to these infantile patterns, to reactivate them at a later time for the solution of tasks for which they are actually not fitted, remains for a lifetime with the human organism. This regressive tendency is characteristic of life. The most general mechanism that brings about regression is failure of higher patterns. When more recent, higher organization fails, the organism reverts to more elementary patterns.

## From the Point of View of Pleasure

The alimentary activity is pleasurable. But it is a complex subject. How, for example, is the pleasure mediated? We do not know. But I think the answer lies in the idea of the entire oral apparatus.

The entire oral cavity, all the senses of touch, sight, hearing, smell, and temperature, all the structures are involved. Perhaps the predominating factor is the kinesthetic sensation, the joy derived from the muscular activity itself. Moreover, the alimentary pleasure experience is not limited to the experiences of the mouth alone because it continues after the food has been swallowed and assimilated from stomach and intestines. Think of the blissful expression on the face of the baby after he has been fed.

All this pleasure enjoyment mediated by the mouth and its components is incomparably greater than the pleasure involved in the mouth. It is merely a preliminary to the real pleasure involved in the sensation called satiation, which I shall call the alimentary orgasm. The word orgasm in this context has nothing to do with genital pleasure events. The nature of this pleasure of satiation in the infant is similar to the climax of genital intercourse in one respect—it involves the entire organism (which is what the word *orgasm* means). This complete emotional involvement is to be distinguished from pleasure experiences that are more or less local affairs, such as pleasure involved in sucking or pleasure derived from stroking. But the pleasure of satiation involves the entire organism. How the pleasure of satiation comes about is not known.

The experience of sucking is further reinforced by the infant's pleasure in cuddling in the mother's arms. This sense of absolute security and safety is a marvelous experience, and the individual will always yearn for it again in later years. In comparison to the struggle animals undergo to get food, the infant is fed by having a nipple pushed into his mouth. This effortless pleasure becomes the mode of wishful thinking. The whole idea of omnipotence develops here. The awareness of being loved entails at least the illusion of alimentary security.

To indulge in speculation, one might say that in the evolutionary scale the alimentary orgasm preceded sexual orgasm because it may be present in species in which a differentiation of the sexual organs is not yet present. It is possible that the amoeba experiences something that is the forerunner of the pleasure of satiation. It is possible that the pleasure of satiation is the first great pleasure mechanism of the organism, one that antedates in the evolutionary scale the appearance of sexual pleasure.

It is a very impressive arrangement of nature that an activity of such high utility value as ingestion should have such a tremendous pleasure value for the organism. Apparently, animals have no insight in the utility value of the intake of food. There is, however, a tremendous pleasure reward that pushes them in this direction. The pleasure experience is the incentive—or an added incentive—that engages the organism in the type of activity or behavior essential for its survival. It has to eat because it likes to eat.

According to Freud, "oral eroticism" related to the mucous membrane of the lips. But he was formulating his libido theory at the time when older physiological theories of hunger and thirst were current. This was that the sensation of hunger could be traced to the contractions of the empty stomach, and the experience of thirst, analogously, could be traced to a drying out of the mucous membranes of the mouth. These conceptions have since proved to be erroneous. Though these local happenings are involved, the sensations of hunger and thirst indicate a want that refers to the total state of the organism, and the mucous membrane of the lips is only one of the many structures and factors involved in alimentary pleasure. Freud himself referred to the pleasure of satiation.

Freud took up this subject of alimentary behavior on the largest possible scale, and the pleasure aspect of alimentary behavior was put into the center of interest. The pleasure derived from sucking and other activities of the mouth he termed oral eroticism, and the psychological need for such pleasure was termed oral libido.

In adaptational psychodynamics, we are calling the oral pleasure just that—oral pleasure. And in this context we will talk of the oral-pleasure drive. The nature of the underlying metaphysical connection between the oral-pleasure drive and the other pleasure drives is something that we do not know.

In the mid-nineteenth century Lindener, a Hungarian pediatrician, observing children sucking their thumbs, developed the idea that the baby gets pleasure from sucking the breast. He stated that sucking must be a pleasure-yielding activity that goes beyond the nutritional value involved because it is continued as thumb-sucking when alimentary values are no longer present. That the baby proceeds easily from sucking his thumb to other pleasant activities such as sexual self-stimulation has also been observed. These findings were published in the 1860s, but made no dent on the medical profession until Freud revived interest in them.

The thumb-sucking habit of the baby is the first example of the falling asunder of the integration of the utility aspect and the pleasure aspect of the alimentary activity. In thumb-sucking, the pleasure-seeking drive is continued even though the infant is already satiated—which means that the utility value of the sucking is exhausted.

Walter Cannon says that when strong emotions energize the organism, the created tension has to be worked off if pathological conditions are not to ensue. The hunger of the baby creates a tremendous tension that has to be worked off. And if the urge of hunger is satiated before the tension is worked off, the baby goes on sucking. The rest of this muscular energy goes on as a pure pleasure pursuit. But once the pleasure-yielding activity is started, it goes beyond the need for working off tension. It gathers momentum and works up a desire for continued pleasure. As you remember, man is never happier than when he gets pleasure without utility.

The continuation of oral-pleasure activity is present in activities such as smoking cigars, whistling, or playing musical instruments. While other factors are involved in all these pursuits, the tendency of continuing the pleasure activity first encountered in sucking is apparent.

Drug addiction and alcohol dependency are related to the pleasure reward of satiation. The thumb-sucking baby separates the pleasure reward of sucking from that of ingestion. By means of drugs, men can steal the pleasure rewards of absorption without taking in food. There is an interrelation between appetite and drug addiction. Some drugs depress the appetite; intake of other drugs is immediately followed by a huge demand for food, especially for carbohydrates.

This, then, is the pleasure aspect of alimentary behavior, which includes oral forepleasure and the climactic pleasure of satiation. The sequence of pleasure that is attendant upon the intake and ingestion of food reaches a climax in satiety, the alimentary orgasm of the infant. The feeding breast becomes the eternal symbol of security. Feeding at the mother's breast remains forever the model of a magical fulfillment of man's wishes in life. Indeed, the individual whose wants have been too readily met at all times as a feeding infant may be unrealistic in his expectations in later life and be impatient. If the mother offers immediate discharge of tension for the hungry infant, he may have no chance to learn patience.

Psychoanalysts were the first to discover that all envious behavior begins as breast or food envy when the young child is presented with a sibling being fed. The feeding situation is the first in which the envious trend is brought out. Envy, however, is not derived from but is shaped by this oral frustration. Impatience in later life, too, can result from the feeding situation. But both impatience and envy are expressions of the primordial egocentric omnipotence.

The feeding schedule is one in which the first conflict arises between mother and infant. Fear and rage may be injected into the whole area and become part of a power struggle. In the earlier literature submission was considered natural and thus not described.

## Fear and Rage in Alimentary Behavior

Now we shall look at the fear and rage that exist in the alimentary situation. There are twin dangers to be kept in mind: that of being starved by Mama and Papa and that of being eaten up by Mama and Papa. Mythologies of all lands are full of stories that exemplify these inherent fears. With the fears come the ideas of mechanisms of defense although I prefer to view these as emergency measures prompted by fear leading to repair.

How does this fear of starvation begin? No matter what approach is used, the feeding schedule will never completely coincide with the infant's appetite. To this discrepancy the baby responds with a number of psychological reactions. Unsatisfied hunger in the infant goes over into rage and elicits adrenalin. Our predatory ancestors managed to survive because that very rage mobilized them to acquire food by killing.

The rage is superseded by exhaustion and panicky fear, which is actually fear of starvation. The child fears he is not being fed because he is not loved. If the child is intimidated, if this rage is attacked by the environment so that the mechanism of conscience is brought into the alimentary activity, the panicky fear is enlarged by the element of guilt, which, in turn, elicits patterns of atonement and self-punishment.

Modern man still has the tendency to react to alimentary frustration with anger, though this is a display of an archaic survival mechanism because we no longer have to kill to eat. And modern man still is likely to go over into a panicky state when he exhausts his rage. This rage and fear can be seen in children, who as a rule, get very irritable before meals.

The second anxiety is the fear of being eaten up. You will remember the story of Hansel and Gretel and the gingerbread house, which depicts the dread children harbor of an evil witch who will come and put them in the stove and eat them up. This fear of being eaten up is a fear of annihilation and death, expressed in the terms and the spirit of this oral phase in which the primary weapon of aggression is the mouth. The child's idea is to annihilate the parents with whom he is angry by eating them up, but if Papa and Mama in turn are angry at him, they will surely punish him by eating him up. This is derived from the overevaluation of the teeth and the mouth as an aggresive weapon. In these early years a pattern in which emergency dyscontrol plays an overpowering part may emerge.

Loss of appetite means the loss of eating pleasure. Loss of appetite is an important area in pathology, and is the consequence of erroneous training methods. Some parents carry the regimentation of eating to such an extreme that apprehension, fear, and resentment prevail in the child. In such an atmosphere the child cannot develop appetite and enjoy the food since he is preoccupied with his fear and his resentment. Instead of looking forward with pleasure to eating, the child awaits in agony, expecting the new maltreatment and torture to come. He can display only defiance as he is caught in a power struggle. The emotional play that should be pleasure is now anxiety, rage, and defiance. The emotions dry up the intestines, dry up the mouth, dry up the stomach, and stop the performance of the digestive tract. Physically, the child now cannot eat and cannot digest because appetite is the indispensable pleasure ingredient of eating and the normal pleasure is missing.

# CHAPTER 9

# *Anal Behavior*

# *and Urination*

## *Anal Behavior*

DEFECATION IS CONCERNED WITH THE ELIMINATION OF BODY WASTES which accumulate in the alimentary tract and especially in its distal portion, the ampulla recti. The feces are primarily composed of secretions from the alimentary tract and such portions of the ingested food as have remained undigested and unabsorbed.

The dangers involved in not getting rid of the contents of the bowels immediately have been exaggerated in human history, and the amount of superstitious belief centering on the idea that retention of feces is a detriment to health and life could fill volumes. For centuries the interest of medicine centered on cathartics and enemas, and popular belief in wide sectors of the population still holds on to these ideas. The preoccupation of a mother with the daily elimination of her baby is an example. Even in recent times, the medical profession has held distortions about the phenomenon of constipation. When I was in medical school, the theory that organisms die because of inability to eliminate damaging products of their metabolism was taken seriously.

### THE MAGIC-MAKING ATTRIBUTE OF THE FECES

Magic thinking plays a major role in the area of defecation. To know the source of this deeply rooted superstition is not possible, but we can draw on the findings of anthropologists and formulate some speculations. In primitive thinking there is a tendency to associate feces and death. That which is dead is like feces, and feces are like that which is dead. How did this primitive association develop? The feces that come out of the human organism are dead as opposed to something alive. And "death" is something that "comes out of" the living human organism when the "soul" departs. Both death and feces are derivatives "produced" by the living organisms, food being alive, feces being dead. Eating something and putting it through the metabolism mill of the organism amounted to killing it, transforming a living thing into a dead thing.

Let us look at the importance that touching and contagion play in primitive thinking. Primitive man was dominated by wishful thinking, which is the belief that he could do magic, and touching was one of his ways of doing magic. If feces are equivalent to death, then all that is needed to "make someone dead" is to smear him with feces. If one brings the enemy into contact with feces, the characteristic of "being dead" will be communicated. If something that is dead is brought into contact with something that is alive, the alive thing will become dead. This identification of feces as a murderous weapon is well documented. How nicely this fits in with man's belief in his own omnipotence! "I want to be able to kill people, so it is wonderful if I can produce all the instruments of killing."

But primitive man had to face the fear this thinking brought him: "My feces are powerful and can kill people: therefore their feces, which must be just as powerful, can kill me."

The archaic thoughts are continued in our own nurseries with their emphasis on how the baby has to be cleaned and how the matter of feces is to be handled. The child inevitably gets the idea that this is a matter of oracular importance as he sees the care with which the adult avoids touching the feces and notices how solicitously they are disposed of. And he observes how carefully the mother figure examines the stool and says, "Fine, Baby made a wonderful thing."

This ambivalent attitude is the way man traditionally views feces— with both fear and respect. The untoward significance attached to the feces is the foundation of the psychoanalytic idea that the child uses feces as a gift to be given only to the most beloved person—the mother. "If this pleases you so much, if this is what you want, here it is." The conduct of the mother reflects the cultural attitude that is rooted in early man's fearful overevaluation of feces as an instrument of aggression and killing.

In ancient times, feces may have been used for purposes of intimidation and social power, and something is still left from the old ceremonials. Overall, it is a representation of the gods that terrifies the whole community. In the magic ritual the dancers appear in ugly paint, which is most likely a substitute for what originally must have been feces.

Let us examine the phenomenon of coprophagia, the eating of feces. In some circumstances it has no meaning: if an unattended child begins to play and put the feces into his mouth, it is simply an expression of ignorance. But it is a different matter if such behavior occurs in the adult. The interpretation of coprophagia is difficult, but tentatively, I suggest two interpretations, each the dramatic opposite of the other. It is possible that coprophagia expresses the idea of self-feeding—the acting out of the grandiose fantasy of a divine self-sufficiency or the delusion that one is a sovereign being, independent of the world. "I need nobody and nothing," this man is saying, a divine self-sufficient. The self-feeding system is a grandiose delusion. My other suggestion is that it is a suicidal mechanism based upon the idea that feces are poison.

### THE PLEASURE ASPECT OF DEFECATION

The idea of the pleasure aspect of the function of defecation was one of the great early discoveries of psychoanalysis. The pleasure attendant on defecation was termed *anal eroticism*. Here we shall restrict ourselves to saying that the organism enjoys anal or defecatory pleasure for itself. One part of the pleasure consists of the sensation of relief from tension. This, however, is pleasure in a negative sense. But there is also a positive pleasure component, an organic or bodily pleasure sensation comparable to alimentary pleasure and genital pleasure, though its intensity is much milder than either of these.

The big question is the mechanism of this pleasure. It seems obvious that alimentary ingestion and satiation must have an alimentary-pleasure machinery. But I am not sure whether an independent anal-pleasure machinery does exist. Because of the anatomic proximity of the anal area to the genital area, excitation originating in the urethra and in the defecatory function can spread to the genital mechanism of pleasure. In the so-called neurasthenia, it is a not infrequent clinical syndrome—the dripping of sperm in cases of severe defecation or ejaculation accompanying acts of difficult defecation. While the pressing and straining may be accompanied by an act of cold ejaculation, excitement reaches the orgasm reflex and elicits this reflex. There are many other signals of the possibility of interreaction.

Is the pleasure aspect of defecation formation due to some unknown pleasure machinery independent of the genital apparatus? Or is the pleasure due to some measure of coexcitation of the genital apparatus because of its proximity to the evacuation organs? Is it one that may on occasion, depending upon the intensity of excitation, be reinforced by a coexcitation of the genital apparatus? At present we can go no further in the understanding of this phenomenon.

TOILET-TRAINING

Now, what is the influence of our culture on anal activity? The interference of the environment with the child's bowel movement activities is created for two motives—the maintenance of cleanliness and the avoidance of alleged dangers to health and life. The whole story of early anal functioning as in other areas of habit training is the tale of a long struggle between a growing and maturing organism that is gradually gaining control of its evacuating activities and the training interferences, coming chiefly from the mother figure. The pressure exerted on the child is for him to achieve early control of bowels.

It takes quite some time after birth before the neural machinery needed for control is ready. This means that early training is inevitably followed by relapses. Neurological data are not definitely established, but the appropriate time to introduce habit-training is probably around two. A child may reach a reasonable degree of bowel control at about two or two and a half years. These are approximate dates only and it is unwise to think in terms other than the individuality of the baby.

The main principle of toilet-training is to achieve it without throwing the child into states of fear, panic, anger, and resentment, that is, without bringing the strong emergency emotions into play. The moment the child responds to toilet-training by becoming panicky or enraged, the training effort has failed. Either it will not have achieved its goal or it will have done so at a cost to the baby's emotional development. Toilet-training should not put the child under emotional strain but should be a slow and pleasant performance, and fear and rage are to be kept out altogether. Remember that it is not the anal pleasure that suffers. Children forced into bowel obedience enjoy the evacuative act just as heartily as do others. The nature of the injury is that the mother hurts the child's pride in having his own way.

Part of the confusion on this subject is that early psychoanalytic literature about it was in terms of the libido. Thus classical psycho-analysts did not examine the fact that certain conditions were the *consequences* of fear and rage injected into the picture. Later, we will examine toilet-training among other types of habit training in the power struggle between the parents and child.

### ABNORMAL ANAL FUNCTIONING

What else is happening to the anal activity while this struggle be-tween the child and the disciplinary authority is going on? What are the consequences of the emergency emotions on the child? What is the impact of fear and suppressed rage on the anal activity itself? One answer is diarrhea, which is produced by the fear, plus the suppressed resentment and rage. How it works is not clearly known. Generally speaking, physiologists have observed that fear quiets the bowels, pre-paring the individual for fight or escape. Yet in the individual with diarrhea we see that fear does the exact opposite—it produces a rush bowel movement or spasm. The salient factor here may be the intensity or volume of fear.

### THE MORBID RETENTION TENDENCY

Traditionally, psychoanalysts have confined themselves to establish-ing the fact that there is pleasure involved in anal activity. One of the early statements by Freud was that the child in time discovers that the harder the feces the greater the pleasure, and in order to increase anal pleasure the child developed a tendency to retain the feces, even to the point of serious constipation. This volitional retention of feces for the purposes of greater enjoyment of the subsequent defecation be-came so much the center of psychoanalytic thinking that all anal activ-ity has been identified with the retention tendency which was consid-ered a biologically established fact. The climax of this theory was pro-pounded by Ferenczi, who stated that expulsion is a urethral function; retention, an anal function; and genital sexuality, the proper combina-tion of urethral expulsion and anal retention.

We now know that there is no such thing as a biological tendency toward retention. What biology presents are the waves of peristalsis and the automatic emptying of the ampulla. What biology has provided is an evacuative tendency. If, for whatever reason, the organism devel-ops a voluntary tendency opposed to this biological function, the tendency is morbid. Normal anal functioning cannot possibly be identical with the retention tendency. The retention tendency does exist but it exists as a disturbance.

How then does this disturbance develop? Usually it is a consequence of the mother's misdirected efforts to train the baby to bowel control. The mother wants to train the child to adhere to a certain time schedule devised by the mother in stubborn disregard of peristalsis in the baby. So the child is put on the pot and urged to defecate in the total absence of a peristaltic wave. If the child wants to please his mother, the element of straining is introduced, and this pleasant performance becomes painful. If the child is defiant he retains the feces. Moreover, there are demonstrable cases of anal fissures that render the act of defecation so painful that the child develops the tendency to avoid the defecation that is painful.

To summarize, this morbid retention tendency is produced by faulty toilet-training and runs diametrically counter to the normal development of the child. It exposes the child to the straining that upsets the natural function of defecation and can drive him into an angry, resentful defiance.

The morbid retention of feces, which is opposed to the evacuative function, is the forerunner of a group of activities that become dominant in grownups who can be described as waste collectors. You have all seen homes that are filled from attic to cellar with stuff because the lady of the house is incapable of parting with anything. You have all known people who collect all kinds of material until they are literally flooded, but will not part with a fragment of it. This is something contrary to adaptation and is the extension of the feces-retaining behavior in a morbid psychological pattern.

### FECES AND MONEY

We have as yet said little about parsimony and money, upon which much confusion and misunderstanding are centered. What is the relationship between feces and money, between anal activity and the accumulating tendency?

Classical psychoanalysts pointed out that feces, the least valuable substance, and gold, the most valuable substance, have always been merged in man's thinking, and that the anal retention tendency of the child is the model for the accumulating hoarding tendency of the grownup, which is "sublimated anal eroticism."

I am in agreement with the basic tenet that in man's unconscious thinking feces and money are frequently associated. I cannot, however, agree with the interpretation that is traditionally put on this fact. From my point of view, the accumulating tendency has only a minor role in the whole matter.

I should like to postulate that the primordial self is the deciding aspect in this behavior of the grownup. The desire to make money is derived from the desire to create something. It is the expression of the desire of the primordial self to be the creator of the instrument and means of power. The first thing the child "makes" is feces. I would suspect that the word *make* occurs in the toilet-training idiom of a number of languages because this is indeed what the child creates. This is the first act of production, and the child thinks it wonderful that he can produce something that is considered to be powerful and valuable.

Later, the grownup discovers that money is as powerful as the feces were once thought to be. The power attached to the feces was a delusion; the power attached to money is real. How wonderful if money, which has the real power attached to it, could be produced the same way as feces, he then thinks. He conceives of the idea of making money not by toil and perspiration but just by "shitting it out." That is the most magnificent ego-pleasing fantasy anybody can invent. The link which associates feces and money is man's fantasy of the effortless and easy way of producing both of them at will.

There is another aspect to the relationship of feces and money. In primitive times, if one laid his hands on something, the best way of protecting his possession was to sit on it. Philology bears this out. The Latin word *possession* comes from the Latin verb meaning "to sit on." You get something and you want to sit on it to play safe. Here the pleasure of the anal zone may be involved.

Let me make one other point. Gold is a good example of an almost useless substance that through superstition all sorts of omnipotent characteristics are related to it and it has become valuable. These superstitions about gold are among the most useful created by man, proving again that *superstition is more far-reaching and gains faster acceptance than the sword.*


## Urination

Let us look at the other evacuative activity, which is urethral functioning. Habit-training means developing a permanent inhibition of the sphincter. The bladder is controlled because it is not permitted to fill up to an extreme degree. Habit-training, cleanliness, and bladder control are important problems of upbringing and education, and the process by which this is reached is not yet fully clarified.

It is generally accepted that bladder control should not be attempted until the neural mechanism is ready and some recent evidence would indicate this is much later than originally thought. The usual consequence of forcing it before this neural mechanism is ready is a defeating of its purpose.

ENURESIS

Enuresis occurs in adults as well as in children although more commonly in males than in females. How does enuresis come about? It seems to me that enuresis in the child comes about as a gesture of defiance, a revolt against overpressure put upon him by an extremely anxious mother.

The fearful child has completely swallowed all or almost all of his anger, his defiance, his resentment. But when the sleep is sufficiently deep and the higher controlling machinery is out of function, this suppressed rage gets its way and the act of urination, performed as a protest, is carried out under the protection of deep sleep.

One perplexing factor is the finding of David M. Levy that the percentage of enuretic children is much higher in proletarian families. In some undiscernible way, bed-wetting can be a reflection of a lack of proper parental care and attention. But how then does lack of care lead to such anxiety and suppressed rage? Or is there another mechanism that brings it about? It may be that different psychological mechanisms may result in the same condition.

SEX AND URINATION

The urinary pleasure, like the anal pleasure, may be derived from a coexcitation of the genital system. Here is a very obscure point in the organization of the sexual system. It is said that the part of the male genital most receptive to stimulation is the glans penis and in the female it is the clitoris and the orifice of the vagina. But this is by no means the whole truth. I am reasonably certain that one part of the genital pleasure of intercourse and self-stimulation is due not to stimulation of the glans penis but to pressure on the shaft, a pressure that ultimately becomes operative on the urethra. All pressure exerted on the penis presses eventually on the urethra, and this pressure on the urethra is an important part in the whole genital pleasure mechanism. In the female, the tiny urethra is also highly susceptible to stimulation and probably yields sexual pleasure. If pressure on the urethra is part of the genital pleasure then the same pressure brought about by urination is pleasurable.

There is also another aspect of a connection between urination and sex. Since watching a little sister or brother urinate is an early exciting experience in life, and may be the forerunner of true sexual excitement in the child, a certain amount of conditioning may occur. A grownup may find that in order to get fully excited sexually, he has to witness his partner urinating. This aberration is not uncommon. Or, the Peeping Tom, the voyeur, may reveal that watching other children urinate was a pleasureful activity in his early childhood.

Urinary activity is important psychologically because of the psychological significance of the child's discovery of the difference between male and female genitalia, which he or she sees as urinating organs at that age. Both the little boy and the little girl are most likely to make this discovery of the differences precisely on the occasion of urination, because it is much easier to perceive the differences in the organs if they are functioning. The boy urinates in an erect position, the girl sits down. The boy is able to direct the stream any way he pleases, the girl is unable to do anything of the kind. The envy and rivalry that ensue is a consequence of this difference. The first stirring in the girl destined to become neurotic may be this desire to urinate like a boy.

Further, the relationship between urination and fire plays an important role in mythology and in psychoanalytic literature in dealing with mythology. One of the speculations is that fire has the effect of stimulating the individual to urination. There is a widespread superstition that children who play with fire before retiring in the evening will wet the bed. I suspect that fire brings about sexual excitement of the variety that tends to be discharged through urination.

### AMBITIOUSNESS IN THE CHILD

In classical psychoanalytic literature the connection between ambition and urinary eroticism was emphasized. Freud suggested that the children who derive substantial pleasure from the urinary act are those who will later on be ambitious enough to distinguish themselves. I am not so sure that ambitiousness itself is acquired from the urinary function. It would seem to me, rather, that children who are ambitious, for reasons not yet discovered, use the opportunity of urination to exercise it. Instead of being the source of ambition, it may be one of the first fields in which this already existing ambitiousness is brought into operation.

This ambition may manifest itself in many ways. The contest between boys who can urinate higher or farther brings ambition and competitiveness into play. The desire to overcome the accidents of incontinence may be another exercise of ambitiousness. Ambition itself is a rare trait in terms of its general occurrence. It is clearly a derivative of the omnipotence of the individual.

# CHAPTER 10

# Sexual Behavior

IN DISCUSSING SEXUAL BEHAVIOR WE ARE DEALING WITH A SUBJECT THAT is second to none in its ability to stir up interest and imagination. Sex was and still is saturated with artistic pleasure, with erotic delights, and with educational anguish. Nowhere else do you find so much mystification, dramatization, and fiction as in the supposedly scientific presentation of sex.

Unfortunately, psychoanalysis limits itself to certain aspects of the question of genital pleasure. Perhaps we would be more helpful if we kept in mind that coitus takes place in a psychodynamic setting and that psychological and psychodynamic factors play a tremendous role in the sexual activity of the human species.

## The Pursuit of Genital Pleasure

The first question is, of course, why does man have sexual activity? One does not have to probe deeply into the mysteries of human nature to be aware that the significance of begetting offspring is rivaled or completely overshadowed by the pleasure aspect. It has been the life practice of man for endless years to engage in genital activity for pleasure as well as for the production of offspring. The human species has a pretty constant orgastic need as distinguished from the lower forms.

The culmination of sexual pleasure in both man and woman is the orgasm. Genital-pleasure function is defined by orgasm, a definite physiological and psychological response. Orgasm, however, is only a gross evidence of sexual pleasure. The total sexual act, including orgasm, varies tremendously in terms of subjective feelings and their duration from time to time and with different people. The afterglow from orgasm and sexual union can be only momentary or extend to an indefinite period. This aspect has been totally neglected by many present-day sexologists.

The huge chapter of sexual pathology can be reduced to the proposition that all pathological varieties of sexual activity—from homosexuality to fetishism—can be described as modified patterns of stimulation calculated to bring about the orgasm, just as standard heterosexual performance is. That which is not calculated to bring about genital orgasm is not sexual.

The next fact of major importance is that genital sex activity begins and ends with a reflex. The two most important parts of sexual activity —preparedness and orgasm—are automatic reflexes. Voluntary action is of no avail. Essentially, orgasm can be defined as a terminal reflex that is elicited by stimulation. What lies between these two reflexes— which is the greater part of sexual activity—is a matter of voluntary control. This is the psychological part. Even in higher animals, sexual activity seems to be a matter of reflexes and chains of reflexes. One reflex is elicited, that in turn elicits another, that one another, and so on. To use Claude Bernard's words, "Little is left to the ignorant will of the individual."

What utilitarian function, other than reproduction, does the orgasm serve? It seems very possible to me that the orgasm is the mechanism by means of which the human being can discharge all of his emotional tensions as well as his sexual tensions. This would mean that by the mechanism of sexual excitation man is able to mobilize all the tensions that may arise in him for any number of reasons. If you assume that the orgasm is an indispensable mechanism for discharge of unnecessary energy, miscellaneous tensions, and all the rest, you can see that the absence of orgasm or the unsatisfactory orgasm inevitably leads to tremendous frustration and difficulties. But this excitation potential is still a mysterious factor. We do not yet know what it is.

Ferenczi was the first to formulate this function of the orgasm and to suggest that sexual activity took on a twofold purpose in man. Recognition of the psychophysiological function of sexual activity and the orgasm is an important contribution of psychoanalysis.

Now this kind of mobilizing and discharge only became possible as more and more emotions were poured into the sexual act. How did this happen? At some point in the evolution of man, a change of immense importance took place. This was the change of the coital pattern of the human being so that the coupling mates were able to lie face to face while engaging in intercourse. The coital pattern then became elaborated into a pattern that included the whole body of each lover in the sexual embrace. I feel that it was because of this change in the coital position that the emotional element began to become so important in sexual activity.

Now what is happening to the organism that is engaging in sexual activity from the psychophysiological point of view? I assume that at any given time an individual has a certain sexual excitation potential. We can also assume that the essence of sexual activity—foreplay and intercourse—is to exploit the excitation potential of the organism by luring it out into the open. The act of orgasm is the discharge of that amount of excitation potential which has been activated into actual excitation, and the satisfaction attendant upon it depends on how much of the latent potential excitation has been transformed into actual excitation. If the potential excitation has been fully transformed into actual excitation, the orgastic discharge is usually followed by a feeling of quiet calm, and the entire sexual need of the organism is completely extinguished.

If, however, only a fraction of the sexual excitation potential has been translated into actual excitation, the discharge relieves only the potential that has already been organized. When this happens, the individual still harbors a good deal of excitation potential after he has experienced his orgasm. He might then feel the need to continue to engage in sexual play and to have intercourse again so that this residual excitation potential can be converted into actual excitation and discharged by orgasm.

This ratio of excitation activated and discharged is not the only factor involved in the experience of sexual satisfaction. As in so many sexual areas, the factors of natural endowment, conditioning, fear, and others are all exerting their influence on the behavior of the organism. If a man fears that sexual intercourse makes him weak, for example, he finds it extremely difficult to work up to a second orgasm because his anxiety increases just as soon as his minimum sexual need subsides through gratification. Whereas, a man who is free from such morbid fears can allow the whole power of his sexual drive to exert itself again to discharge the residual excitation.

We do not understand how this excitation discharge operates in the female, who tends to have multiple orgasms as a result of one sex act or in a series of sex acts. Certain women experience only one orgasm; other women can have twenty orgasms during one sexual experience. The natural variability of the female is so tremendous that it raises many unanswerable questions.

Clinical experience shows that the more prolific the sexual excitement generated through mobilizing all latent and open pleasure resources of the organism, the more satisfactory and the more healthy in its consequences to the organism is the sexual activity.

## The Central Sexual Motive State

To achieve the end result—orgasm—the individual must allow the central sexual motive state to emerge within himself. The central sexual motive state is an affirmative attitude toward sexual excitation. While this motive state lasts, the sexual motive takes precedence over all other motivation and behavior, with the exception of responding to any intruding signals, such as outside noises, that would trigger the emergency function overruling all behavior.

An almost immediate consequence as the central sexual motive state crystallizes is the development of sensory needs. This means that the individual's attention will be directed toward sexual stimuli, which will be selectively taken out of context. In his comings and goings, the sexually excited man will be primarily interested in the available sexual stimuli. If none is there, he will imagine and project them into nonsexual environmental situations by means of symbolization, because of his need for a sexual partner.

Another characteristic of the central sexual motive state is that the organism has the tendency to mobilize as many of his extragenital pleasure resources as he can so that he can enjoy gratification through the stimulation of sensitive areas of mind and body while using these satisfactions as powerful stimuli that increase the genital longing and desire.

After preparedness occurs, the individual begins to feel a need for motor activity, which is analogous to the sensory need. This is a characteristic that is also common to the central alimentary sexual motive state.

## Initial Sexual Excitation

Let us go back and analyze the phases of sexual activity. It begins with the rise of initial sexual excitation. It is even possible that the body reacts to a sexual stimulus (real or in fantasy) by secreting a highly powerful chemical compound, something like a hormone, which circulates in the blood and affects the cerebral cortex. It would be simpler perhaps if this stimulation of the cortex were exactly translated into sexual excitation. But nothing of the kind exists. The development of sexual excitation depends upon the way the total cortex reacts to this stimulation. Psychologically speaking, the self decides whether or not it wishes to be sexually excited. If it does not wish to, it seems to have the power to suppress sexual excitation completely. Thus, the amount of sexual excitation is primarily proportional to the desirability of the individual, which can be cultivated within a certain range. The greater the desire is, the greater the excitation. And when the desire is absent or when strong reluctance to entertain desire exists, the development of excitation may be completely blocked. The most decisive factor is the individual's desire to be sexually excited.

## Forepleasure

The mutually consenting couple indulges in forepleasure, which is the mobilizing of the extragenital pleasure resources under the primacy of the genitals. The purpose is to obtain the pleasure of gratifying the local resources and to build the excitation so as to activate preparedness. Local gratification is always eclipsed by the still greater tension and genital desire that the partial gratification tends to create. In standard heterosexual performance the local pleasures of forepleasure do not diminish the genital desire because the organism at this point is integrated under the leadership of the genitals.

Take, as an example, the mouth. We know that the pleasure generated by activities of the mouth is rooted in the alimentary function. But if oral pleasure is experienced by an individual in the central sexual motive state and integrated into a genital-pleasure pattern two things will happen. Oral pleasure, as on the occasion of eating, will be experienced, but at the same time this pleasure satisfaction achieved by the mouth will be eclipsed by its serving as a powerful stimulus to the genital organs. Kissing gives pleasure and also increases genital desire.

Actually, forepleasure can utilize anything pleasurable that happens in a sexual setting. Looking at the partner or listening to her voice or being fondled by her can give pleasure and heighten the sexual excitation. Forepleasure can include local stimulation of the genitals, of adjacent parts, and of other parts of the body. Theoretically, any part of the body that is capable of sexual excitation is entitled to be included in sexual forepleasure. Every individual starts out with the same pleasure modalities in his body and mind, just as every male starts out with the same anatomy. If the central sexual motive state is sufficiently intense, every part of the body can become a sexually sensitive spot, though, of course, the erotic sensitivity of the various parts of the body is physiologically different. From this, we begin to see that the sexual excitability is not so much a property of certain erogenous zones as it is the interpretation put on the stimulus that emanates from those areas. If there is a great sexual excitation in an intense central sexual motive state, any kind of stimulation is able to promote the sexual excitation. The mental stimulation is all powerful. The consequence of this is that the individual has a tendency to develop a complicated stimulus and procedure pattern.

So long as this genital excitation prevails without discharge, none of the local areas can be satiated. The kissing goes on and on, and all the other activities are recharged, so to speak, by the stronger genital need. But as long as this pressure from the center exists, all these peripheral desires continue. Otherwise all these activities would come to a natural end.

The relationship between these extragenital sources of pleasure and the genital pleasure was a brilliant discovery of Freud. It was he who named this complicated mechanism *forepleasure*.

Let me remind you at this point of a few basic considerations. You can inflict pain on a person regardless of his wishes and can make somebody suffer whether he wants to or not. But this is true only of pain. It is important to remember that you cannot make anybody enjoy pleasure unless he is willing to have that specific pleasure.

It is equally important to remember that each individual develops an outlook about sexual activity that is the result of culture, society, religion, family, education, social forces, and all other influences that affect every human being. Sex cannot be discussed in a vacuum or outside of social forces. The desires of one person, of course, differ in a considerable way from the desires of another. What the individual finds pleasurable will result from the interaction of his sexual outlook and his available local pleasure resources.

The way an individual integrates his genital-pleasure pattern depends on the life history of that individual. Accordingly, he will have utilized his natural pleasure resources by developing corresponding desires or will have inhibited his natural pleasure resources by developed anxieties or reactions of disgust. This is a question of the struggle between the desire for pleasure on the one hand and the inhibitory action of anxiety on the other. It is an interplay of given natural pleasure tendencies in conflict with inhibitory cultural influences, represented by fear, disgust, and other factors. The individual's capacity to use potential pleasure resources in his body as resources of pleasure, then, depends upon the attitude he has built up in his mind toward that particular function as a source of pleasure. If any activity arouses fear or disgust for some social or personal reason, that pleasure resource, though it may be present as a potential, cannot be admitted into the genital-pleasure pattern of that individual.

With these considerations in mind, we can raise the question, What is "normal" sexual forepleasure? What does and does not belong in this integrated genital-pleasure pattern? What makes the answer difficult is that there are usually two persons involved.

Let us look at two examples of forepleasure activities. In Western civilization, because of the influence of the Church, there was a tendency to frown upon forepleasure activities and reduce intercourse to procreative activity, which was the union of the genitals proper. Therefore, the mouth-genital contact was considered a sinful and extravagant activity in the eyes of the Church. Any number of people have grown up with a fear of mouth-genital activity because they view it as condemned, unaesthetic, and unpleasant. It is almost unnecessary to say that the male or female who has this outlook cannot enjoy mouth-genital contact as one of the preparatory forepleasure activities. But another individual, one who does not share this prejudice, can utilize this activity as a source of great excitation.

"Is cunnilingus or fellatio a perversion?" There is hardly a question that I have heard more often than this one. As the cultural prejudice disappears, the natural pleasure tendencies break through and include the once forbidden modality in a new genital-pleasure pattern. It is hard to see from a medical point of view just why the mouth-genital contact should be more objectionable than the contact of two bacteria-filled mouths.

Even though we try to be as objective as possible in estimating these things, we must not forget that we all have been conditioned by our culture and our upbringing. Even when we are striving for an honestly objective and impartial investigation, we can never be sure that we are not ourselves victimized by the special conditions of our own upbringing. We have all been raised from an early age to suppress the enjoyment of urinary and defecatory activities. Yet many people include pleasure derived from urinary and anal activities in the genital pattern. The organs of urination and defecation are in the closest anatomic vicinity to the genital organs. In spite of our tendency to romanticize sex, anatomy remains.

From the practical point of view, it is all-important that the special leanings and desires of the two partners should match. If one partner strongly wants something that awakens aversion in his partner, there is trouble. Any change brought about in the sexual behavior pattern of the individual will consist of setting up or removing the culturally derived inhibitory forces. You cannot lift the individual out of his culture. In most instances, however, the task of the psychoanalyst is to remove the barriers and emancipate some of the potential pleasure resources.

I am discussing these variations within the framework of forepleasure, preparatory to coitus. When any of these contacts displaces coitus and itself becomes the end result, it is a matter of sexual pathology. (This will be discussed later.) No matter what the variations, the end of forepleasure should be the same. Eventually the total excitation generated in both mates will effect a powerful state of preparedness and will heighten and make imperative the desire to penetrate or receive.

## Preparedness

At a certain point, all the preliminary activities of wooing, arousal, and forepleasure climax in both man and woman in a preparedness for coitus. The act of preparedness is an automatic reflex that is not within the voluntary control of the organism. In the male, the organ of copulation has to be created by erection. The erect penis is a copulating organ developed especially when and if there is need for it. After the purpose is served, it reverts again or is retransformed again into a different organ. This fact is of great significance.

Though the initial reflex of preparedness is less conspicuous in the female than is erection in the male, it nevertheless takes place. The signs of an initial excitation and a normal desire in the female are lubrication, erection of the clitoris, the so-called erection of the small labia, the so-called erection of the nipples of the breast, and other physiological changes which need to be better understood.

But the female, unlike the male, does not have to undergo preparedness for intercourse to occur. She can be subjected to it without any emotional participation or she can voluntarily undergo it without desire or feeling. And she can be used for intercourse whether she wants it or not. The male can penetrate the female unless, for example, she develops vaginism, a muscular cramp that prevents entry.

## Intercourse

After preparedness occurs, the individual begins to feel a need for the motor activity he is prepared to execute. This is accomplished by local stimulation of the genitalia as they unite in coitus. The mutual friction provides each of the partners with a sensation of pleasure and satisfaction at the same time as such stimulation increases the need for motor activity. The conversion of the excitation potential into actual excitation continues to occur and increases until orgasm is elicited. Every bit of pleasure gives rise to a still greater need until the individual arrives at orgasm. The rhythm of the stimulus is a subjective matter, and two partners who are adjusted to each other manage to synchronize this whole pattern of stimulation.

This increasing of the motor activity is an indispensable component in standard heterosexual performance. When this does not function well, the individual may have to resort to modified patterns to achieve orgasm. We will be talking about these substitutes when we come to disordered behavior.

## Orgasm

If all goes well, both partners achieve orgasm, which is the end purpose of sexual activity. I can do no more than touch on one or two aspects of this immense subject. First, I want to say emphatically that the clitoral orgasm of the female is just as respectable and desirable as any other kind of female orgasm. Discriminating between the vaginal pleasure machinery and the clitoral pleasure machinery is an arbitrary business. God created both, if I may say so, and it was not stated on the tablets of stone which ranks higher than the other. Many a woman with tears in her eyes has told me how ashamed she is that she can only come to orgasm if her clitoris is manually stimulated. "Oh, what a terrible thing that is." When I ask her why this is so terrible she does not know why but she is convinced that there is something terrible the matter with her. Some women have orgasm through stimulation of their breasts or by fantasy. Is this so awful? An orgasm is an orgasm.

Although all parts of the female genitalia are sensitive from the earliest time on, more stimulation reaches the clitoris and the introitus than the inside of the vagina, which is closed by the hymen. So conditioning brings that very sensitive clitoris earlier into play. Moreover, the sexual inhibitions and sexual fears that are instilled into a woman's mind center on the vagina and penetration. Relatively speaking, it seems accurate enough to say that the clitoris remains free from the intimidation derived from education and that all intimidations center on the vagina.

This unfortunate attitude toward the clitoral orgasm is, ironically enough, one of the sins that can be charged up to psychoanalysis, which injected new prejudices and errors into public notions. It adopted the tenet that in the normal development of the female, the site of orgasm shifted from the clitoris to the vagina. This standard of vaginal eroticism made it a requirement that either a woman have orgasm by way of vaginal stimulation or she was not a "mature individual on the genital level." This dictum has engendered needless inadequacy feelings.

The whole phenomenon of orgasm itself is very variable and has a wide range. This spread seems to be greater in the female than in the male. The male can have a more satisfactory orgasm and a less satisfactory orgasm, and he can even have ejaculation with no accompanying pleasure whatsoever. But in the female the differences in the quality of orgasm are very great. The rhythmic contraction that is the essence of the female orgasm may involve the introitus region, the small labia, the clitoris region, and the whole vaginal passage which may behave indeed like a bellows. In a more intense orgasm the contraction may involve a good many adjacent pelvic structures below the vagina and even the lower part of the rectum as well. In a very intense orgasm all the voluntary muscles of the whole abdomen might be involved with all the preceding structures. Ranging from the minor throbbing of the clitoris region to the explosive phenomenon that involves the vulva, the vagina, the lower abdomen, and all the pelvic structures, the female can experience all shapes and grades of orgasms. It is possible that the female may experience a greater release of tension and a sense of greater relaxation after she has had a vaginal orgasm as compared to a clitoral orgasm but it is probably a quantitative rather than a qualitative difference. But we must keep in mind the variability from one female to another.

## Summary of Sexual Behavior

Much human misery has been caused by sexual misconceptions. It would seem to me that the only technique of genital union that can be considered superior is the one that succeeds in bringing into play all the pleasure resources of the organism and that discharges most completely the maximum amount of sexual and nonsexual tension. Every human individual develops a certain amount of sexual inhibition, and a large amount of sexual inhibition exists in our culture and is "normal" or pretty close to normal in terms of our culture. It is impossible to pigeonhole these things sharply into "normal" and "pathological."

Some individuals specialize to such an extent in the most culturally condemned type of pleasure activity that their capacity for genital enjoyment may depend on the presence of such features. These are the so-called perversions—a word which should disappear from psychopathology or from the scientific study of sex because it includes moral condemnation. If we permit moral prejudices to creep in, we cannot proceed scientifically.

However, one element is pathological when injected into sexual activity, no matter how or when it is allowed to take place. I refer to the abnormal genital pleasure pattern that is organized to include the intentional production of pain. The intentional inclusion of pain or painful experience, such as anxiety, as utilized by the so-called masochists and sadists in the genital pattern is morbid per se. I will talk about this when I analyze disordered sexual behavior.

## Reproduction

We must not lose sight of the fact that the main and original purpose of sexual activity is propagation and survival of the species. The terminal reflex which we call orgasm (the supreme pleasure of the organism) coincides with or is identical with the act of insemination by the male. The male orgasm, then, which is dependent upon the reproductive act of insemination, is the pleasure aspect of insemination, which has a pivotal function in reproduction. Sexual pleasure is plainly integrated with the reproductive function, and sexual pleasure cannot be separated from reproduction.

Consideration of the sexual-pleasure function does not allow us to coin a new concept of sex. You can separate the practice of sex as a pursuit of pleasure from the reproductive intent, but the machinery and the whole content is of necessity the same. Sex in the sense of genital pleasure is rooted in the reproductive function and is part and parcel of it.

Now if man engages in mating without the reproductive intent and calls that sex, then we should simply say that sex is the utilization without reproductive intent of the reproductive machinery for the sake of the pleasure attendant upon it. Let me remind you that we have encountered this practice before. When we discussed thumb-sucking in alimentary behavior, I suggested to you that man was never happier than when he managed to get the pleasure without the utility activity.

## The Nature of Sexual Attraction

How does the individual go about finding his sexual partner? I think sex attraction should be analyzed as a purely physiological, sensual phenomenon, as separate from the "in love" context. How then is sexual selection and sexual response to be explained? Why is it that at times a male and a female respond to each other sexually with strong desire? Or with very slight desire? Why is it that at other times there is no response at all? How does that work? How is this sexual response elicited? The woman or man who will arouse in any given individual sexual reaction is said to be sexually appealing to the other, but is this sex attraction?

Very little work has been done on this important question of sexual excitability. Psychoanalysts have not spent much time examining the question because it was hidden under the problem of conditions of love and they have focused their attention on the question of love. But the formula of so-called love was used to include also the sexual response, and Freud's idea was that this is an unconscious phenomenon. Certain unconscious conditions or requirements are set up in any given individual, he said, and if and when an experience meets these unconscious requirements, a favorable response is elicited.

What are those unconscious requirements? My observations are that on the sensual level this selective sexual response depends on the conditioning sexual experience in the previous life history of the individual. The essential point is that this previous sexual experience that shapes the individual's sexual desire without his being fully aware of it is of two kinds—actual experience and imaginary experience. In this shaping or molding or specifying the sexual desire, the imaginary sexual experience eclipses the actual experience.

Suppose a young boy has a pleasurable genital experience from stimulation by his nurse. This may happen accidentally (while she is giving him a bath, for example) or it may be intentional on the part of the nurse who wants to keep the boy quiet. The boy's sexual response may then be molded by the features of his nurse. On the basis of conditioning, those features will become the preferred stimulus pattern. When these features appear he gets sexually excited because he has been conditioned by having had a pleasurable genital experience earlier. He does not even need to know that. The sexual responses of the boy may be conditioned by any feature of this partner on whom the boy's attention is selectively centered. These features will modulate or shape his sexual desire. In a sense sexual desire is the desire of the individual to find those features, because the moment the feature is there, the individual will experience sexual desire. So the individual emerges from his childhood history with preferred stimulus patterns that he does not even know about. When this preferred stimulus pattern appears, his immediate reaction is an explosive sexual excitation.

Now while the conditioning influence of all the actual early ubiquitous sex experience is enormous, it is still eclipsed by the conditioning power of subsequent daydreaming or fantasies. Especially is this true in the teens, when the sexual taste of the individual is shaping up.

How is the individual conditioned by this imaginary experience? The sexually excitable boy goes to the movies and sees a beautiful actress and melts away. Now he goes home and a million sexual fantasies will be formed about that actress. The result is a conditioning of his sexual desire by those given features which he happened to see in her. So these puberty fantasies, some of which can be self-stimulation fantasies, shape the taste and the unconscious responsiveness of the individual by resulting in the preferred stimulus pattern. Usually, the boy in puberty is guided by popular sentiment. In our time, he was told that Garbo was the most beautiful woman in the world so he was conditioned to some aspect of her though he did not know this was happening. Then a few years later he met a girl and she turned out to be his preferred stimulus pattern. When an individual suddenly finds another individual sexually exciting, he is actually refinding a preferred stimulus pattern that has been built up in his mind through his life experience. In this life experience, the imaginary experience by far outweighs the real experience. The same conditioning takes place in the female. Certain features are taken and hammered in, and by means of this fantasy formation the conditioning occurs.

This is not the complete solution to this question. Still, it is perhaps too sober and disillusioning for us to accept the possibility that the much debated mysteries of sexual response are principally the outcome of conditioning established primarily through the activities of the imagination.

## Maleness and Femaleness

Let me end this chapter on sexual behavior with the most basic questions of all. What is maleness? What is femaleness? In many ways this is like asking "What is life?"—which no biologist would attempt to define at this time.

Prehistoric man discovered that man and other species exist in two editions marked by contrasting characteristics. To these two editions were given the name male and female. This distinction was developed apparently from the recognition of pregnancy, childbirth, the female's nursing of the baby, the structural differences of the external genitalia, and the different kind of participation in the sexual act.

With the advent of the microscope, the gonads and the germ cells were discovered and the essentials of reproduction were found to be the egg and the sperm. The egg-producing gonad was the ovary; the sperm-producing male gonad was called the testicles. And now, in a typically cellular-biological manner, a definition was concocted: the female is a female by virtue of her having eggs, and a male is a male by virtue of his having sperms.

Now let us compare the merits of these two approaches. Prehistoric man defined sex on the basis of the reproductive function as a whole. The cellular-biological definition, on the other hand, defines sex, not on the basis of the reproductive system as a whole but on the basis of one single component, the germ cell, of the whole system. Moreover, prehistoric man, having defined sex on the basis of the reproductive system as a whole, based his definition predominantly on function—mating, childbearing, and the rest of it. Cellular biology, on the other hand, based the definition exclusively on structure—the microscopic picture of sperm versus egg. Orgasm in the male is always male, and orgasm in the female is always female. Male orgasm rests on male structures and female orgasm rests on female structures.

As far as I am concerned, the cellular-biological orientation means a retrogression from a much more mature, realistic type of thinking to a one-sided scientific outlook. Modern scientists lost sight of the many things that prehistoric men already knew. Instead of defining sex on a functional basis, on the basis of the whole function, modern man proceeded to define sex on an anatomic token, namely, the sperm and the egg.

You will find literature in which the writer gives the percentage of so-called male and female hormonal output, or the proportion of so-called male and female hormones in the blood, and arrives at conclusions regarding the maleness or femaleness of an individual. When we come to disordered sexual behavior, I will talk about this troublesome notion of bisexuality in some detail. The presence of a certain percentage of female hormone in the male blood cannot confer upon that male any ability to function in a female way since he does not have the organs for it. Nor can the presence of any amount of male hormones in a female confer upon that female the ability to function with organs which she does not have.

Maleness and femaleness must be defined as the capacity to function in the male way or in the female way. From my point of view, sex is not determined by the kind of germ cells that are produced. Originally the germ cell was bisexual. But sex is not a tissue; still less is it a group of cells. Sex is the reproductive system as a whole, and it embraces structures and physiologic functions that appear in the other systems of the organism. Once the original cell has became male or female, there is no evidence that the other possibility still exists.

# CHAPTER 11

# Respiration and

# Other Behavior Areas

ORDINARILY, THE RESPIRATORY FUNCTION IS AN AUTOMATIC ONE, REGU-
lated by lower centers in the central nervous system. But inasmuch as it
is under voluntary control and can be affected by the emotions, it is a
behavior area that concerns us.

## Respiratory Behavior

The automatic pattern of breathing is not so uniform as one might
think. From the outset it is modified by the spontaneous expression
of continually aroused emotions which influence the frequency and
depth and other aspects of breathing. Crying and sobbing are deepened acts of inspiration. Laughing is an explosive act of exhaling. In
similar ways, the various emotions influence the automatic pattern of
breathing. In addition, the natural rhythm of automatic breathing is
modified and regulated for the purposes of speaking, singing, and like
muscular exertions.

The breathing pattern is subject to morbid changes due to the injec-
tion of anxiety, which has a truly massive effect on breathing. The
problem is how to adjust breathing in the presence of anxiety or how
to eliminate the anxiety or how to adjust breathing and thereby cope
with anxiety.

Now, is there any pleasure value in breathing? My personal inclina-
tion is to believe that there is. When you walk out into the air after

being shut up, the first thing you find yourself doing is taking a deep breath with enjoyment. Going into the mountains or into the country away from crowded conditions in the cities immediately makes you conscious of a pleasure that you have been missing.

Look what happens when you are sleeping. When it is hot and humid you cannot sleep. Then you open your window and the cool air comes in and you sleep wonderfully. You enjoy the breathing and it puts you to sleep, and you maintain a state of deep sleep.

Observation, in addition to complicated chemical factors, leads me to feel that we can make the very crude subjective statement that sometimes we feel happy because of pleasurable breathing, though we can only faintly suspect how and what goes on.

How does the intake of oxygen in the narrow sense influence our well-being, our sensations of pleasure, our emotional expression, and our mood? We can answer this by examining anoxia, which occurs as a result of the diminished oxygen pressure of higher altitude. First of all, not all individuals respond to increasing anoxia in the same manner, though the reaction can be divided into a more or less constant part and into a more or less variable part.

The constant part is that every individual, when anoxia occurs, appears to suffer some change in the self-control, memory, judgment, coordination, and function of the special center. These seem to be the direct psychological expression of local changes in the brain cells which, however, are temporary and reversible.

The variable is the euphorizing action of anoxia. Like alcoholic intoxication, anoxia causes some people to develop self-confidence and to lose understanding of danger and threat. The danger of this state is that the victim does not know what danger he is in. Tending to overestimate his own power, he plunges into disaster. It is like the drunken driver who has a feeling of exaggerated self-confidence and does not suspect that he has impaired his motor skills.

Some people get drowsy; others get very belligerent; and others are subject to panic. The emotional response to this impairment is primarily dictated by the intrinsic tendency of the individual, but it may be modified by the environmental setting. If one man in a group begins to laugh, the others probably will laugh too.

It may seem that euphoria from anoxia is an exception to the rule that behavior is guided by sensations of pleasure that have survival value. Actually this is not so because only with man did animals ever get high enough to go past the relatively prolonged discomfort and pain in anoxia that always precedes the euphoria.

In the infant breathing goes on for a long time in a completely automatic fashion, and then the baby finds himself laughing or crying. These emotional responses of the organism are more or less reflex. The first influence in the infant is perhaps the parents' effort to persuade the child to control the expression of the emotions. The first real voluntary control comes into the picture of breathing by the child's effort to control the expression of the emotions because Mama says, "Don't cry."

I believe that the way a child is taught to control the expression of emotion in early life is an important influence that shapes the individual in certain respects for life. In certain circumstances, the pattern of efficient breathing is interfered with and the result is the psychopathology of breathing.

Asthma is by no means the only neurotic change in breathing. There are neurotic complications of breathing of the inspiratory type in children. They suddenly get the feeling that they are not getting enough air. Prompted by anxieties, they gasp and try all sorts of contorted acts of inspiration.

Higher demands are made on the child when he starts to talk. He gets all kinds of instructions. "Don't swallow your words, don't do this. . . ." Various speech difficulties have much to do with the action of anxiety on breathing.

The inability of some individuals to engage in athletic activity is a result of the action of anxiety on the breathing function. Sometimes a young boy with a perfectly healthy body cannot run because he has no wind. He is unable to engage in any activity in which breathing has to be adjusted to the requirements of that activity in order to achieve a higher rate of efficiency. The solution is to eliminate fear, thereby freeing the breathing function again so that the child can be adjusted to the requirements of the activity.

The most important aspect of swimming is the regulation of breathing. To teach a child to swim involves teaching him to breathe free from fear and to learn how to breathe evenly in the water. Swimming instruction that concentrates on the various movements of the body often loses sight of the central problem, which is avoidance of anxiety. The influence of anxiety on breathing can be so disastrous that the individual cannot stay above water and will drown. A large percentage of drownings may thus be due to anxiety phenomena or the consequences of anxiety.

The importance of breathing in terms of omnipotence and magic and the illusory evaluation put on it by the primordial self is second to none. Since ancient times, breathing has been somehow connected with the soul. People hit upon the idea of the soul as separate from the body when they saw the differences between the dead and the living. The only visible thing they could see was that the breath of the alive man was coming in and out and the breath of the dead man had stopped. Hence we have the idea that the soul is somehow the breath and that the soul is what makes the body a living human being. All mythologies and cosmological theories of mankind contain the item of man being created by an act of breathing. "And the Lord God formed man of the dust of the ground and breathed into his nostrils the breath of life, and man became a living soul."

The superstition attached to breathing is substantial in primitive man. Superstition means delusional or illusional evaluation of things from the point of view of omnipotence. There is always a possibility of survival of such ancient superstitions whenever it is possible to do so under a rational disguise. What happens is that a certain reaction that seems to be reasonable and justified is then seen to be exaggerated because of the unconscious reinforcement.

An example is the halitosis campaign of today. Manufacturers want to sell their mouthwash so they make people conscious of their bad breath. But this campaign would not be so successful if it did not evoke an unconscious fear. This panicky fear of bad breath is somehow associated with death. If breath is the most potent instrument of creation, then a perfect breath is essential!

I should like to make a brief reference to hyperventilation, which may lead to catatonic convulsions through lowering the calcium and carbon dioxide levels. The psychologically significant fact is that some neurotics can cultivate fainting spells by this machinery, although they do not usually know what they are doing. Anybody will faint or throw a fit if he engages in forced inspiration for a few minutes. This is one mechanism that can be beautifully exploited by the hysteric.

### Thermal Regulatory Behavior

I shall make just a few comments on thermal regulatory behavior. This is not a subject I have spent much time or thought on. The most important thermal regulatory organ is the skin: the second is breathing. An example of thermal regulatory behavior that is voluntary is behavior calculated to warm one in cold weather—slapping oneself to get warm. But there is also behavior in which the thermal regulatory aspect is present, but eclipsed by the presence of other motivations.

Housing, naturally, has many motivations, but one of its most important is the protection against excesses of heat and cold. The only thermal regulatory behavior is to be taken into Mama's arms and embraced, the body of the mother serving as a stove. The situation in the womb and in the arms of the mother has become a model for all building activity. All the early buildings in tribal life started with this duplicating of the human body with a cavity in it—the uterus of the mother. Of course, architecture has many other motivations, such as art, the prestige element, and the display motive. The thermal regulatory situation also plays a tremendous part in attachment to the home: first the arms of Mama and then the warm fireplace around which family life gathers. The warmth of the fireplace becomes symbolic of the whole situation and leads to attachment to the place of birth.

Another item in thermal regulatory behavior is clothing. Here again the thermal regulatory aspect of clothing is complicated by other motivations; the chief ones being dressing for social prestige and for sexual effect. I shall not discuss the prestige aspect except to observe that in former times, unlike our age of informality, people of higher standing had to distinguish themselves by dressing accordingly. Some remnants of that still exist today. We expect the military and the clergy, for example, to follow the clothing rules in their public appearances.

The sex aspect of dressing is more complicated. The anthropologists used to argue about why our ancestors in the subtropical climate of Africa and Asia started to wear loincloths. Sexual drive in man had become a permanent phenomenon; it was no longer an oestrus phenomenon that came every few weeks and then stopped as in animals. The sight of the naked genitalia of the opposite sex was an extremely strong stimulus, and ancient people were wise enough to hit upon the solution of covering up. This is a hypothesis, just as everything about ancient man is guesswork.

Clothing also has the antithetical purpose. It serves as a sexual stimulus to focus man's attention on sex. Female clothing is almost exclusively a means of sexual attraction, sex appeal, and display. Covering up became artful in the sense of being an invitation to undress, which can be sexually stimulating. Children love the feeling of nakedness as do most adults who are not too inhibited. It gives them a sense of freedom. A dream of nakedness may have this meaning or it may be a fear of social exposure.

# CHAPTER 12

# Group Behavior

*The Pattern of Group Activity*

THE FATHER-MOTHER-SIBLING GROUPING IS A PATTERN FOR ALL ORGANized and integrated group activity. Every such group, involving collaboration, division of labor, and integration of activities, is based upon the family setup in which one father rules over the siblings. This arrangement is a social necessity.

This does not mean that the arrangement of all social units is based on the family. The fact is that the family unit itself is merely an example of the general principle of organization that can be seen at every stage of organic development. Wherever we see division of labor between different types of cells and tissues and organs, we find that integration means the establishment of a gradient. The situation requires that one unit become dominant as compared to the others that remain submissive. Without the relationship between domination and submission, no organization is conceivable.

The most striking example of this is the cerebral cortex which holds an almost complete dictatorship over the organism. The family setup, with a father in charge, repeats on the social level the same principle of domination and submission. This organic law goes astray in society because the moment somebody becomes the foreman, he is likely to exhibit the tendency not only to work for the benefit of the group but also to get advantages for himself, which amounts to varying degrees of exploitation of the group.

The reduction of the primordial self leads to the development of the less impressive but more objectively true real self which is surrounded by a shell of illusion. This illusion is sometimes displaced from the individual to a group unit, and by being shared by all the members of the group it acquires a sort of reality. The man who would not say, "I'm a wonderful guy," is often willing to say these things about his own tribe or his own nation. Then it is called nationalism.

So-called national sovereignty, of course, is a delusion and an absurdity in a world in which people are constantly influencing each other, a world in which almost anything a nation does can encroach upon the so-called sovereignty of other nations. Just as it is a world in which no individual can do anything without thereby influencing the situation of others. Such tenets as national sovereignty are the greatest stumbling block in the way of the development of a world community.

## Privilege and Prejudice

Let me begin by pointing out that every individual, in his developmental history, wanted privilege. It is only for want of privilege that he settles for equality. This theory is fundamental for all social behavior of mankind. The demand for equality is a highly unstable product and the temptation to revert to the struggle for privilege is always present. It requires strong insight and a high cultural level not to yield to this temptation but to maintain the society on the basis of equality.

In the mutual struggle of people living together two facts are always present—competition and collaboration. Inherent in every collaborative arrangement is the element of trying to get the greater advantage. Since time immemorial some basic trends have been present. For example, once advantage has been gained through superior achievement, by whatever means, the tendency is for the individual to try to hold onto the advantages throughout his own life and that of his descendants.

Every arrangement by which advantages gained in fair competition are perpetuated to another generation works against equality of opportunity and is diametrically opposed to the principle of equality of opportunity. Inherited wealth, which has a beneficial effect on the development of an economy, is not inalienable and can be lost. If you inherit an estate, you have to manage it or lose it. This, then, is the psychological background of ancestor worship. If I owe a privileged position to my ancestor, I shall be only too happy to worship him.

Related to this perpetuation of advantages gained is prejudice and discrimination, in particular against other nations and minority groups.

Now what is the psychological operation of prejudice? Prejudice is one of the illusory devices by which the self rescues some of its infantile vainglory and holds on to the illusion that he is enjoying some privilege.

The simplest way to cultivate the illusion of privilege in myself is to invent somebody who is lower than I am. The tendency of man is to single out a minority group and say, "I am better than any of them." It secures something for nothing. If this prejudice is followed by discriminatory practice, then prejudice instead of fair play becomes operative and the members of the group discriminated against can be excluded from full participation in society.

The greater the insecurity feeling or the greater the sense of inadequacy or the greater the shakiness of the self, the more reliant and dependent that person will be on such auxiliary constructions. He will be the greatest nationalist, and will cherish all sorts of prejudices. He will be the fiercest bigot. What this self-love of the primordial self does to the human being is extraordinary.

### Religion, Science, and Art

The idea of a divine father is an extension of the idea of the real father. It is a clinging to the infantile idea that the individual has an omnipotent father who can be counted on to perform for him. If one person alone cherished the abstract conception of a divine father, he would not get far with it. But it was the fact of common need that led to the development of this collective illusion of the tribal god, and this joint belief endowed this illusion with a semblance of reality. Eventually, the concept of an invisible (as separate from a man-made idol) God became universal. "We are all equal before God" is the psychological transposition of the idea that we must all be equal before Papa. This is the basis of democracy.

When a man reaches the limits of his self-sufficiency, he turns to God. You must understand this role of religion—enhancing security wherever man's own power to provide for himself reaches its limitations. Whenever it comes to problems incapable of solution because our knowledge is not yet advanced enough, the individual is tempted to fall back on the infantile mechanism of security, turning to Papa, turning to God. Moreover, there is little interest in how Papa or God brings about the desired result. The whole infantile attitude culminates in a psychological technic of "how to keep myself in God's good graces."

All during the Middle Ages, when this infantile attitude prevailed, there was extreme hostility toward all natural science or inquiry and research. With Galileo came the development of technology. "I cannot rely on Papa and I cannot rely on God. I have to improve my own resources and find out about the world around me." This is what natural science does, and the scientific development is therefore emotionally diametrically opposed to the religious orientation. But the individual, no matter how scientific he is or how realistic or how much he knows, retains the residue of paternal attachment in his mind, an attachment too deeply ingrained to be completely removed.

Like religion, art and science are based on infantile omnipotence. All science started out with rebellion, with the scientist placing himself in the role of God who prescribes laws for the universe. By prescribing scientific laws for the universe, the scientist shows an unconscious identification with God. Although science is based on reality testing, the underlying psychological excitement is directly derived from the thirst for knowledge, and the true scientific spirit is the spirit of omnipotence.

The artist does it another way. He re-creates the world in symbols of his own fashioning. This behavior is also fundamentally based on an identification with God and the idea of omnipotence.

## Wealth and Possessions

Hoarding is the first step in foresight, exemplified in the biblical legend of Joseph who used the crops of good years to feed his people in the lean years. The psychological principles that underlie attitudes toward possession and wealth are inexhaustible. All wealth enlarges the self, merges somehow into the self, and becomes part of the self. Under normal circumstances there is a complete identification of the individual with his possessions, and the threat of damage to his possessions affects him in the same way as any threat of damage to his own body. Possessions become an extension of the self and are taken into the organization of the self.

Wealth and ownership and possessions increase or inflate and enlarge the ego. Here wealth means power, security, and an enlargement of the self, while lack of wealth, or poverty, establishes insecurity and fear of the future. There are many serious neurotic difficulties related to this sense of ownership and possession.

Some people of wealth are neurotically prevented from enjoying their affluence, because they are unable to carry out this natural identification. One young man I treated had inherited a huge estate from his father, who had been a strict man, demanding, and very disciplinary. Fifteen years after his father's death, during which my patient had managed to take good care of this fortune and even increased its value, he was still having recurring dreams in which his father returned and demanded his money back. This patient had not acquired the sense of ownership and pleasure in that money because of his feeling that it actually belonged to his father. Rationally, he knew he could write checks and buy things and use the money for his own purposes, but emotionally that money still belonged to his father.

The poor, like the rich, suffer neurotic difficulties related to the sense of ownership and possession, among which are lack of a sense of ownership and overevaluation of the security to be derived from it. The vast majority without means do not suffer from that feeling of insecurity that would be objectively justified on the grounds of their actual economic situation. Reliance on the strength of his arms, on his skills, or his ability to provide for himself allows the healthy man to maintain a better state of subjective security than one might expect.

The moment the individual starts to enlarge the self, new responsibilities, new fears, and new anxieties start. Here we are including possessions in the aggregate organization of the self—one's home, for example. As soon as man acquires a new possession, he suffers fears of losing it, of being deprived of it, of its being injured. There is some measure of truth in the dread of the wealthy man that everybody desires to take his possessions away from him, because everyone who has anything is potentially the target of the greed and envy of other people. When this situation is neurotically magnified, the man sees others as potential invaders.

What is the psychodynamic source of the wish to possess? The original incentive toward accumulation does not come from anal experience. The first thing ever accumulated by living organisms is food. It is certainly not a sublimated anal interest that causes animals to put away food supplies—the drive is rooted in the biological need of the organism to eat food.

Each individual is motivated by his basic need for survival. Therefore he struggles for power and possessions as a means of safety and security. That power means, "I want to have my way." It means the strength to exert influence. It means the desire to be respected and feared and if possible admired. This same set of intentions collides with those of the other person. He in turn is motivated by the desire to get for himself what the other man has attained. Today, this struggle is relatively submerged so far as the individual is concerned because he has delegated their representation to the national unit. So the matter goes on, not only between individuals but also between nations.

It seems reasonable to talk about acquisitive behavior in the context of group behavior because the individual develops this trait in terms of his society's attitudes toward it. Our society places great importance on possessions and wealth, so that ownership is a value we all grow up believing in. After that, it is a matter of motivation, ability, willingness to sacrifice, and the many factors that determine how economically successful an individual will be. Some primitive societies value a man in terms of how much he can give away, and his sense of stature and security, accordingly, depends on the reverse activity.

In behavior concerned with safety and security, it is necessary to distinguish between the period of growth and the period of adulthood. During the "sanctuary" period the individual gets protection and support from the parents and absorption of love. During the adult period he derives protection and support from membership in the community. Acquisitiveness, hoarding, competitiveness, and cooperativeness, all contribute to the individual's feeling of safety and security.

## Technology

Modern technology presents a new aspect with which man must come to terms. The nature of these technological installations is their tendency toward ever larger units of production. The model for this organization of production is the pattern of the human organism that we have already analyzed. In industrial hierarchies all over the world we invariably find a system as dictatorial as the control of the cortex over the human organism. Large-scale industrial production is organized pretty much like the human organism in that the highest executive levels have an almost complete control over the whole pyramid. Industrial production is also military preparedness of the national state, part and parcel of the emergency function of the nation. The emergency function of the individual has precedence over other functions.

Remember that we cannot be too onesidedly psychodynamical. We must always consider the nature of the man-made environment we live in, in which the nation not only is the sum total of individuals but is also the sum total of these highly complicated installations, such as the production plant.

Perhaps at some future time there will be such a terrific abundance that nations will no longer need to feel enmity and will work out a system of industrial production based on hierarchic levels of integration and controlled by a democratic machinery. Whether that is possible I do not know. The road to it is very long because it presupposes such an abundance that we could afford the luxury of not producing at all while we are organizing. The prerequisite would be that there should be no more need for emergency function. So long as there is the other guy who has a gun in his hand you cannot do without it.

# CHAPTER 13

# Love and Marriage

WHAT IS THE ESSENCE OF LOVE? YOU REMEMBER OUR BASIC PRINCIPLES OF psychodynamic reactions—that pain elicits the riddance mechanism and pleasure elicits a tendency to absorb the pleasure and retain the source of it. This principle can be operative in terms of any animal need. In what we call love, the individual is motivated by the desire to hold on to and retain the source of pleasure, no matter what that pleasure might be. Love, then, is a response to the source of pleasure.

An individual can be valuable to another as a source of many different kinds of pleasure. All love situations include extragenital pleasures, but they need not include genital experiences. The infant loves his mother's breast and tries to keep it in his mouth. There is no genital involvement in this emotion. When an individual is a source of genital pleasure to another (which is the strongest kind of pleasure one person can give to another) the love relationship is the being in love state that I will be talking about.

The phenomena of sensual craving and the affectionate relationship called love are so completely merged with each other that even in scientific theory, such as the Freudian theory, the two were taken to be manifestations of one and the same thing. Accordingly, the psychoanalytic theory distinguished between the tender or affectionate trend and the physical or sensual trend, both of which derived from the same sexual drive. The tender current was love; the sensual current was the drive for intercourse.

I doubt that love is a manifestation of sex. I suggest that love is a much more primitive mechanism and much more widely distributed than sexual feeling. It has important connections with sex and is often found in combination with it, but it is a phenomenon in its own right, which is apart from and independent of sex.

## The Being in Love State

In my opinion, the phenomenon of romantic love, which I call the being in love state, is made up of three merging elements: sexual attraction and need, a relapse to the dependency adaptation (which offers emotional security of the infantile type), and self-love. When one individual finds the person who triggers and integrates these three emotional forces in himself, he is going to have an explosive experience. Sexual intercourse in the being in love state is obviously an experience much superior to a sexual experience outside of the being in love state. All our drama and fiction for the last two thousand years has revolved around the problem of romantic love and of executing this love in the sex act.

The first love relationship that every human being experiences exists in the relationship between the infant and mother. This is also the relationship that allows him to experience the feeling of security. From a biological point of view, this love and these extragenital pleasure modalities are the means by which the security of the infant is safeguarded. It is a matter of life and death for the infant to get the ministrations of the parent, and in order to secure this constant contact between the baby and mother, any and all aspects of this contact have been made sources of pleasure. The pleasure modalities involved in kissing, embracing, and the like are primarily the executive of this love which is rooted biologically in the need of the baby. This experience of the baby becomes the pattern for security in two senses. In the emotional sense, he gets the experience of feeling secure. And in the objective, factual sense, he actually is secure because he is being taken care of. This is the dependence adaptation.

The dependence form of security is the organism's original experience of security. But as he grows up, the individual has to change over into an independent and self-sustaining creature whose security will rest on his own activity. The yearning for this earlier type of security will always remain with him in the form of a dependence craving. Almost all neuroses are based on this craving.

In the being in love state, the grownup places himself in an illusory state. The male believes that his girl friend is in the same relationship to him as his mother used to be. He has revived his infantile dependence pattern because he believes he has found a substitute. The female has the same illusion, of course. Being in love gives the individual this marvelous illusion of security that is derived from the regressive revival of that ancient dependence pattern.

The delusion of security that is derived from this mutual emotional response is so fantastic that Freud states the being in love state is actually a psychotic state. Because it is so common, he says, we hesitate to call it psychotic. It is psychotic because the lovers entertain this delusion that "if I have you, darling, the rest of the world doesn't matter." Each of the partners is the baby who is enjoying the security of being loved by the mother and each is getting this wonderful feeling of safety and security. Each is experiencing this unique feeling that, thus far, has nothing to do with sex.

Freud said that being in love was dangerous business, and I agree. It is paradoxical that the individual should feel his greatest security at the very time that he should be steering his way most cautiously, but the trouble is that he does not realize the illusory nature of the experience.

First, the security that the lover feels does not coincide with the facts of the matter. In his childhood he had every right to feel this security because the mother was taking care of him. But all the love in the world does not enable the girl to take care of the man or the man to take care of the girl in the sense that the mother took care of the needs of the infant. The security the lovers feel, I repeat, is an illusion.

Second, the price is too high. To the extent to which an individual actually sinks into the being in love state, he renounces the status of being grownup and tends to behave like an absolutely secure baby who is relying on his parents to take care of him. The result is a crippling of the personality of the individual. You cannot be both fully adaptively mature and fully in love at the same time. If he indulges himself in the being in love state, it may actually weaken his powers of adaptation and survival and reduce his adaptive machinery. From the point of view of survival, the being in love state is, as Freud states, a pathological phenomenon.

The third circumstance that lovers lose sight of is that most of the needs of the adult are of such a nature that another person can never satisfy them. Most needs can be satisfied only by the individual's own efforts. Thus, in spite of this dependence craving, there remains in the grownup person the urge to be independent and mature and self-reliant. This regressive yearning is always accompanied by the completely antagonistic striving: "Nonetheless, I want to remain a grownup and I want to have all the privileges of being a self-sustaining creature."

The fourth is that one ignores reality at one's own peril. In the proverbial situation, the lovers permit themselves to submerge in their enjoyment of sexual contact and feel no need to pay attention to what is going on around them because they possess this marvelous sense of security. Without this illusion they would not dare to be so indifferent to reality and perhaps harm themselves at times.

This basic phenomenon of falling in love is complicated. It is equally true that the enjoyment of sex—like other activities in which pleasure is involved—requires a security arrangement. You cannot be on call for an emergency and at the same time give yourself over in a carefree manner to enjoyment. The fact remains, however, that the security arrangement brought about by being in love is illusory and emotional rather than actual.

These are a few of the perils. Think of the tragedies to which this emotion has led. Think of the situations in which this dependency becomes a one-sided phenomenon, as when one of the two partners is madly in love and dependent and the other has ceased to share the feeling!

How an individual falls in love is indicative, in a very general way, of the degree of insecurity of the individual and of the extent of his need to seek security by infantile means. The greater the individual's insecurity, the greater his desire to fall into the being in love state. His need is to remedy this condition through being in love, by conjuring up a supporting and protecting agent. The more self-sufficient an individual is, male or female, the less capable will he or she be of falling violently in love, and the less inclined will he or she be to renounce self-sufficiency and independence for a form of dependence. In more self-reliant individuals, there usually will be a more equal relationship, characterized by mutual admiration and respect.

Of course, such a statement must be qualified. Some individuals who derive great pride from their self-reliance and self-esteem nonetheless seek this phenomenon as a sort of sanctuary where they can relax from the struggles of daily life, from the pain of striving for a self-assertive existence. Falling in love also depends on the individual's ability to form loving attachments, which, in turn, depends on his trust, security, and past experiences in loving relationships.

The being in love state satisfies a tremendous desire. It removes from life the burden of self-preservation. It throws the individual back into that early dependency state when he felt such a sense of security, and thus it produces a fulfillment of desire. When these emotions are combined with the pleasure attendant on the release of sexual tension, there comes a complete merger between what is a relapse to an infantile dependence adaptation with a grownup desire for sexual gratification.

These two components of the being in love state can fall asunder to such an extent that they can be in conflict with each other. It is as subject to disintegration as anything else. The being in love state contains a third factor, which is self-love. The satisfaction derived from one's ability to provide oneself with so much security and genital gratification is extraordinary. Self-esteem and self-confidence go up high if the individual loves and is being loved, which provides the enjoyment of the self that in classical psychoanalytic literature is described as narcissistic gratification. This reward of ego satisfaction plays a tremendous role in the phenomenon of love.

As you recall, the mother and father were the objects on whom the child shaped his or her ambitions. They were viewed as the models for that very perfection the individual was seeking for himself. The child was yearning for those features he believed were actually the features of Papa or Mama. Later on, he discovered them to be missing in the parents, and eventually he discovered them missing in himself. But the struggle to get and possess those features still continued.

This is the source of the tendency to read features of perfection into the love object that the individual wanted to have for himself. It is precisely because of this ego aspect of the state of being in love that the strange feature we call idealization of the love object occurs. Love paralyzes the individual's critical judgment. He cannot see the faults and shortcomings of his beloved because part of his enjoyment is derived from the act of making himself believe that the beloved is uniquely superb. By means of wishful thinking, the lover brings about the illusion of perfection, thereby satisfying his need.

Let us consider one other aspect of the being in love state. If love originally means a craving for dependence, how does this integration of the desire for security and the desire for a sex partner come about? The individual yearns for the one partner who will be at the same time a source of security and a source of sexual pleasure, because he has already experienced the pleasure of this combination in his childhood.

Originally, the manifold pleasures that the infant derives from contact with the mother have no genital orientation and even less genital content. The genital impulse is not yet sufficiently awakened to influence the relationship to any considerable extent. The whole pleasure-seeking pattern of the infant is organized, if at all, around the alimentary function and is under the primacy of the mouth.

But as intellectual maturity and over-all growth proceeds, around the age of four, five, or six, let us say, the genital need puts in its appearance sufficiently strongly to produce definite sensations of desire, especially in the boy. Along with this is the underlying natural phenomenon of attraction between the sexes, which is a fundamental law that is not yet fully understood. Seeking a gratification of this genital desire, the boy quite naturally turns to his mother, who has been the source of gratification in regard to any other need. Freud says that the mother has proved herself such a source of gratification that it is small wonder that the boy retains her as an object of desire for purposes of the Oedipus complex.

Since the genital need puts in its appearance in a very powerful manner during the period of factual dependence of the boy on the mother, this need for a genital partner merges with the early infantile need for a patron. This is a tremendous complication because he is forced to relinquish the forbidden genital impulse toward his mother. The integration has come into being only to be torn apart. The difficulty is to achieve this integration once again after puberty. To obtain it, one must get a partner with whom actual genital union is possible and with whom one can revive, in an illusory fashion, the features of the mother as a factor of security. The mother, who was a real factor of security, was a forbidden sexual partner. Later on one gets a real partner for sex and tries to bring about an illusory revival of the mother image as a factor of security.

Now here a complication arises in regard to the girl. The girl's first security is also derived from her mother so the early pattern is that the mother provides early emotional and factual security for both sexes, for the girl as much as for the boy. In the development of the girl, it is a turning point when the pressures of the genital need and the underlying natural phenomenon of attraction between the sexes makes her turn away from her mother and toward her father. By this she establishes the second model for security, based on her attachment to her father, in which a merger of security and sex is now possible, just as it was for the boy who did not have to change his partner to bring about this merger. The emotional security of the girl has switched from her mother to her father, and in our culture this corresponds to the factual situation. Her mother is her security model for bodily care. And her father, as the family provider, is her security model for overall security. This factor, of course, plays a role in the boy, too, but in our culture it is more emphasized in the case of the girl because girls are educated toward dependency, whereas boys are educated toward a self-sustaining existence.

By a selective process we do not understand clearly, the sense of security in the male is attached to the hair color of his mother, to her eyes, to the shape of her face, to the tone of her voice. Any conceivable feature may play a dominant role and become representative of the mother. A pattern is created that is representative of the mother. This stimulus pattern will certainly not correspond to an anatomic description of the mother. Rather it will be a result of collective attention and will thereby mirror the constitutional trend of the individual. Falling in love for security reasons, as apart from the pressure of sex, seems to be a mechanism organized similarly to the one that operates in sexual attraction.

A preferred security stimulus pattern representative of the mother will be constructed, and the dependency craving will actually be a search for refinding this pattern that exists in the unconscious. The total sexual phenomenon of falling in love comes about from a merger of these two patterns—the preferred sexual stimulus pattern and the preferred security stimulus pattern.

This explanation of the being in love state does not answer all the mysteries. There are the unconscious requirements in the individual that have to be satisfied. They too are the consequence of life experience; they too rest on the previous experience, both actual and imaginary, of the individual. By the time he is grown, patterns of favored and desired features and traits have established themselves in the individual.

## Marriage

This is a boundless topic. It is impossible within the confines of this survey course to do justice to any of these complex subjects. It is not easy to define marriage. Briefly, in the complex integrated unit that we call marriage, the individual seeks to get for himself emotional security, economic security, sexual gratification, and the privileges of parenthood.

I believe that psychological enlightenment, even a little better understanding of the underlying psychodynamics, may considerably improve marriage. Surely we would have less emotional trouble than we have now if the man and woman entering marriage knew how essential it was that there be constant compromise and adjustment of mutual conflicting interests, if they knew better than to expect of a human partnership that their interests would completely coincide, and if they knew what the advantages and the sacrifices are.

Recalling that human behavior can be integrated on the lower emotional level or the higher thought level, one of the outstanding phenomena in human life is the pleasure derived from love, behavior completely on the emotional level. Nonetheless, we are faced with the problem of subjecting these human feelings to intellectual guidance, of fitting them into a rational frame. The moment we view the rational frame clearly, we at least have a chance. So long as this intellectual rational frame is not clear, people are at the mercy of emotional impulses. The situation can become dominated by the basic pattern of love, frustration, and resentment. Then the problem is let loose completely in terms of emotional regulation and the intelligence has no chance of doing anything about it. But analysis of this situation actually becomes a tool whereby we can improve this whole institution and help to give people a better chance in marriage.

This integrative scheme—the effort to combine emotional and economic security needs with sexual needs and parenthood—seems to be the superior solution despite its handicaps. How to work that integrative scheme out in detail, where to make concessions and allowances, what liberties are to be secured, are other questions. This scheme can be carried out in patterns so widely different that they can hardly be recognized as still dealing with the basic integrative scheme of uniting a man and a woman to satisfy basic needs.

#### MUTUAL DEPENDENCE

In marriage, as distinguished from the romantic phenomenon of the being in love state, the individual seeks to gratify his emotional security needs and his factual security needs by making the marriage into an economic union. The two people want realistic security in addition to the emotional security. The individual wants marriage to provide him with an approximation of his early relationship with Mama, who gave him factual as well as emotional security. Insofar as the partners are able to fulfill these basic needs of each other and provide each other with sexual gratification, they are living in the state of mutual dependence that we call married love.

The ideal formula or requirement is that a self-reliant mature adult must not undermine his actual security by renouncing the basic privileges of being an adult. This is a sound requirement. Complete dependency of one partner on the other makes the dependent partner a child who functions with the helplessness and insecurity of the child. Accordingly, he will be precisely as dependent and lacking in independence as the intensity of the attachment is. The tendency to grow extremely dependent on the mate is unhealthy and dangerous.

Some measure of mutual dependence is a tremendous relief and blessing. The security derived from the presence of the other party should complement the individual's security. If a marriage is to be psychodynamically good, it must be capable of a range of flexibility and fluctuation. If for some reason the independent existence of the man is reduced and his dependence on his wife is increased, in sickness for instance, the wife is expected to devote more of herself to the service of the husband. In other circumstances the husband would help the wife through a crisis.

Marriage has a golden middle road that can be followed. The extreme absolute, self-relying, independent behavior which abhors the slightest degree of dependence on the partner is absurd, and, the complete dependence which abhors the duties and responsibilities of self-reliance is impossible. Why must human beings tend to extremes of behavior? This tendency is a fact, but it is also a mystery. Most of the difficulty in marriage is caused when each individual tends to go to the extreme and tends to avoid the complications of the middle road which means compromises and intelligent adjustment. Anthropology teaches us how many times man has evolved patterns for the institution of marriage that have actually been based on these extremes.

In an ideal marriage, husband and wife must be able to play any and all roles toward each other, within the general requirement that each should retain a certain measure of basic independent human self-reliance. This is the general frame: they must be able to become mutually dependent for transitional periods and again be more independent. This is highly complex. All conception of marriage in terms of any one rigid pattern (he wants his wife to be mother, she wants her husband to be father) is too one-sided to take care of the actual complexities.

As the "good" marriage goes along, it is almost inevitable that mutual dependency will increase and the sexual factor will gradually fade out. By the time a couple reaches the age of sixty or seventy, each may be so dependent on the other that they are like two babies. In a way, the more ideal and perfect the marriage, the greater the loss of independence on the part of each partner. I am spending time on this because our cultural values tend to obscure this fact.

If one is securing the advantages of mutual dependence, one cannot at the same time have the security derived from self-sustaining independence. If the man or woman indulges in extreme dependence, he cannot retain self-sustaining independence, simply because dependence and self-reliance are mutually exclusive. People want the impossible. They want the blessings of being taken care of and the privileges of independence. This is the reason the institution of marriage is such an extremely difficult one. To solve this problem is no easy job.

### COOPERATION VERSUS COMPETITION

Let us look at this emotional and economic security from another point of view. The essence of this security is the exclusion of competition and the accentuation of cooperation. Therefore the basic tendency of mutual competition, which characterizes our world, is suspended within this union. If two people form an economic unit, it follows that they cannot compete with each other. If the unit is to be successful they must cooperate and complement one another. And indeed emotionally and economically the marriage unit can be considered a sanctuary in which the individual seeks and finds relief from the daily competitive struggle in the community. When he comes home, he expects to find cooperation, not competition. And to the extent to which he finds it, the marriage is happy or not.

Now suppose the competition in the marriage outweighs the cooperation. The more egotistic, self-centered, self-loving, and narcissistic the partners, the greater is the danger that the marriage will go to pieces on grounds of mutual competition. Self-seeking people who indulge to a high degree in self-adoration, actors who are married to each other, can become hostile if either one is more prominently featured. They call it their artistic temperament. But if she is the first star and he is only the second leading man, murder is likely to result.

When the opportunity for entering into competition with each other is great, especially if the partners are unenlightened, problems arise. They are engaged in a murderous competition instead of a cooperative marriage. Competition is possible under any and all circumstances. There are girls who must compete with the male under any circumstances because they themselves want to be boys and can never give in to the fact that they are not. Or, when husband and wife are engaged in the same pursuit, in a competitive way, the temptation and the opportunity for competition between them may be greater.

### OFFSPRING

A strong positive factor that works to the advantage of marriage is the mutual interest in the offspring. The subject of parental love is so vast that I can take time here to make only a few observations. First, what is the difference between the maternal and paternal function? In the mammalia, at least, the first bodily care is for the female of the species who carries the fetus, gives birth to the child, and provides the newborn infant with food. In those early years the baby is chiefly there for the enjoyment of the mother.

This is by no means true of all species. Biology is indeed the realm of unlimited possibilities and there are many species in which the main burden of caring for the young is assigned to the father. In the early years of the life of the child, the chief role of the father is to be the head of the household and the main provider. But after infancy the father begins to participate more actively in the responsibilities of rearing the child.

Whenever we find such a situation of mutual dependence in nature, we see that the parties to the arrangement are bound to each other by ties of strong affection or love. We have seen that the baby's love for his parents is actually a life and death matter. These findings corroborate the common life observation that the baby needs parental love. All the abilities of the child are brought into being and developed by the sunshine of interest expended upon him by the father and mother.

Now this overwhelming interest that the parent feels for the child is derived from parental love. What is the nature of this reciprocal affection that the parents feel for the child? Does the thing that has been called maternal love, the maternal instinct, the maternal drive actually exist? I am prepared to maintain that all mammals, including the human being, have a very powerful parental drive.

Let me remind you that every variety of human behavior is subject to disturbances, and there are certainly disturbances in the manifestations of the parental drive. Do we know anything about maternal behavior as a driving force that can be linked up with other forms of behavior? Until we learn more about these "drives," all discussion about them and all analysis of the relationship between them are speculation.

Clinical observation tells us that we are not dealing here with simple quantitative relationships. We see that the maternal interest may rise and fall as a consequence of vicissitudes in the sex and love areas. A mother may love her child more because she adores her husband, and a mother may love her child more because she hates her husband. Maternal love can be intensified by a happy, healthy life on the part of the mother, and it can be intensified, in a morbid way, by the mother's frustration.

The desire to reproduce is made up of many motivations, in addition to the basic biological significance of survival of the species. This is one of its utility values. In egoistic terms, it has other utility values. On one level, especially in primitive societies, offspring represent old-age security for the parents.

Offspring are connected with so-called narcissistic interests. Your sons and sometimes your daughters can fulfill your desire for immortality by carrying out your dynastic interests. They can carry on the rule, carry on the estate, carry on the enterprise, carry on the name, and so forth.

# CHAPTER 14

# Mores of Sex and Marriage

ANTHROPOLOGY HAS ADDED MUCH TO OUR KNOWLEDGE OF SEXUAL AND marital mores. My comments about sexual mores have just one purpose, to save you from considering those things in the midst of which you live as *the* natural. We are all conditioned in a certain way. But many other varieties of culture have existed and do exist, and the vast majority of human beings live in entirely different cultures.

## Sexual Morality

The sexual mores of our present-day American society are going through a revaluation. In its monolithic form Victorian sexual morality was undermined by the work of psychoanalysis. One of the great cultural feats effected by Freud was to break down these mores. Prior to that, sex life was not even dealt with in textbooks of medicine and physiology. Prudishness went so far that the discussion of reproduction began with the fertilization of the egg by the sperm. It was only a couple of hundred years ago that an obstetrician was not permitted to examine a woman except under a blanket.

Sexual liberation got a new push through psychoanalysis. Today, sexual attitudes of all kinds are being rapidly changed. We know that history seems to move in cycles. World War I and its aftermath were forces that aided the undermining of Victorian morality. In the 1920s came the first demand for enlightened education and greater sexual freedom. In this postwar period women attained an independence and sexual freedom that had been unthinkable a generation earlier. The main problem of contraception was alleviated about that time with the introduction of birth control devices for the woman. There was a

period in the defeated countries, such as Germany, Hungary, and
Austria, when the pendulum swung to the opposite extreme and an
excessive libertinism replaced the former rigidity. In that generation,
sex was completely reduced to unmitigated sexual pursuit, and attitudes destroyed almost completely the possibility of merging it with
love. Sexual promiscuity was the order of the day.

This swing toward freedom was again accelerated under the influence of World War II. War brings a breakdown of the existing morality. The soldier who does not know whether he will be alive tomorrow
thinks he has the right to have a good time. After the war is over,
much of the changing attitudes persist.

The mores that existed in Victorian society were allowed to develop
because we live in a male society in which the male, as the more powerful, bends the moral law to his own ends. Three sets of sexual mores
usually go hand in hand. These are the attitudes of the society toward
sexual activity in children, including self-stimulation; toward premarital
sexual experience; and toward marriage as a monogamous arrangement.
If the requirement of premarital chastity goes, sooner or later the sex
freedom permitted children will increase and the interpretation of
monogamy will become liberalized. In one society you will have an
extreme suppression and regimentation of sex in all its phases. In
another you will have liberty, and then freedom permeates all the
phases. You cannot, in other words, exercise regimentation in one
phase, liberty in another, regimentation in the third, and so forth.
So the natural tendency is either to have an extreme regimentation of
all three sets of mores, as exemplified by the Victorian era, or complete
freedom, as seen in so many preliterate societies.

But this is only the tendency. Anthropology and social history show
that sexual mores contain an example of everything. The range of
sexual mores is infinite. Here you are a little more restricted, there
you are allowed to do this but not allowed to do that. So it goes.
In all monogamously structured societies, the sexual temptation emanat-
ing from the presence of other possible sexual partners is very strong.

Many societies have some sort of escape vent. Frequently, promiscuity is sanctioned under religious auspices during certain limited periods.
The Mardi Gras carnival is a derivative of an old custom.

Victorian society was not wise enough to arrange socially sanctioned
outlets. It would inevitably happen that one of the partners in an
unsatisfactory marriage just could not carry the burden of such mis-
placement and would break out in some way or other. The more di-

vorce was rendered difficult by the law or by the presence of a large number of children, the more these problems were solved by clandestine love affairs. The emphasis was on hiding everything from the community, which, nonetheless, naturally knew everything.

The net result was that regardless of what the marital setups were, the sexually most endowed male and female or the most demanding people eventually got together. It is entirely possible to define adultery as the right man or woman in the wrong place. In the early days of psychoanalysis, books were filled with discussions of neurotic difficulties due to sexual frustration.

At best, the demands of monogamy cause complications. But all this was accentuated by the way young people in Victorian middle-class society went about choosing a mate. Because of the requirement of premarital chastity, both parties bought a cat in the sack. Knowing nothing about themselves, their mates, their sexual endowments, tragedies of sexual maladjustment were inevitable. The so-called love match was an exception. Generally, the selection of a marital partner was guided almost exclusively by economic considerations.

### INCEST AND THE OEDIPUS COMPLEX

In the development of sexual morality, the outstanding factor, the root of all sexual morality, is the incest taboo—the prohibition against the mother's sleeping with her son, the daughter's sleeping with her father, and the siblings sleeping with each other. Sexual morality appears to be more or less an extension of this fundamental taboo. A study of sexual mores must actually begin with an anthropological study of the incest taboo.

The fact that incest taboos are taken far more seriously by primitive peoples than they are among civilized communities indicates that these prohibitions are no refinements that come with increasing civilization and literacy. The early anthropologists were amazed to find that in many primitive societies incest was punished by death and that the incest taboo was in the very center of legislation.

The observers of higher vertebrates—monkeys and apes—tell us that apes brought up in the same cage lose their sexual desire for one another, and it is difficult to arouse them to engage in sexual activity with each other. How, then, can there be maximum sex desire on the part of the child for his parents?

A penetrating psychoanalytic study of this question—the first attempt to bring depth psychology into an anthropological study—is Freud's *Totem and Taboo*. Freud says that in all primitive societies this dread of incest is understandable in the face of such primitive legislation, which could begin only after human beings started living in families.

The old incest taboos must have started in religion because there could have been no separation between religion and jurisprudence in the codes of early man. The incest taboo seems to be included in the Decalogue. It appears in two places in the Bible. In Exodus it reads: "Honor thy father and thy mother that thy days may be long upon the land which the Lord, thy God, giveth thee." Then again in Deuteronomy, it reads: "Honor thy father and thy mother as the Lord, thy God, has commanded thee, that thy days may be prolonged and that it may go well with thee in the land which the Lord, thy God, giveth thee." The striking thing about this ruling is that this is the only one of the Ten Commandments that talks of a reward. This may be a camouflaged version of the incest taboo.

The most important point in the development of incest taboos, I hold, is the superior power of the male, and that male jealousy created the sexual morality. The superior physical power of the male is responsible for the fact that through the ages of human development, sexual morality and legal institutions have been shaped to suit the ends of the stronger partner.

Male jealousy was the foundation upon which he erected sexual morality and made it into religion and law. "No son is to be allowed to sleep with his mother. The mother belongs to me." Only much later did it come to prohibiting the father-daughter incest because the father was not anxious to restrict his own freedom of action. It follows that he had an interest also in restricting sexual contact between brother and sister among his children.

That incest is a question of power is shown in the social customs which developed under the influence of family relations, such as the right of the overlord to have the virginity of the serf girl. The incest problem, however, is far from solved by pointing out the influence of superior power on the shaping of law, morale, and order.

The claim that incestuous events are the cause of neurosis was overstated. For the most part, I see them only as precipitating causes. The topic of incest is of particular importance because in the early years of psychoanalysis all theories about neuroses were simplified to the statement that the incest temptation in contemporary society is tremendous. For a while, it was believed that many cases of psychoneurosis were due to actual incest. Freud later modified this position and says that these patients were experiencing incest fantasies that they purported to be real.

Classical psychoanalysis defined the so-called Oedipus complex. It held that the cultural necessity of suppressing the incest temptation is so heavy a burden that a large number of people fail in its execution. Freud went so far as to say that human beings found it difficult ever to be fully happy again, once the incest barriers were driven into human sexuality. This holds to the tenet that the failure to suppress successfully the incestuous desire is the nucleus complex of every neurosis and the source of all neurotic disorders. The affectionate and nonsexual relationship between child and parent was called the Oedipus complex, and the whole phenomenon of infantile dependence on the parent was expressed in terms of a sexual language.

The theory that infantile dependence consists only of a desire to have the mother or the father as a sex partner is an unfortunate generalization. But Freud, in one of his less quoted papers, says that this fundamental tenet should be modified and suggested that the preoedipal phase of development also has to be considered in the development of neuroses.

We cannot understand the neuroses as a consequence of only the cultural regimentation of the sexual drive. As I see it, the error in the Oedipus complex doctrine is the attempt to explain everything in terms of a genital drive. Rather, the nucleus of every neurosis is infantile dependence.

## Polygamous Marriage

Let us look briefly at the polygamous society. Every new lover or mistress of course means polygamy in any society. But polygamy in the anthropological sense means simultaneous marriage between one man and several women, marriage between one woman and two or more men, or one group of women and one group of men having sexual access to the members of the other group.

In most polygamous societies, the arrangement of one male with many wives has prevailed. In these societies, the all-powerful male has the power to subjugate women into complete slavery. We know very little about the psychology of women who have been kept in harems although it has been rumored that much homosexual contact existed among these women.

Group marriage is the arrangement in which a small group of women have sexual privileges with a large group of men in one large household. Ralph Linton says the Marchesa Society lived under this social system for centuries, the basis of it being an unusual ratio of two and a half men to one woman. The alternative is female infanticide. This practice is an historical fact, but it is hidden. They are forced to do something like this because the food supply on the island where they live is so limited. At some point the wise men must have figured out that one means of population control was to limit the number of childbearing women.

In group marriage, how do they manage to control the most elementary male instinct of jealousy? The economic factor seems to be the answer. The ambitious boy wants to marry an attractive girl who seems likely to be able to attract more and more auxiliary husbands. This is to the boy's interest because all the auxiliary husbands work for him. There is premarital sexual freedom in this society, and marriages to come are foreshadowed by the gangs that are already formed in puberty.

There is no emotional factor involved in the physical sex. How could there be? If this man were in an emotional relationship with this woman, he would kill the others. So the whole arrangement of rationed physical sex is maintained at the cost of the emotional side.

# CHAPTER 15

# The Primordial Self

～～～～～～～～～～～～～～～～～～～～～～～～～～～～～～～～～～～～～～～～

THE CONSCIOUS ORGANISM'S AWARENESS OF ITSELF IS THE CENTRAL PHE-nomenon of human existence. I believe that self-awareness emerges from and is sustained by proprioceptive sensations. Perceiving his mus-cular activities, the infant discovers *himself* as the one who acts. This circular pattern can be interpreted as the psychodynamic expression of innate nervous circuits of the brain. The infant's most vigorous and gratifying muscular activity is sucking at his mother's breast. Thus, in our mammalian species it is through sucking that the organism first achieves awareness of itself.

The circular pattern of self-awareness and willed action is the founda-tion upon which the organism develops its systemic self-image, called the action self. By combining kinesthetic and other sensory in-formation in communicative exchange with its human environment, the organism learns to recognize itself as a cohesive and enduring being, separate from its mother and the rest of the world about it. The self-image is formed as the organism's attention focuses on the equipment it uses for controlling its environment. At psychodynamic levels, the action self thus comes to represent the total organism in action.

The action self undergoes profound developmental changes. En-chanted by its success in sucking, the young organism attributes un-limited power to its willed action and pictures itself as an omnipotent being. Its early self-image is called the primordial self. We now skip a number of years to the grownup individual. The primordial self is now shrunk to a residual primordial self, and removed to the nonre-porting process where it exists for the rest of the individual's life. From a reality-tested picture of the organism the action self then separates a thought picture of what the organism desires to become (ego ideal).

However, the dividing line between the thought picture of what one is (tested self) and the blueprint of what one would like to be (desired self) remains precarious throughout the life span. No human being has an accurate estimation of himself. A little bit of illusion is always cherished. The primordial or infantile self remains within the individual as a revivable potentiality.

This illusory conception of himself by the individual is a corollary to the remarkable biological situation—that of being taken care of—in which the baby finds himself. It is an adaptation product, an adaptation to the unique situation of being taken care of.

The moment the responsibility for survival is lifted from the shoulders of a living creature who possesses the intellectual and emotional instrumentality for developing mental life, maximum expansion, unlimited by any reality testing, can occur. The realities of the infant's life are all assumed by the parent. Thus the infant, unaware of the role of the parents, probably nurtures the illusion that whatever happens does so by virtue of his own wishes. Paradoxically, it is in a sense realistic for the baby to consider himself omnipotent.

Surrealistic art renounces the coordination and integration which is characteristic of the adult mind and proposes instead to depict the activity of the nonreporting mind and express the infantile way of looking at life. Since infantile impressions are more ancient and stronger than any later impressions, they represent, in a psychological sense, the most "realistic realism" man is capable of, and constitute a wonderful reality. Never again is the extreme pleasure value of this love of self attained. The self loves itself, appreciates itself, and thereby becomes both subject and object of this emotional phenomenon.

In the classical psychoanalytical literature this self-love is called narcissism, a term originally used by Havelock Ellis. It was used in connection with the adult whose behavior was conspicuous, almost to the point of aberration, in its extreme attention to his own bodily self. Freud later discovered that this apparent aberration is only one of a tremendous number of manifestations of an attitude common to all mankind, and he considered self-love the fundamental condition with which the human being starts out in early life. Freud also established the connection between narcissism and love for other people in his concept of object libido.

The child's illusion is that he has only to wish things and they will happen. Or, he has only to raise his hand and signal for something and it will appear. Gradually, the child begins to understand that these occurrences are not the result of the magic power of his wishes and gestures. He begins to see that it is not the omnipotence of his thoughts and signals that bring the desired results. It is his parents who provide the fulfillment or realization of his needs.

During alimentary behavior certain behavior tendencies are brought into play. One is impatience. This is an expression of the underlying omnipotence belief. "If I am omnipotent, I want it at once." To have to wait is an offense against one's omnipotent conception of oneself. Impatient people get frustrated at waiting and immediately react with rage. This stems from the omnipotence idea of oneself that one never quite discards.

The interaction of the omnipotence idea with an alimentary situation may lead to the development of envy and rivalry. All envy is primarily breast envy. It is the reaction of the child to the feeding of the younger sibling who now has the breast. More generally, breast envy means all the special attention an infant gets. Wanting bitterly to retrieve privileges once possessed and now lost, the child puts up a desperate fight. In psychoanalytic literature envy was described as sublimated oral eroticism. But let us go beyond the breast and recognize that envy and rivalry both derive from the egocentric megalomaniac conception of the self that says, "I and only I can have it. If she has it, I want to take it away." "If it is something I had before and now he has it, I want to get it back." The feeding situation is merely the occasion that brings this egocentric-rooted drive into play.

Impatience, envy, and rivalry are all practiced, learned, and developed in the feeding situation. But they are not derivatives of the oral drive— they are derivatives of the egocentric outlook.

## Delegated Omnipotence

At some point the infant begins to realize that all is not the result of his magic power, and a significant change takes place in the infantile delusion of omnipotence. He now begins to ascribe omnipotence to the parents. Strictly speaking, the delegated omnipotence is only loosely held when the child goes through the oppositional stage, but to some extent the child may fall back on it all his life, the way he does with his dependency on parents or parent substitutes. You have heard children say, "Mama knows everything." "My daddy can do anything." The clue to what is happening lies in the child's emphasis on the pronoun my. What the child does is to change the construction of his belief in his omnipotence. He has not abandoned his belief in his own omnipotence as irrational or absurd. He has not renounced his belief in his own omnipotence. What he does is to delegate his own omnipotence to his parents, by means of which he can sustain that old belief against refutation of the facts.

The omnipotence of the parents is recognized on condition that they are going to exercise their magnificence for the benefit of the child. The outsider sees a helpless and dependent creature thrown on the resources of the mother. The situation the baby sees is that of delegated omnipotence—illusion that the mother is like an extended arm because she is an agent of omnipotence who performs for the baby.

The parent is considered omnipotent only as a proxy because he is the almighty agent of the really almighty self. The parents are considered omnipotent, not for the sake of their own glory but for the egotistic reasons of the baby. The ages for these stages are not known, but by the stage of oppositional behavior the child realizes the parents will not always do as he wishes. There is evidence that the child no longer feels omnipotent around one year when he becomes anxious at separation from his mother.

This construction throws an important psychological light on religion. Man derives security from the idea of being taken care of and having almighty agents at his disposal because he had this situation in infancy. Throughout history people have developed religious ideas, deities, whose most important feature is their omnipotence. These deities are all venerated with the emphasis placed on the pronoun my. My God is the One who will perform for my benefit, who will help me, and who will be, in other words, the executive agent of my omnipotence.

It requires a highly developed level of thought and an understanding of the findings of science to renounce the idea of a personal God. Such sacrifice cuts into the flesh of human beings. When emergencies and problems beyond scientific solution occur—old age, sickness—then the miracle is needed and the nonbeliever finds it desirable to have a God to whom to pray.

## The Dependence Adaptation of the Child

The infant is dependent for his survival on the services of the parents. This situation is unique in that the human infant is born into the world in a lesser state of perfection and development than are the young of other species. So great is the necessity for parents, particularly the mother, in this first period that the relationship is safeguarded by all sorts of natural arrangements, the most important of which is the strong tie of affection that attaches the baby to the mother and the mother to the baby. This affection binds them one to the other. The baby has an insatiable demand for affection, and the mother has a great need to expend affection on the baby.

Unquestionably, for the child to survive he has to be fed constantly by affection, which the baby is equipped to absorb and by which he is able to proceed in a state of healthy development. That the unwanted and unloved child dies is a long known fact. In psychoanalytic literature it was first emphasized by Ferenczi, and in recent years many investigations have validated this subject.

Biologically, this relationship is a security arrangement for the baby. Psychologically, it is an emotional situation—one of affection. The security during the early period is characterized by reliance and dependence on the parents. The child gets bodily care from his mother and the needs of the family are provided by the father. During this period, the child is not self-sustaining. He lives on the labor of others, the hosts being the parents. The significant aspect of this period is the child's attempt to get the parents to do everything for him the way he wants it.

This situation extends into the grownup who retains the craving for dependency, the reliance on a superior authority, the belief in the existence of a parental agency that is going to perform for him. In sharp contrast is the situation of the adult without a Papa and Mama, who has to sustain himself by his own efforts and who, in order to bring about the desired changes in the world, must acquire a materialistic technique in conformity with the laws of nature.

The whole period of growth and development sees the human being living in two different environments. The first is the nursery—organized for the child's benefit, dominated by the psychological techniques of ingratiation and expiation and administered by the superior person on whose benevolent cooperation the whole system depends. The second —to which the growing infant and the adolescent must shift—is the environment of the adult where all the laws of self-sustaining existence come into operation. Now in this adult world he must be self-reliant and function under a set of rules about sex and assertion different from those under which he grew up.

This transition from a world in which one's omnipotence has powerful agents, namely, one's parents, into a hostile world in which one has to fend for oneself is painful. So much so that few men are able to effect the change consistently. Every human being may get into a psychological situation in which he reverts to this earlier pattern of dependence adaptation. The adult never relinquishes the possibility of falling back for security on the resources of childhood, of calling on and invoking parental care.

Neurotic behavior is saturated with the unconscious presence or relapse to the infantile patterns in which security is based on the ministrations of the parents. The neurotic is living in the nursery, calling on the resources of Papa or Mama, tending to forget and negate his own resources. He neglects the grownup attitude toward the world which requires a materialistic technique (technology) in favor of psychology (ingratiation and expiation). By resorting to ingratiation and expiation he hopes that the authority figures will do the rest. In treatment of these patients and in all neuroses, this tendency to relapse to the infantile pattern is a central phenomenon. Neurotic behavior and behavior under treatment are characterized by this strong tendency to revive the pattern of escape through delegated magic. In neurotic or overreactive behavior, the following triad occurs: dependency adaptation, excessive emergency emotions, and loss of self-reliance.

## Delegated Identification

In human beings the process of learning is probably based on delegated identification. The child admires what the father does. He has an inkling that it is not I who does that. From this delegated identification, the child moves to imitative identification. The core of the human being is so illusional that what we admire enough to learn appears to be only what we already know. The line of development is from the primordial self through delegated identification to emulative identification and actual imitation. The emulated omnipotent parent representation is the ego ideal. The tested self is gradually built up in the process of learning, plus motivation and direction, which come from his desired self. Whenever the individual's desires are fulfilled through his own action, he has a sense of self-reward or satisfaction and feels self-reliant. Self-reliance is the characteristic of the normal adult.

# CHAPTER 16

# The Training of the Child

# and the Power Struggle

No MATTER HOW PEACEFUL THINGS ARE ON THE SURFACE, EVERY HOUSE-hold is the scene of a tenacious power struggle between the child and the parents. The parents are determined to civilize this unbridled little being and train him for adult living. The child is equally determined to retain his pleasures, to express his self-assertive tendencies, and to convert the prohibitive parents into obedient servants.

Ideally, the child should be gently coaxed or persuaded to do what the parents want, but all the while feel independent, self-reliant, secure, and spontaneous. Naturally this is impossible. If the parents make few demands and give much love, the struggle between parents and child will be mild, though this again depends on the constitution of the child. The child, of course, has to accept most of the rules and regulations of society to live with other people.

The initial struggle for control is usually waged over toilet-training, but the struggle can begin over anything that the child and his parents differ about. It can start over eating habits, over going to bed, or over putting away toys. Freud built up his theory of the "anal character" on the idea that the behavior modality developed on the toilet can extend to other areas of behavior in the life of the adult.

I will use the battle of the toilet to illustrate the workings of the power struggle. The struggle begins when the child is forced to defecate regardless of his own peristalsis. He may respond in one of two ways—either with fear or rage or else with a submissive or a self-assertive manner. If he responded in a fearful, submissive way, he will try to defecate and regiment his bowels according to his mother's wishes. This happens when he is too afraid of the consequences to resist, thereby losing the mother's love and facing punishment. So to avoid punishment and loss of love, and gain the pleasure of receiving love through obedience, he accepts the time schedule and other conditions imposed by the mother. The anxiety reaction to her demands leads to the submissive policy of trying to placate her and retain her favor.

The defiance policy, rooted in rage and leading to temper tantrums, is self-assertive. "No, I am not going to do what you want me to. I am going to have my way." The reward for the defiance is pride in having his own way. It expresses itself in all the negative and self-willed behavior that is characterized by the answer, "No!" What the child wants is to be loved by the parent and yet have his own way. "Mother should continue to love me and let me do what I want." This rage and anger leading to defiant behavior is actually not a hostile impulse but a coercive impulse, the aim of which is to dragoon the mother into submission.

Actually, this is not an either/or matter. What usually happens is that the child's toilet behavior oscillates between submission and defiance, between fear and rage. Over and over again, the cycle is played out. The child tries to rise against the pressure of authority. He fails and is dragooned by fear into submissive behavior. His rage gets strong again and he makes another defiant attempt. Even if the child is successful in his defiance, a breakdown sometimes occurs, and an intermittent picture ensues of alternating anxiety-controlled and rage-controlled behavior. Even in instances where anxiety seems to prevail, the rage is not completely out of the picture—it is suppressed and ready at any time to take over.

Freud assumed that bowel obedience forces the child to relinquish evacuative pleasure by "sublimating" the desire for it or by stemming its tide by "reaction formations," and that these developments were then reflected in the shaping of obsessive symptoms. Bowel defiance, he thought, increased the child's evacuative pleasure. The fact is that children forced into bowel obedience enjoy the evacuative act just as much as other children, whereas bowel defiance is often enough initially an effort to avoid pain rather than insure pleasure. This occurs when the act of defecation is rendered painful by an anal fissure, constipation, or some local disturbance. With her insistence on bowel regularity, the mother hurts not the child's evacuative pleasure but his pride in having his own way. Also, one sees the obsessional patients whose bowel training has been uneventful, but who are nevertheless marked by the same conflict between guilty fear and defiant rage.

The all-important phenomenon is that while the battle of the chamber pot is going on the emphasis and interest of the child is actually in the fight itself. The fight with the disciplinary authority is started by the child's desire to evacuate when he pleases. But as the fight goes on it becomes an end in itself. The child is interested more in this struggle for control than in what started the conflict. This is a very important psychological feature, which has been strikingly demonstrated in animal experiments by Jules Masserman. Animals hitting and fighting each other for the breast later continued fighting and forgot all about the food. The child too may get in a power struggle with one of his siblings with the same result as with an adult.

The emotions the child experiences in the battle of the toilet and in other habit-training areas will have a great influence on how the so-called anal character leads his life. I refer here to the individual who reacts in an extreme way to extreme environmental pressure. The result brings about a morbid preoccupation with the authority of the parent. The persistence of the power-struggle attitudes prevented him from developing into a normally self-reliant adult. If his fear is the stronger emotion, he will exhibit submissiveness, overcleanliness, orderliness, punctuality, regularity, pedantry, and the like in his adult life. If his rage was greater, he will act in negative, untidy, negligent, unreliable, and defiant ways. What the actual symptoms are depend on what the parents stress. If the emergency emotions were both very strong, he will continue to vacillate between submissive behavior and defiant behavior, depending on the relative weight of the guilty fear and the defiant rage at the moment, just as he did as a child.

Now the insight into the adult who is still oriented in terms of toilet behavior or other habit-training struggles is brilliantly indicated in Freud's observation that all these qualities come out "in the performance of petty duty." These are the individuals who do not acquire a mature scale of values, those who unwittingly and unknowingly continue to act as if the items of the nursery are the most important things in life. For them, going or not going to the toilet, soiling or not soiling one's pants, being on time or not being on time, are the all-important issues. For the adult so oriented, the whole sphere of childhood in which this demand for obedience is established continues to motivate him, like an anachronism, in grownup life. These people remain orderly in all those issues that were issues in childhood. They do not see that they are no longer the primary matters in grownup life.

If the pattern of defiance continues in adult life, the individual's development is hampered because he still uses the yardstick of the nursery, still believes he is under infantile discipline, still behaves as if his major interest in life were defying authority figures and thereby obtaining freedom for self-assertive activities. Such people will inevitably respond to demands made on them in the performance of small duties with an automatic note of defiance—but in the major concerns of life they may be very obedient and subservient. Their self-assertive defiance is reserved for the issues of the nursery.

In obsessional neuroses, this is the source of magnificent symptoms. All pedantry and all orderliness, all interest, in fact, is concentrated on those matters whose execution has become mechanical in most grownups, and all essentials are permitted to fall by the wayside, because all attention is still concentrated on the item around which the toilet struggle in the nursery was fought.

One example of the behavior of the so-called anal character is that he handles money in a manner said to resemble alternating diarrhea and constipation. Fits of avarice and fits of prodigious spending alternate with each other, both violating the requirements of the sane, rational handling of money. So far as I am concerned, the hoarding-splurging pattern has nothing "anal" about it. Both activities are consequences of those same emergency emotions that produce the phenomenon of constipation or diarrhea in the anal sphere. If we keep the emphasis on the emotions where it properly belongs, we will recognize a spending bout as the anxiety phenomenon that it is.

In summary, the so-called anal character is not a grownup still dominated by anal eroticism but an individual still reacting with the emergency reactions of the child—the anxiety and rage, the submissive and self-assertive responses—that were brought into play on the occasion of the power struggle waged between the child and his mother over habit-training. The anal area is one battlefield on which this battle can be fought out, but the essence of the struggle is the pressure of the mother on the one hand and the emergency emotions of the child on the other. Behavior developed by the child on the occasion of toilet-training can become a model for behavior in related areas. This I view as the meaning of the construction of the "anal character."

In the constant interrelationship between child and parent, the power struggle is always present, depending on factors in parent and child for its mildness or severity. In this atmosphere the individual forms his attitudes toward cooperation, competition, domination, and submission. He also develops his sexual and ethical values. More important, the power struggle and conscience, the weapons of the parents, have a great deal to do with the image the child forms of himself and the rest of the world.

CHAPTER **17**

# The Development

# of Conscience

IF A SOCIETY IS TO SURVIVE, IT MUST IMPOSE MORAL SELF-RESTRAINT UPON its members to increase their fitness for peaceful cooperation with one another and with the group as a whole. The essential thing about conscience is that it is a combination of the interplaying automatic mechanisms of self-restraint, self-punishment, and self-reward. The mechanism of conscience must be looked upon as an operation of the emergency function, which is built on the principle of anticipation. Just as the emotions continue the trend established on the hedonic level of anticipating impending injury, so the mechanism of conscience anticipates objection, restraint, and punishment from the parents. It is both rational and emotional. The mechanism of conscience is shown schematically in Table 2 below.

The story of conscience is one of the most confused in psychoanalytic literature. We can hope to bring more clarity into this matter, although we cannot match the unrivaled beauty and emotional impact of the theory of the superego. Freud's view in *Civilization and Its Discontents* is that "There is a voice of conscience that is the voice of the father." The connection of the development of conscience with the particular aims of incestuous desire makes a fascinating story. It is to Melanie Klein's credit to have shown that there is development of conscience long before there are incestuous desires; conscience probably starts at about age one year and a half.

Conscience originates in the child's relationship with his parents and other disciplinary authorities. It continues to grow and operate in the individual's relationship with his society. Originally it prevents and repairs damage and anticipates requirements of the parents. Later it automatizes responses through the cumulative effect of repeated experience. Much later it aids in setting standards for the young and in fostering community mutual aid. The continued function of conscience is to facilitate peaceful cooperation with society by helping the individual become an ethical person and a law-abiding citizen.

## TABLE 2 The Restraining Mechanism of Conscience, Failure, Repair, and Miscarried Repair

The Restraining Mechanism of Conscience:
fear of conscience (fear of inescapable punishment) → self-restraint mirroring prohibitions imposed upon the child → obedience (law-abiding behavior) → rising self-respect and moral pride → parental (social) reward.

Failure and Repair:
temptation plus defiant rage overrule fear of conscience → disobedience → guilty fear → falling self-respect and moral pride.

Dynamic Composition of Guilty Fear:
awareness of guilt + agonizing suspense of inescapable punishment + longing for parents' loving care + venting retroflexed rage upon self

Repair:
guilty fear → expiatory behavior → parental (social) forgiveness → rising self-respect and moral pride.

Miscarried Repair:
retroflexed rage in guilty fear → defiant rage over repressed guilty fear (guilty rage) → reproachful behavior.

The prohibitions and requirements imposed on the child by his parents form an integral part of the social and cultural system under which the family lives. These parental rules, while varying in different societies, must be and are enforced everywhere by reward and punishment. The parent forbids the child to do certain things that the child likes to do and commands him to do some things that he does not like to do. "Don't do this. If you do, I won't love you, and I shall punish you." The warning can be interpreted as a threat of restraint and punishment.

By means of anticipation, the warning of the authority becomes self-warning. So the child makes an anticipatory move. When he again wants to play with the china he has been forbidden to play with, he now hears Mama's "no, no, no" inside himself. Self-warning leads to self-restraint or self-control, and self-restraint can lead to self-reward, the enjoyment of being a "good" baby. Our own civilized behavior is based on this mechanism. It is what I call the prophylactic branch of emergency control because it prevents the individual from getting into trouble.

Reward puts a pleasure premium on behavior, making it attractive and desirable; punishment puts a pain sanction on unwanted behavior. The whole reward and punishment system is based on the fundamental hedonic regulation by the pain-pleasure principle.

## Punishment

Let us examine punishment first. All punishment amounts to saying to the child, "I shall not love you." It is a threat, since love is a guarantee of services forthcoming from the parent and assures the security of the child. If this threat is not effective, the child is spanked, thereby adding infliction of pain.

Punishment is applied in two types of cases. The first occurs when the child is ordered not to do what he himself wants to do. He is forbidden to tear up his brother's book or break his sister's doll. The second situation arises when a child is ordered to do what he himself has no desire to do, such as going to bed. The latter situation is the more important from the psychological point of view. The parent sets up a threat of punishment. Between the opposing forces of the desire and the punishment, a conflict is set up in the child. The outcome depends upon whether fear of punishment or desire to perform a certain act is stronger.

As long as the child's fear of punishment remains contingent upon being caught, it operates as a fear of detection. Hence whenever he yields to the temptation, augmented as a rule by his defiant rage, he will try to "get away with" his disobedience by hiding from authorities. An adult who never rose above this mechanism of self-restraint will behave in much the same way. Self-restraint through fear of detection is not yet a mechanism of conscience. We may call it a mechanism of preconscience. On the other hand, the self-reward of self-respect and rising moral pride is already a mechanism of conscience.

At some point, the child arrives at the conviction that punishment is inescapable because his parents see, hear, and know everything. The stronger the child's primordial belief in his own omnipotence, the more powerful this idea will be. The automatized version of this fear of inescapable punishment must be recognized as the fear of conscience. The fear of conscience is the most effective and socially the most valuable mechanism of self-restraint.

The philosopher Kant was overwhelmed by the existence of what he calls "moral law within." Our analysis shows that such a law can exist because the fear of conscience is a fear of inescapable punishment. While hiding it from himself, Kant nonetheless gives this secret away in his famous passage, "Two things fill the mind with ever new and increasing admiration and awe, the oftener and the more steadily we reflect on them, the starry heavens above and the moral law within."

Poetry and folklore praise the sun and the stars as the eyes of God. For instance, in the sonnet "Shall I compare thee to a summer's day?" Shakespeare calls the sun the "eye of heaven." The two things juxtaposed in Kant's conscious thought may have been casually connected in the nonreporting forephrase of this thought: "With those all-seeing eyes above me there must be the moral law within me."

Belief in divine omnipotence strengthens the child's fear of conscience but is not necessary. With progressing automatizations, obedience tends to elicit at once the self-reward of self-respect and rising moral pride leading to self-reliance. This mechanism must be reinforced from time to time by parental reward.

Temptation may release the child's repressed rage or elicit a rage of frustration and thus make him defiant. By defeating his fear of conscience, this combination may drive him to disobedience. However, he soon discovers that it is one thing to override a fear of detection and quite another to override a fear of conscience. Although both satisfied a prohibited desire, the difference is that fear of conscience leaves no hope for escape. Here there is no problem of detection; the child knows he did wrong and punishment is inescapable. The pain of awareness is intensified by his desire to reinstate himself in the good graces of his parents. Even his defiant rage recoils and turns inward against him, causing him to heap self-reproach upon self-reproach. We call these feelings of self-reproach, which are motivated by a desire for forgiveness, *guilty fear*. The phrase is taken from Shakespeare.

The child is taught by his parents what to do about his guilty fear. He must make a confession, show remorse, receive his due punishment, and ask forgiveness. Thereupon his parents take him back into their loving care. We call this sequence *expiatory behavior;* it is an emotional mechanism of repair. Accordingly, guilty fear is not a preventive signal but a reparative one. By successive stages of anticipation and automatization the expiatory pattern becomes firmly fixed. In one of its versions, the child seeks forgiveness by self-punishment, which he may execute automatically without conscious knowledge.

Guilty fear consciously is the feeling of self-reproach. In the nonreporting process, guilty fear contains the following elements: the anticipated criticism from without, which has become self-criticism; anticipation of the punishment; the desire to restore oneself to good standing with the parents whose love is the guarantee of all; and retroflexion of rage upon oneself. This guilty fear leads to expiatory behavior.

What is the difference between fear and guilty fear? Fear excites and elicits behavior of the escape pattern. Guilty fear, in the relation between child and parent, elicits behavior of the expiatory pattern. Because the authority knows everything and is omnipotent, no escape is possible. Because the authority is needed, the child cannot resort to escape. His survival depends on the ministrations of his parents and their love. So for the sake of survival, he must restore himself to their good graces.

The simplest form of guilty fear is rue. This is a reaction on the magic omnipotence level. "I wish I hadn't done it," the child says. Then he has the magic idea, "I can undo it." When the child realizes that what is done is done, the rue is transformed into remorse or guilty fear. Guilty fear leads to the need for confession, to self-criticism, and to the need for punishment.

Emotional tension can exist in the individual without conscious awareness of emotion. In the same way, guilty fear, the need for confession, the drive toward self-criticism and toward self-punishment may exist without the individual knowing it. Automatically brought into play, it becomes a reflex. But its driving force remains the same with the result that this pressure to expiate, which operates against the conscious self, may break through.

Take the example of a culprit giving himself away with a slip of the tongue, thereby unwittingly confessing. He unintentionally carries out this whole pattern of expiatory behavior, and discharges this terrific tension, of which he is not aware, by doing something that is self-punishing. Or, a guilty man may get into an accident or cut his finger.

The result of the self-punishment again is a relief from unconscious tension. These so-called unconscious tensions must be eliminated and the simplest way of discharging them is by carrying out self-punishment. It is another facet of what is commonly called conscience.

The relief that guilty fear seeks is punishment or self-punishment, not for its own sake but for the sake of forgiveness and the recapturing of the love of the parents. Clinical experience disproves the classical theory which envisaged only a "masochistic need for punishment" and a corresponding "sadism of the superego." The retroflexion of rage or self reproach is one of the brilliant findings of Freud, who describes it as "sadism (aggression) turned upon the self."

The "voice of conscience" is an inner experience of high dramatic effectiveness. Why does conscience need to resort to this dramatic effect? If in order to defeat temptation, conscience must speak in a loud voice and repeat time and again "don't do it!" this shows that its automatic restraining power is inadequate. Self-restraint is achieved by the inner reproduction of the original auditory experience which should have led to this response in the first place. In general, the more automatically conscience works, the finer an instrument it is from the point of view of social cooperation.

The automatization of conscience, however, has limits to its adaptive usefulness. Overautomatization produces the untoward mechanisms of nonreporting fear of conscience, imagined guilt, nonreporting guilty fear, automatic self-punishment for imagined guilt, the mechanism of pain dependence, in which the pain of advance punishment is sought as a license for the fulfillment of the prohibited desires.

We have seen that both preventive signals, fear of detection and fear of conscience, may be overruled by defiant rage. The same applies to the reparative signal of guilty fear, but the mechanism is different. The crucial force in guilty fear is retroflexed rage; it is the component which humbles the self most. If this rage once again becomes environment-directed and defiant, the self turns from self-reproach to reproaching the very person he guiltily fears, from expiation to attack. "You are to blame (not I)." The self then believes it is acting purely in "self-defense." Actually this is a mechanism of miscarried repair. I call it rage over guilty fear or guilty rage. Here expiatory behavior is superseded by paranoid behavior. Expiatory behavior always has a depressive coloring; paranoid behavior, if it has any coloring, has a hypomanic one. Rage, as compared to fear, is more pleasing to the ego and has a higher stature value. Fear is usually humiliating and leads to submissive behavior, while rage leads to self-assertive behavior. Thus expiatory behavior can be shifted into paranoid behavior, which means that the conscience will not work as it is supposed to.

In the development of conscience a large percentage of children are damaged, leading to lifelong feelings of low self-reliance, fully automatized self-punishment, pathological inhibitions of sexuality and assertion, pain-dependent behavior, hypochondriasis, obsessive behavior, and depression. During conscience-formation these disorders, or predispositions to these disorders, may develop if the parents are too restrictive, use a preponderance of punitive measures to obtain obedience, or give the child too little love or care in return for obedience. Also, these disorders may develop if the child's frustration tolerance is low or his assertiveness great; both of these disorders probably are on a constitutional basis, genetic in some cases. When the child's defiance is intense and the demands of the parents high, the child will build up a negative image of himself only made worse by his continual need for expiation. By emphasizing reward instead of punishment some of this can be avoided.

The device of reward accomplishes a pattern formation that is similar to the development of the automatized mechanisms of self-restraint and self-punishment except that the process is positive. The child learns to anticipate the reward promised from without, and the process leads to the pattern of self-reward. The individual pats himself on the back. He is proud and satisfied with himself because he expects the father and the mother—and later the community—to admire him and accord high prestige to him. These phenomena were also described as contributing to the formation of a desired self, fulfillment of which gives the individual tremendous satisfaction.

Let us revert here to the problem of psychogenic or cultural pleasure as distinguished from bodily pleasure. The mechanism of bodily pleasure is poorly understood, but even less well understood is the mechanism of purely psychological pleasure. One thing we do know is that psychogenic pleasure results from desire and is the fulfillment of that which is desired. If there is no desire, there is no psychogenic pleasure. To a certain extent, desire must also be present if bodily pleasure is to be gained. Without appetite you cannot have the pleasure of satiation.

The reward system sets up desires to a point where the individual himself does not sense his desire. This can be distinguished as self-desire, or stature desire. By doing some things, he will become an admired citizen, one to be looked up to. It may be that the reward augments, intensifies, quickens an existing desire. The reward system is the other part of the action of conscience. Conscience is not only an automatic mechanism of self-restraint and self-punishment but also a mechanism of self-reward.

There is a loophole here. That which has been previously condemned as a crime can be set free and glorified into being a virtue if it is set up by one's group as a duty to be rewarded. This is how mankind destroys itself. The crusaders who set out to spread the religion of love by massacring the Mohammedans, the Bolsheviks who set out to make mankind happier by massacring the aristocrats, the Nazis who tried to make the supreme crime of genocide into a supreme virtue—these are examples of how ideology has distorted crime. When an evil has been decreed a virtue, the inhibitory impulse is dissipated. There is a quickening of the desire to commit once-forbidden deeds because of the reward.

Conscience is the very foundation of society. It is a transmissive mechanism that ties the individual to the group. However, guilty fear and purely emotional repair work of expiation have little value in adult life. The rational response to one's wrongdoings is to apologize, pay damage, and be satisfied with learning one's lesson. Conscience need not be dominated by the mechanisms of the stern punishment system. Thanks to the same processes of repetitive anticipation, parental reward creates in the child the automatic mechanisms of self-reward known as self-reliance and moral pride. By shifting the emphasis from inhibition to facilitation, the reward system builds a healthy conscience. The child learns to give himself rewards. For the child, and later the adult, there is no substitute for self-reward. It is the emotional experience that makes man self-reliant.

The "voice of conscience" may have inspired the concept of the superego which Freud outlines as follows: Arising from an internalized replica of the father, the superego uses its "borrowed power" to keep the ego under control. The ego welcomes this development, which will help it to withstand and defeat the incestuous desires of its id, so firmly prohibited by the father. In this concept of the genesis of conscience, the internalization of the external father-son relationship is the dramatic event. In order to arrive at this climax, Freud internalizes the whole triangle. It is unmistakable that in this intrapsychic drama the id's relationship to the ego is the same as Jocasta's to Oedipus or that of Potiphar's wife to Joseph.

Freud's thesis is that the individual is ruled by his conscience from

within in much the same way and for much the same purposes as
he is ruled from without by the patriarchal institutions of our Western
civilization. Freud insists that in both the species and the individual,
use of conscience is to be traced to the father's sexual prerogative.
The parents' perogatives, through delegated omnipotence from the
child, however, would seem to be more consistent with the facts of
both history and clinical observation. Freud thought that the superego
was formed by the repression of the oedipal complex because of castration fear. Again, when conscience is formed through reward rather
than fear, the child develops a positive picture of himself.

Disorders of conscience very frequently occur, leading to overreactive
behavior. The child can grow up feeling he is bad and not lovable
because of too strict or too punitive a conscience. The child's conscience can be automatized and be too rigid for adult behavior or
contain too much nonreporting guilty fear from defiant rage. In the
latter case, the individual is constantly expiating on a nonreporting
level, which only makes him feel more worthless and dependent with
low self-reliance. On a nonreporting level the individual often punishes
himself without consciously knowing what he is doing.

Moral pain dependence is a chronic disorder of conscience and requires the individual to adopt a self-sacrificing way of life. He has become so fearful of doing wrong that he cuts down his activities and
takes pride in being overly moral. At the slightest temptation, he
excessively expiates. This disorder is an outcome of restrictive upbringing and genotype. It may be observed in the context of any disorder
and in mild forms can exist alone.

I used to be quite unsuccessful with the treatment of such patients
until I decided to abandon the former concepts of "masochism" and
try to think afresh on the matter. The gist of what I said to the
patient, using the many clinical illustrations he gave me from his own
history, is as follows: "You're overconscientious. Who benefits by that?
No one. Who is damaged by it? You, and very often others. I can assure
you that you were not born to behave this way. This pattern was forced
upon you in your childhood under such and such conditions until it
became your second nature. Underneath, the resources of a healthy
person are still available. You can learn how to shed your second nature
and develop your real self."

It is a difficult task, but with psychodynamic understanding this
often sets the patient on a new track. Such patients remain caught in
or have regressed to the pattern of infantile dependence. They cannot

endure life without the illusion of being perpetually loved and cared for. They are incessantly atoning, by automatized mechanisms or self-punishment, for their temptations and their imagined sins. It is usually true that in the early years of childhood such a patient's defiant rage was excessive. At the same time, he realized the value of keeping loving parental care for his welfare. His fear of being abandoned was even stronger than his excessive rage. The result was that his fear turned the bulk of his defiant rage into retroflexed rage, which was directed against himself, and forced the rest of it to become deeply repressed. The pride the patient now takes in his overmorality is compensation for the pride he originally took in his overassertiveness, which he was forced to renounce. This moral pain dependence is only the skeleton of the patient's pathological conscience, which is difficult to understand and neutralize.

A graphic example of this process is supplied by a patient who, as an adolescent, was prohibited from visiting a house of ill repute. He avoided it as ordered, then felt compelled to avoid the street in which the house was located, and eventually avoided the entire section of the city. Subsequently he had to move to a town where it happened there was no such house, but unfortunately, in that town he discovered a former schoolmate who had since acquired an unsavory reputation. Step by step the patient developed the same series of precautions as before. The experience of the house of ill repute became the hidden content of an obsessive ritual. This case would not be called a phobic avoidance because many other forms of obsessive behavior are present.

Since the human organism cannot stay alive without satisfying its minimal hedonic requirements, the person is forced to find solace and high moral gratification in the fact that he is a "fine man." He discovers more and more opportunities to "fulfill his duty," imposing upon himself burdens and sacrifices which often enough do no good to either him or anyone else.

## The Role of the Parent

All the social usages of child-raising reflect the same situation that is characteristic of life altogether, with law and social custom on the side of the stronger party. Many a rule of child-raising has no other goal than to protect the interests of the parents. What the child should do or should not do is frequently decided in favor of what is in the best interests of the parents, for example, not touching a vase. We must free ourselves from the hypocrisy of pretending that everything the parent does is in the best interests of the child.

Generally, it is of great importance that the child grow up in a homogeneous environment, that the father and mother abide by approximately the same principles. The combination of a severe and austere father and a completely indulgent mother cancels each of them out. The result is that the child cannot get a clear picture of how he should behave and how the world around him behaves.

I am no expert in matters of child psychology. But I should like to disclose a few fundamental considerations that I believe are valid. Let me first remind you that all the basic utility functions are combined with pleasure in the human being. So the parent should work out the details of raising the child in terms of pleasure orientation.

First, the parent should, whenever possible, avoid implanting anxiety in any of the pleasure functions. In trying to regiment pleasure activity, it should be done so as not to scare the child. Second, the parent should, whenever possible, prevent the child from becoming fixed to an early, primitive, infantile form of gratification, since this renders him incapable of further development.

Third, the parent should, whenever possible, use the appreciative reward system rather than stern punishment in developing the child's conscience, thus creating in the child the automatic mechanisms of self-reward known as self-respect and moral pride.

Furthermore, the parent should, whenever possible, teach the child to avoid social conflict. Let me give you an example. Parents ask how much nudity the child should see, and other related questions. Nowadays, the nudist upbringing is perhaps the prevailing attitude of parents. The home is a nudist colony—the parents go around in the nude, the children go around in the nude. Then the child goes out into a society which is not yet nudist. He visits an uncle where he causes consternation when he runs around naked. So the conflict begins. The thing is to forestall social conflict by teaching the child about the habits of the society in which he lives. Why expose him to conflicts he cannot handle because he assumes that the whole world acts as he does at home?

Also, the parent should try, whenever possible, to facilitate the development of higher desires, so that the child can get pleasure from socially useful cultural activities. (This is the "sublimation" of classical psychoanalysis.)

We live in a civilized world, which means that we must engage in activities we did not have to bother about in the jungle. We must learn to develop appropriate desires and take pleasure in those activities that our culture demands, such as learning to read and write. In order to endow these culturally useful and necessary activities with pleasure, it seems inescapable that some of the free pleasure indulgence of the baby should be restricted.

If the basic primitive pleasure desire of the baby is given free rein, and these simple and easy methods of pleasure gratification are constantly kept open, education will have great difficulty in developing pleasure drives of a higher and therefore less intense type. The higher the type of pleasure indulgence, the less intense is the pleasure. Nothing can compete with the pleasure of orgasm. Next comes pleasure of satiation, and then other varieties of bodily pleasure. How far away that is from reading a good short story. Freud says that the higher the pleasure the less it shakes the belly, and he states that culture was developed at the cost of the suppression of the sexual instinct. I suggest substituting the phrase "primitive pleasure activities" for the Freudian "sexual instinct." In order to restore the natural harmony so that the human being can learn to take pleasure in activities that originally did not yield same, it may be necessary for the human being to forgo some of the pleasure indulgence he derives from elementary biological activities.

This is not to say that the child should not engage in self-stimulation or thumb-sucking. What I am saying is that this very difficult problem is handled in a pseudoscientific manner today, which is just as bad as the previous completely unscientific attitude. Complete freedom does not benefit the child, but no attitude which intimidates the child and causes anxiety can be beneficial.

The mother can neglect or overprotect the child; either condition is a major factor in the development of the neurotic individual. What is the golden road in the middle which will do the most good for the growing child? The most important thing is for him to develop independence and self-reliance. His needs must be supplied in such a manner that there will be no interference with the child's ability to fulfill his own needs in the future.

If the child gets too much freedom, he is undersupplied, and damaged in his development. If the child is oversupplied or overprotected in his needs, his development toward independence is retarded and we find the dependence and helplessness characteristic of a very young child.

The motivation leading to neglect or overprotection is complicated. No matter how much maternal drive a woman possesses, she is also subject to the same conflict of interests that exists in every human relationship. When the mother is tired and the child begins to cry, sheer human discomfort engenders the mother's hostile, angry, vindictive impulses. She may suppress them, but the accumulated hostile impulses may come out in a variety of ways.

When experiencing the baby's pleasure appeal, the mother responds with love, and when experiencing the baby as a frustration she responds with rage. If the love grows weaker and the rage grows stronger, neglectful maternal behavior results, with consequences to the baby. If the love prevails over rage, and the rage is suppressed for the sake of love, the result is the typical overcompensatory behavior that tends toward overprotection. In order to keep that anger in check, her love is overdone. It is as if the overprotective mother were trying to protect the child against her own hostility. The pattern is overcompensatory love and, underneath that, hatred.

The child depends upon the parents' loving care, and the parents insist that whenever he is disobedient, he should mollify them by expiation. By the operation of this educational system, the child's defiant rages and resentments are in part repressed, in part turned into self-reproaches. The latter mechanism transforms his sexual fears into guilty sexual fears. The child then vents self-reproaches on himself in an effort to win back the love of his parents. He confesses, takes his punishment, is forgiven, and returns to the fold.

Sexual pathology, then, is essentially an inhibition caused by pathological development of conscience. Freud felt that castration fears ended the Oedipus complex in boys but began the sequence in girls. I believe that the Oedipus complex in both boys and girls is terminated by parental demand through delegated omnipotence.

# CHAPTER 18

# Sexual Development

≈≈≈≈≈≈≈≈≈≈≈≈≈≈≈≈≈≈≈≈≈≈≈≈≈≈≈≈≈≈≈≈≈≈≈≈≈≈≈≈≈≈≈≈

THE LIFE CYCLE CAN BE DIVIDED INTO SIX PERIODS FROM THE POINT OF view of the development of the sex function: (1) the period up to three years old; (2) the period from three to seven; (3) the period from seven to puberty; (4) puberty; (5) maturity; (6) the change of life. It is likely that both sexes are sensitive to sexual stimulation from birth on.

Let me remind you of the basic psychodynamic law that pleasure experience leaves behind it a tendency to repeat it. But in order to do so, some power of discrimination has to be developed before the growing baby is able to grasp that he has pleasure and under what conditions. Even if the baby experiences pleasure, the sexual push or drive to repeat it is not differentiated. It takes some time before the baby grasps the idea that he has this pleasure, and a still longer time to understand that some kind of stimulation is highly desirable.

The shaping of sexual desire and the awakening of sexual behavior depend to a large extent on chance or intentional stimulation on the one hand and intellectual growth on the other. It is difficult for this sexual drive to come into operation before the child is three or four years old. Given conditions such as systematic stimulation, the child has a perfect sex drive. What happens between the ages of four and seven is that the child achieves enough intellectual maturity to take cognizance of and handle this desire. The apparent emergence of the sex drive in these years occurs because the child now has the previously lacking intellectual machinery to discover or handle the sex drive he seems to have been born with.

By the age of four the child enters the period Freud describes as the "early flourishing period of sex in infancy." By then, in most instances though by no means all, an intense autoerotic activity sets in. This infantile masturbation is by no means always digital stimulation. (I happen to dislike the word *masturbation* because it is a moralizing word.) Many times it takes the most complicated forms, depending upon the chance experiences the child has. It usually consists of an over-all rubbing, since the child has no idea what is essential in the performance. Knowledge of how to apply the stimulation in the most effective manner is usually missing.

Let us start with the self-stimulation of the girl, which is more complicated. First, in one way or another she has discovered that certain actions bring pleasure, and she repeats the actions to get this pleasure. Generally, the patterns set up for the pursuit of genital pleasure by the little girl are infinite; among these digital stimulations is the exception. These infantile forms of self-stimulation will influence any later neurosis.

Self-stimulation often begins with cleanliness. Mother gives the little girl a bath and a rubbing to clean the external genitalia, and the child discovers this is pleasant. Frequently, the self-stimulation of the little girl consists of pressing her thighs together, which probably affects the clitoris. Sometimes she learns to elicit pleasurable sensations by rubbing herself in bed. She gets pleasure when her genital organ is rubbed against some object.

For the boy, the situation is much simpler. Here it is practically the rule that cleanliness procedures—the bathtub procedure in which the penis is cleaned by the mother—lead to the discovery of pleasure. Again, the boy's self-stimulation is not limited to handling of the genitals, although it is unquestionably much more frequent than in the female.

Boys are much more exposed to genital stimulation. All female personnel in charge of boys, starting with the mother, take a vague and often unrecognized delight in handling the genitals of the boy, and this unwittingly may degenerate into an almost intentional masturbation. Nonetheless, in the boy you find forms of self-stimulation that are counterparts of the self-stimulation of girls. Boys, too, may go in for all sorts of maneuvers, of rubbing themselves against things in order to produce the sensation first experienced with chance activities.

In psychoanalytic literature, these self-stimulating activities were connected with incest fantasies. It was speculated that when the boy plays with himself, he is imagining having sexual relations with his mother, and the girl is imagining the same with her father. Freud, however, says from the outset that the self-stimulation of the child in the beginning was a "pure organ activity," which does not yet have the psychological function. I think this is absolutely true. I think classical psychoanalysis exaggerated the construction that infantile sexual activity was connected with incest fantasies and was the outlet for the Oedipus complex, although there are, to be sure, plenty of cases of this kind.

Prohibition of self-stimulation, accompanied by all kinds of threats, amounts to injecting fear into the pleasure context of genital pleasure activities and is at the root of many disturbances of the sexual function. The anxieties injected into that area at such an early age can almost never be completely driven out. The discovery of the anatomic differences between the two sexes only intensifies the anxiety already present.

## The Primal Scene

What else is happening during this flourishing period of infantile sexuality? The direct stimulation of the child, intentionally or otherwise, is one of two factors that stimulate his sexual activity and arouse his sexual appetite. The other stimulant is the observation by the child of sexual goings on between adults and between animals. Freud makes this observation, though he first said the stimulation stemmed from oedipal interest in finding out where the new sibling came from. My feeling is that the arrival of the new sibling stirs sexual curiosity, which plays a great role in the development of intellectual curiosity. But it does not stimulate sexual desire.

Psychoanalysts began to focus on one particular part of sexual observation. This, usually called the primal scene, is the inadvertent observation by the child of sexual intercourse between his parents, who usually think he is too young to know what is going on.

The primal scene was once charged with the responsibility for practically every form of neurosis. But gradually psychoanalysts concluded that while it is important, it cannot have any specific responsibility. The significant thing is that the child may misunderstand the experience because he is in no way prepared to understand it. He does not know what sex is, but he does know what violence is. The child's typical misunderstanding is that this is a fight. Papa is attacking Mama. The reaction is a terrific panic. This mistaking of sex for violence is only one part of the child's reaction.

Usually there are kisses and embraces first, so on the basis of natural responsiveness of the human organism to sexual stimulation, the child too becomes sexually excited. So the confusion begins. The child thinks this is an act of violence and becomes appropriately frightened. At the same time, his body becomes sexually excited. The sexual excitement can be so intense that it can actually lead to orgastic excitation (not of seminal fluid, because that is not yet present). Many times the excitement leads to a derailment of excitation and discharge through an act of urination or defecation.

If such an experience is repeated, and if the pleasure aspect begins to come to the fore and the fear lessens, the child may acquire a notorious insomnia, the result of lying there quietly and waiting for the chance to see it. This is a frequent cause of insomnia.

The discrepancy between the behavior of the father during the daytime and in these nocturnal scenes impresses itself deeply upon the child. Next day he is again the sweet and lovely man who is known to the child, and then again at night he goes wild. The impressions of this period are reflected in later dream life—dreams of drunkards and madmen and people going up or down stairs in a strange and irresponsible manner. Or, the typical dream symbolism of catastrophe—earthquakes, floods, thunderstorms, houses crumbling and collapsing, and so forth. I hasten to remind you that all dream symbols must always be related to the emotional situation the patient is in and do not always refer to sex. The significance of the primal scene is that it exerts great influence on the shaping of sex interest and sexual desire and preferred stimulation. Many more people have experiences of this kind than is commonly realized.

### Sex Education of Children

I would like to make a few comments about providing sexual information to children. How much information about intercourse and reproduction should be given to the child raises some interesting questions. If the fundamental position in our society is that of preventing children from sexual play, then it follows that you cannot feed them information to increase their desire for such activities. Progressive teachers have failed to realize this elementary connection and thought that they could provide children with information and still keep them away from early sexual activity. But when the child learns about intercourse, he thinks, "I would like to try that." The more satisfactory the information is, the more the child wants to try it out. Educators have had to become aware of this. Whether free sexuality among children and adolescents is desirable for the individual and our society is anybody's guess. Now that we are in the midst of a sexual revolution we may have no choice.

### DISCOVERY OF THE TWO SEXES

Almost as soon as the child begins to talk, he learns that he is a "boy" and she learns that she is a "girl." But the child does not know what is meant by that. The child may think of this state as having to do with any superficial characteristic he happens to notice, such as articles of clothing.

At some time or other, however, the child discovers the anatomic difference between the sexes. Freud believes it to be of extreme significance in the development of every human being. Experience corroborates this opinion. One qualification we might make to the Freudian theory is that the impact of this traumatic event depends upon the cultural climate of the nursery. Rigid sexual hypocrisy of the old type increases the severity of the shock. Modern and progressive attitudes diminish it. It is dangerous to overdramatize and simplify this discovery.

Every child has an innate tendency toward an egocentric outlook and therefore tends to ascribe its own organization and features to every other human being, to every animal, and even to inanimate things. It is quite natural for a child to see the railroad engine "urinate."

### THE CASTRATION SHOCK OF THE LITTLE BOY

The discovery of the genital difference does not occur when the boy sees the girl for the first time. This difference may be overlooked many times, because the little boy tends to reject the impression. He forgets it or he does not believe his own eyes or he pretends it was there. Or he concocts explanations, "It is too small yet and it will grow out." In other words, the little boy, guided by the pain-avoidance principle, denies the testimony of his own senses. But this goes on for just so long.

That egocentric little boy experiences a terrific shock when he actually "discovers" that this organ, which he has already learned to appreciate highly as a site of pleasure sensation, is missing in the little girl. Erection occurs with or without stimulation, and the little boy so dearly loves all the performances of urination and activities with this organ that he is stunned by its absence in another human being. What he sees is something that looks like a wound in place of where a penis should be. And he may remember that he has been told if he plays with his organ it will be cut off. He rapidly concludes that here is another child who has actually been mutilated. Therefore, one had better not fool around with self-stimulation.

It is a fair guess, substantiated by some case histories, that the "discovery" is likely to occur when the little boy's interest in his own genitalia is increased because he is actively engaged in self-stimulation. It may even be that the "discovery" occurs *because* of the self-stimulation.

The threat of genital mutilation in the context of the self-stimulating activity, on the one hand, and the discovery of the child who looks as if she were the result of the execution of this threat add up to what is called *castration shock*. That these two experiences become significant in terms of each other is, I think, a well-validated contribution of Freud's.

To understand castration shock we must see how these factors interact. It is because the little boy has been exposed in one way or another to the so-called castration threat that the actuality of the little girl's genitalia registers, although he has probably seen it many times before. It is in the light of this threat to him that the little girl's external genitalia resembles a wound, and it is because he is enjoying the sexual pleasure of self-stimulation that his genital organ is so precious to him.

Yet it seems that every little boy reacts at some time to the recognition of the little girl's genitalia with castration fear even if he has never been threatened or has grown up under permissive sexual attitudes. However, our society still has punitive attitudes towards sex. Is there some additional hitherto unobserved factor that guides the imagination of the little boy to his castration fear? It may be that it takes only a slight hint to precipitate the fear in some children.

The information that the female organ is just as complete and perfect as the male's is not available to the little boy of that age. The little boy reacts to the discovery of two sexes with pain and agony, for it is a threat to his masculinity. From this time on, according to the intensity of the fear of mutilation the little boy suffers, the vagina will be a reminder of the "reality" of the castration threat. It will be associated with anxiety. It will act as a stimulus pattern that arouses dread. And it will take time for him to overcome this castration shock.

Yet the sight of the genitalia of the opposite sex is one of the most powerful sexual stimuli. Under the conditions we are discussing, however, the vagina is deprived of this power, and instead arouses panic. But it may arouse both—excitement, complicated by the presence of panic. The dread of the sight of the vagina, interpreted as a wound, may remain with the man for life and interfere with his normal sexual pleasure activities in many ways. This is because it has become a stimulus pattern that elicits anxiety rather than pleasurable excitation.

## PENIS ENVY

In the development of a little girl, she, too, may behave as if she has been in some way or other mistreated. She may feel that she does not have something that the other child does have. In the Freudian construction, the outstanding reaction of the female child to the discovery of the sex difference is penis envy. "He has it. I don't have it. I would like to have it myself. Why don't I have it?" The child at first does not realize that this is a characteristic of her sex. She believes it is her personal condition, and it may take some time before she discovers that no woman has this organ.

Because the girl does not want to accept this condition, she creates all sorts of fantasies. "Mine is too little yet. It will grow out." If the self-stimulation guilt already exists, the girl will develop the fantasy that once upon a time she too had possessed such an organ but that she was deprived of it as a punishment. If she is guilty about self-stimulation, she may feel that is why she lost it, or why it was cut off or removed while she was sleeping.

I now find the Freudian construction of penis envy untrue. Freud assumes that the clitoris of the little girl is a crippled penis. From this he went on to say that the little girl is actually a little boy with a crippled penis. According to his theory, all the excitations of the little girl come from the clitoris, and this leads to penis envy. I feel that this theory disguises basic problems of a cultural phenomenon with that of a biological significance. Whatever it may be, the so-called penis envy is not biological. Now we cannot deny that penis envy does exist in the woman who envies the prerogatives of a man. But this is cultural and is only possible in a male-dominated society. In such a society a woman would want all the male privilege power and status. But she does not envy him his penis. Indeed, when the little girl, who knows nothing about male privilege, first sees the little boy, she feels something is wrong with him because he drips down in front. Clara Thompson saw this clearly, before most male psychoanalysts did.

In the discussion of pathology you will see that it has tremendous importance if a girl remains dissatisfied with her own sex, revolting against it, and insisting that she is going to be a boy or is a boy. There are some women who try to assume masculine characteristics and lead their lives as if they were men.

In such instances there is no doubt about the presence of penis envy and the confusion this envy causes in sexual function. For no free sexual activity, no absorption of sexual pleasure is conceivable if anxiety interferes. The clinical experience that has accumulated since Freud gave the outlines of these significant developments demonstrates that the presence and role of anxiety behind the penis was overlooked.

The castration fantasy has its corollary in the idea that the penis is a weapon of attack. The woman is thereby prepared to interpret intercourse in terms of violence, an assault perpetrated by the weapon penis on the defenseless woman, whose vagina is nothing but the absence of a penis. This outlook is deposited in an endless variety of dreams wherein men persecute women with all kinds of weapons and guns and where the penis is symbolized as a snake or other dangerous animal. All these ideas derive from the thought, "Not only have I been castrated, genitally mutilated, but having lost my penis I am rendered defenseless." The other child, who is now discovered to be the boy, has the instrument of aggression.

The discovery of menstruation corroborates the idea that the one who has been deprived of a penis is exposed to further injury. The idea of defloration and intercourse now appears as a corroboration of that fear; likewise, the fact that there is blood and injury involved in childbirth. Once this erroneous outlook is established, the normal facts of biology simply become corroborations of this outlook.

What needs to be added to the construction is that the envy is overcome with increasing intellectual development and maturity in all those girls who become approximately normal. In those girls in whom this envy remains and plays a great role, it does so because of the fear behind it—the fear of repeated genital mutilation or injury, the need for a defense against that, leading to a strengthening of the penis envy, and a desire to have this organ as a defense.

On another level penis envy is destructive as it leads to feelings in the woman of being inadequate and dependent if she does not have the penis and its strength. These women dream of finding or taking a penis as a means of repair. This is the castrating woman.

In little girls, too, the discovery of the male sex is most easily made at the period of life when they masturbate—not by any means on the first occasion when they observe sexual differences. There are histories of girls who were put into the same bathtub with their little brother, and it took years before they made the discovery. When the child begins to masturbate, the discovery is made. The period in which the little girl fools herself, thinking "Mine is still small but it will grow out" is the source of all sorts of fantasies that may remain for life. For example, "I have to eat something and then it will grow out."

Many tales about feeding can eventually be traced to the idea so beautifully expressed in the following story: The mother or nurse warns the girl child not to eat some fruit and not to swallow the pits because if she does, a tree will grow out of her. This is the negative version of the underlying idea that if one eats something special a penis will grow. The next stage in the development of this fantasy is, "If I eat something, a baby will grow," one of the common primitive misconceptions of pregnancy found in children.

Parents, to maintain the traditional puritanical view which aimed at establishing the monogamous life, had to frighten the child sufficiently to repress the child's defiant rages and resentments about sexual expression. These fears come to play a crucial part when the orgastic desire invades the child's dependency relation to the parents. There is a powerful, though unrecognized, sexual undercurrent in the parents' own attitude toward their child. Giving him, as she must, her natural love and affection, the mother unwittingly also arouses her son's sensual desire, and the father courts his daughter's favor. The father then tends to become hostile to the boy, and the mother becomes hostile to her daughter. Actually, each parent is punishing the child for what are the consequences of the other parent's unrecognized temptation.

Eventually, the explicit or implied threats of genital degradation force the child to renounce or inhibit his incest temptation. In later life, this temptation may still influence the choice of mate. Or, if the individual shies away from sexual contacts, and yet desires the emotional security of a mate, his incest temptation may be reactivated as miscarried repair.

When the child develops an orgastic desire for the parent of the opposite sex, the parent of the same sex whom the child would wish to replace inevitably becomes the target of his jealous resentment. This emotional constellation of the child is designated the Oedipus complex by Freud.

The child's experiences in the family group lay the foundations of what will later emerge as his adaptational patterns. This includes the individual's attitudes toward cooperation and competition, his proneness to domination or submission, his aspirations, social fears, and resentments. This lasting adaptive organization has, of course, profound bearings on the individual's sexual behavior as well.

# CHAPTER 19

# Thinking and the Self

It looks to me as if the varieties of thinking are a privilege of man. Only the human being has the privilege of indulging in varieties of thinking that are not realistic, that do not deserve the description of trial action, and are obviously governed by processes other than the urge to imitate, anticipate, and understand reality. The most typical of this sort of emotional thinking is daydreaming and dreaming in sleep.

## Mankind's Varieties of Thinking

Every human being has daydreams. As we grow older we tend to do this less and less, but around puberty and the younger years we all have plenty of them. The daydream and realistic thinking are markedly different from each other. Realistic thinking consists of figuring out ways and means toward desired ends. Daydreaming ignores the ways and means and shifts the emphasis to pleasurable anticipation of desired ends.

The adolescent boy is walking along the street thinking to himself, "How can I get to know Miss Jones, the movie star?" Suddenly he finds himself walking a little bit faster and the whole story starts to take shape in his mind. It so happens that Miss Jones is crossing the street and a car is bearing down on her and at the last minute he jumps out and protects her from being run over. Miss Jones is very happy and says, "Oh, Mr. So and So . . ."

Or, think of the man who is applying for a job. On the way there he already imagines himself sitting in the office, holding down the job, rising every six months to a higher rank. By the time he arrives in the reception room and is waiting to be interviewed, he is probably already the executive vice-president, having married the boss' daughter.

In this and a million similar dreams you see that the emphasis is not on trial action, not on figuring out ways and means, not on making a blueprint for motor action. It is a contemplation and pleasurable anticipation of desired ends. This is the so-called wishful thinking, which is emotional thinking. It is driven by expectation of pleasure.

There is also the fearful and angry fantasy. The guiding interest there is never to find out what the reality is. The behavior prompted by the emotion is simply anticipated in imagination, and the ends are those indicated by the emotions concerned. A man who is seized with fear will interpret the events surrounding him in terms of possible injury to himself. He will not be able to evaluate the realistic chance of being hurt and of getting away. He will specialize in figuring out the ends dictated by his emotions. He will consider only the threatening aspect of the experience and will have fearful fantasies of injury and pain.

In daydreams we indulge in more or less strongly emotional thinking. Normal individuals have almost only wishful daydreams. Their daydreaming is dominated by the pleasurable type of emotions. Disturbed individuals also have the so-called terror fantasies. The so-called anxiety neurotic will skillfully select from the environment those features that seem to justify the expectation that something terrible is about to happen to him. And all his thinking is dominated by this singled-out element that shows the selective influence of fear.

It is perhaps better to think in terms of a spread, with realistic thinking at one end and emotional thinking at the other. It is not a black or white alternative of realistic thinking or emotional thinking. Between these opposites, we can observe all shades and grades of in-between states. Sometimes it is difficult to judge how realistic our thinking is or to recognize the extent to which we are being influenced by an emotional expectation.

In the relationship between the unemotional-thought level and emotional levels, the unemotional-thought level is not to be considered a new level of integration that has completely superseded the emotional level. On the contrary, the unemotional-thought level is incapable of independent existence. It is superimposed upon, but to a very large measure dependent upon, the proper functioning of the emotional levels. There would be no hedonic regulation on the unemotional-thought level without the participation of the emotions.

The main problem in life is to train the emotional levels to adapt to the guidance of the unemotional-thought level. The unemotional-thought level should hold sway, and emotion should function under the guidance of rational thought. The individual who has accomplished this may be looked upon as the ideal normal person. When the emotions, with their infantile past, disturb the individual's thought processes and make them the servant of the emotions, the individual suffers from neurosis. The struggle for dominance between the unemotional-thought level and the emotional level is one of the main problems in the psychoneurosis.

Another important aspect of the varieties of thinking is indicated by the contrast between egocentric thinking and objective thinking. I have already talked about the egocentric omnipotence of the baby. Every human being starts out with this self-image and undergoes a painful process in which these grandiose ideas are liquidated. Eventually the individual arrives at the discovery of the bitter truth—that he is a tiny nobody in a large universe, in which very little, if any, attention is paid to him. This is a very, very, long road. Some individuals never reach that point.

It requires a high level of scientific thinking to be fully aware of the nothingness of ourselves, and there are all grades and in-between stations between these two self-conceptions. The tendency to think in a strictly egocentric manner is intrinsic in every human being. That all emotional thinking is in a sense self-centered goes without saying. What I am emphasizing at this point is the egocentric aspect of emotional thinking as distinguished from an objective point of view of the environment.

Obviously in every human being the varieties of thinking change with the passage of time. This is a developmental process. In infancy and childhood, thinking is egocentric and highly emotional. Later on, as time goes by, it becomes more objective and realistic.

But we are not dealing here with the kind of development in which one stage follows the other and automatically supersedes the preceding stage. We are dealing with the very curious type of development in which all stages remain as potentialities. The development of thinking means that, although new techniques and modalities of thinking are constantly being evolved, the possibility of lapsing into thinking in one of the old ways always remains. This is of fundamental importance. No matter how highly the individual has developed in ways of thinking, he can never be certain of this acquisition. The greatest philosopher may catch himself daydreaming, and everybody dreams at night.

Another aspect of thinking that bears examination is its logical quality. It takes time before the growing individual acquires the automatic handling of the laws of logic, before he arrives at the point where he can make immediate appraisals of non sequiturs and illogical sequences and a proper evaluation of logical conclusions. When we study the speech of children and the dream life of adults, we see the highly imperfect thinking that goes on. It is different from adult realistic thinking, not only in the sense that it is emotional and egocentric but also in the technical imperfection of the processes.

Let me give you an illustration. A gentleman comes in with a black bag and looks into the baby's throat and the baby cries because it is unpleasant. Next time, a lawyer comes in. He is an entirely different person, but he also happens to be carrying a black bag. The reappearance of the black bag is enough to make the child display the same fright and reaction that he experienced after the doctor's visit. The power of discrimination—the keeping apart of things that do not belong together—is very poor. Freud calls this type of thinking a *primary process* and he calls rational thinking a *secondary process*. These are tentative distinctions, and I am inclined to think that it is impossible for us to simplify matters to that extent.

It is a terrific struggle for the child to grasp what yesterday is and what tomorrow means. This whole ordering of our experience in categories of time is an extremely difficult and long development. And there are all modalities and varieties of thinking in which there is no ordering in terms of time as yet. The same process occurs to a lesser degree in the ordering of space—what happens here and what happens elsewhere and how many elsewheres there are, as distinguished from here and now.

Let me return to my suggestion that this matter of all shades and grades of nonrealistic thinking is a privilege unique to man as distinguished from the rest of the animal world. From a technical point of view, this is possible only to man because he alone has some means of language. Whatever other means of communication exist among many species, they seem to be fairly primitive. Because language has the virtue of permitting conceptual thinking as distinguished from visual images, it has vastly increased the possibility of dealing with symbols instead of the things themselves.

When I think of tables, I can use the word *table* instead of having to think of images of what I have seen. Therefore the presence of language makes it possible for me to go off in my manipulation of these symbols from realistic pathways. But the fact of language only explains how it is possible for us to do such things. This is not the real reason why man can indulge in nonrealistic thinking. The real reason is biological.

Now how does man significantly differ from all animals? The so-called care of the young is, of course, a widespread biological phenomenon. But in all other species this care of the young by the parent exists only for a very limited period, after which the mother gives a few pushes and the offspring moves ahead. By and large, the survival of the organism from the earliest moment is actually dependent on what the individual himself can do. Behavior of the individual and survival of the individual is one and the same thing. If he wants to survive, he must so behave as to keep himself alive. But this is not true of the human being.

What does the care of the human infant consist of? No species known to us comes to this world in such an immature state of development as the human infant. Accordingly, the period of maturation of the human species is incomparably longer than that of any other species noted. During all the years of incompleteness and immaturity, a situation prevails that has no counterpart in the animal system.

This is the situation of the sanctuary. The basic fact, which is of fundamental significance, is that the human infant survives not by virtue of what he does for himself but by virtue of what his mother does for him. The baby's behavior is not penalized by immediate death if he goes far away from the necessities of realistic self-adaptive behavior. He is exempt from the responsibilities of adaptation and survival.

Because the mother will do the right thing, the baby's behavior, especially his thought behavior, can go as haywire as he pleases. Because his needs are provided for, he can develop varieties of thinking and motor behavior that are governed by interests other than survival. Whatever he does, whatever he thinks or feels, he is as free as a singing bird in the forest.

This is the unique thing about the human being that causes so much trouble. It is because the human infant grows up in a sanctuary that he can indulge in such delusions as his own omnipotence, that he can indulge in egocentric thinking and in absolutely emotional thinking, and that he can afford to disregard reality.

It is a very slow process for the child to learn to talk, to think, and to reason. It is a constant effort of the environment gradually to teach him to grasp what is real and what is not and to enable him to learn the ways of logic so that he will be able to make a more realistic appraisal of himself and the outside world. Small wonder, then, that in neuroses and psychoses the adult relapses from a realistic type of thought and motor behavior into strange varieties of thinking and behaving that can be identified as infantile. They are the product of a stay in a sanctuary.

If you visualize the life cycle and the years of developmental growth, it seems reasonable to suppose that what we are calling an unemotional-thought level of integration is in itself composed of many component strata. The top level that outstanding individuals of the species can reach today would probably be some kind of scientific thinking, perhaps mathematical thinking. It is realistic, objective, discriminatory, and critical to the highest degree. And at the lowest thought level is the type of thinking that is completely egocentric, emotional, prelogical, and preverbal. It is thinking that is characterized by visual or perceptual images, for example, by auditory images and tactile images.

Now it is obvious that not every human being reaches the level of mathematical thinking. The rest of the population reaches various lower levels as their own respective top level. So a characteristic of every individual is the item of what top level of thinking his mind has developed to. What are the substrata in his thought apparatus or his preparedness for thinking? With the exception of idiots, everybody reaches the language level, but above the language level there is still much entirely egocentric and emotional thinking.

There is another peculiarity. Even those individuals who have reached the highest level yet attained by man do not choose to spend all their lives sticking to this type of thinking. When the greatest mathematician takes a walk in a beautiful forest or goes to the seashore and sees the wonderful world about him, he comes down to a more human and emotional level. The moment he engages in a daydream, he comes down from the top level. When he dreams in his sleep, he goes down still further.

Now what happens to the highest stratum if a man goes down to lower levels in his thinking? That we do not know. Possibly these higher levels of thinking represent potentialities, which are sometimes actualized in the human being. Imagine a tall building. In the evening all the hundred odd floors are lit up. Then suddenly the top ten floors are darkened. It is as if those darkened floors did not exist at all. When the lights go on again, they are visible again.

I suggest that in order to get higher and higher in the levels of thinking, we must make additional efforts. It seems likely that some energy threshold has to be passed to reach the next higher level. If we do not force ourselves to rise above the threshold of our highest level, we almost automatically sink down to a lower one.

If you are asleep and awaken partially and have a dream, your consciousness goes down. If you are daydreaming, your consciousness is somewhere down. You are always conscious of the kind of thinking that represents the top thinking at any given time.

Here let me say a few words about a highly speculative kind of thinking. What actually is the factor of creativity? We do not know. It enters the psychodynamic picture as a given entity. I feel that all current psychoanalytic explanations of such factors are unsatisfactory. For instance, it was believed for a time that all scientific interest derives from the child's question Where do babies come from? Curiosity does not arise when the child begins to wonder about this, but rather it is the occasion of the birth of a sibling that develops the *existing* curiosity. A dull child will not be so curious about this. The keen child will be more interested, and his mind and interest will be wound up and set to work.

This is one of the occasions when a natural interest and endowment are brought into play. Such a natural endowment always needs provoking or precipitating situations. This is true all over the field of biology. A situation that is a proper stimulus sets an already existing latent trend into motion. The child who has the raw material out of which scientific curiosity may develop will immediately take a tremendous interest in the problem of where babies come from.

What the source of this curiosity is, we do not know. But I suspect that all curiosity aims at control of some kind—thought control or technological control. "I would like to know how it works because I want to control it." This is surely relevant in the child's curiosity about where babies come from. The child wants to prevent other babies from coming.

## The Nature of the Self

Now you cannot talk about such things as thought and consciousness without finding yourself face to face with the eternal mystery of mankind, which is the nature of the self. Let us look at this entity that is so hard to get at from the point of view of adaptational psychodynamics. Who is that, me, or I? How is that self related to the machinery of the mind? If we trace the development of the self perhaps we can come up with a few fundamental ideas that seem reasonable assumptions.

Stanley Cobb said, "Everybody has a pretty good idea of what he is." For clinical purposes, this is perfectly good. We can say that the self is the picture that the whole individual has of himself. This is a tautological statement, but you cannot get behind that.

How does this self come into the picture? All that is conscious in the individual under normal circumstances is considered to be part of the self. This is a natural feeling. I have suggested that consciousness is linked with the top strata. So is the self. It is likely that the self is composed of at least two parts. One may represent the temporal continuity of the individual, and the other may be the level on which thinking takes place. This would mean that the self, like consciousness, moves up and down when thinking goes up and down on the various levels. Part of it is constant and part is assimilated in the respective thought level.

How does this representation of the individual to himself come about? My observations have led me to believe that the essence of this self is action. So do not think of a structure when you think of the self. You are better off to think of it as something functional. Try to think in terms of thought processes, processes of feelings, processes of volition, and processes of experiences, of perception, and of activity.

The uniqueness of self and consciousness is such that we cannot hope to explain it by tracing it to something more primitive or to something better known. What we can try to do is to show how it works, how it comes into being, how it develops. It would seem to come into being as a result of the sucking activity of the infant. If the earliest form of the self is an action self, I would be inclined to say that the earliest form is the mouth self, because it is derived from the activities of the mouth. The mouth may be the origin of the whole experience of self.

It is interesting to follow the development of the self. Out of these emotionally charged proprioceptive sensations, the infant develops the sense of power and might. One more step and it becomes almightiness. This is the source of omnipotence. Charles Sherrington defines the mind as "the manager of muscles."

The omnipotent infant feels he is a giant surrounded by a little something that is the universe. Later on, when reality testing has done its destructive work, the imagery undergoes complete reversal. The self is then the little nothing and the universe about it becomes the giant. Every human being begins to associate at a very early age the idea of power with these images of bodily size. On the primitive level the child has attained, he cannot think in such functional terms as power, so the greatness of power is always represented by great size.

This way of thinking has some interesting pathological consequences. The self has a size and stature that are visualized in vague images of bodily size. Concepts of power or omnipotence are difficult for the primitive mind to deal with, so they are translated into visual images, just as they are in the child. Mankind has been doing this since its earliest days. In Gulliver's Travels, a tiny addition in size gives the Emperor such prestige that he awes his beholders. Darwin's description of pride reads, "He is haughty—haut, or high, and makes himself appear as large as possible so he is said to be swollen or puffed up with pride."

In omnipotence, the illusion is that everything that takes place in me is in some way produced in me. I am the responsible author. Language expresses this beautifully. We speak of my sensation, my view of a river. Psychologically, the emphasis is the word my as if I am responsible for the fact that I can have sensations.

Under pathological conditions this is no longer the case. In schizophrenia the consciousness of the individual is struck by feelings and thoughts from the lower levels that the individual is incapable of incorporating in himself because their content is so strange. He denies ownership of them because he does not accept them as ideas and feelings and thoughts of his own. The result is that the field of self and of consciousness are separated, because the field of consciousness is wider than the field of self. The point is that the individual is experiencing conscious phenomena that he cannot assimilate into the self. So he believes they are part of the outside world, and these are the hallucinations.

There are other less serious pathological states in which the oncoming thoughts cannot be very well assimilated. These are the strange obsessive thoughts. The individual knows this is not I. "I don't want to kill my child, and yet here is that impulse to take a knife and kill my child." Obsessional ideas of this kind are obnoxious to the individual who has them. But he cannot deny that they pop up in his mind. The individual can deny authorship, but he cannot deny that the thought is a part of his self. He can only say he does not want to have these ideas.

All of us have some experience of this sort when we dream. The self disappears, the connections between past and future, the sense of identity are all gone. When we are asleep and dreaming, we do not have the historical continuity of ourselves. The self has shrunken to such an extent that almost all the dream content is located outside of the self. They are hallucinations, experienced as outside realities, though they are part of the activities of our own mind.

Now the infant goes on to a gradual discovery of various parts of the body. At first it is in an illusory fashion, but later on it becomes more and more realistic. The infant begins to know that these are parts of his body—this is me and this is not me. Gradually, the individual begins to learn about his psychological features—his nature and capacities. All that becomes the content of what we refer to as self. And the continuity of the past and the future becomes part of that self.

As the individual grows up, his experiences of self are gradually filled more and more with grownup, objective, realistic elements. Who am I? What am I? What do I look like? What are my limbs? What is my body? What is not my body? Critical thinking begins to reduce the illusory features and gradually produces a picture of self which is the result of reality testing in the grownup sense.

The reduction of the grandiose self requires two things for its accomplishment: one is self-observation, the second is the sharpening of self-observation to self-criticism. All self-observation and self-criticism are derived from being observed and criticized by others. Initially, the individual discovers he is being observed and criticized. Then in anticipation of forthcoming observation and criticism, he begins to do it to himself. Self-observation and self-criticism are social phenomena. Neither they nor conscience would exist outside of the group.

Slowly and gradually the individual is forced to reduce his megalomaniac conception of his own self to a more objective level. This is a painful process, and of necessity, it is spread over a decade or more. To execute this operation quickly might crush the human being. Little by little, a reduced ego emerges and the individual's ideas about himself eventually may approximate objective truth. With this painful reduction in the size of the self, what happens to the affection and love the self used to expend upon itself? And what happens to those old primordial ideas—the self's conceptions of itself?

The individual's original primordial idea of his own self is indestructible. When it is renounced as reality, it is not completely eliminated from the mind but is retained as the goal of future attainments.

It becomes the desired self. In a sense, all advances of science and technology can be considered realizations of this human longing because they vastly increase our powers over nature and bring us closer to a state of omnipotence. Advances of modern technology, notably the bomb with its lethal potential, seem to bring closer an approximation of this state of omnipotence.

Medical science has permitted us to increase day by day our vulnerabilities to the attack of all kinds of infection. Medical science and technology are prolonging our lives, so that we are getting closer and closer to immortality and invulnerability, though we can never reach the heights envisioned by the primordial self that once dwelt in each of us.

But this is too slow a progress for the individual. His solution is to make a regressive revival of his own omnipotence and set out in the world to realize it. The lust for omnipotence is a powerful element in human society. In the psychotic, the delusions of grandeur, the megalomania of various psychotic conditions, are straight revivals of the omnipotence of the primordial self. This characteristic of the psychotic is commonly known. But not so commonly noted are the non-psychotic, normal manifestations of that ancient primordial lust for omnipotence. All science aims at increasing man's power over nature. Science in itself is a bid for omnipotence.

The most important thing about the self is that it is also the site of our love. The one most dearly loved is the self. In addition, it has social aspects. The self is one point through which the individual is integrated into society. This happens because pride and vanity and prestige express satisfactions of this desire for self-love. We have a self-love, we love ourselves and want other people to love us.

The effort to realize the self gives the individual a tremendous feeling of self-love, which we call drive or ambition. Just as a baby wants to be loved by his parents because their love guarantees their forthcoming services, a grownup wants to be loved by the community. He wants the attention, the recognition, and the admiration which bring the satisfaction that comes from realization of the desired self. The temptation to declare yourself a god, as so many rulers have done in bygone days, is thus easily understood.

Self-realization provides the general frame for all of man's various behavior areas. It is unique and characteristic of the human individual. Every behavior modality is an item in the over-all picture of self-realization. Self-realization always means the fulfillment of an ideal.

If the individual fails to realize his ideals, he experiences a loss of pride and a keen desire to recapture the lost stature. The level of prestige is vital to the individual's mood because it produces various degrees of elation and depression. Every fulfillment of an ideal, if it comes at the end of a long struggle or in spite of great difficulties, is realized as a great triumph and effects a growth in the size of the ego which is a state of elation. And the contrary, failure or frustration, leads to a shrinking of the self and to depression and to longing for a retrieval of the desired stature.

The growing self has a conception not only of itself but of the world. Accompanying the development of the various stages of conception of the self (from primordial through tested self) is a gradual development in the individual's inner picture of his outer world.

The picture of the outside world held as an infant is experienced in the dream life. The realistic world picture one gradually gains is the product of the higher thought level of the adult. In the adult, these two entities—the action self and the world—are in a reciprocal relationship to each other. In the aura of omnipotence or self-inflation, the action self is tremendous and the world is its negligible appendage. In a state of depression, the action self is but a small speck in a gigantic world.

These phenomena are not static. They are dynamic; in constant flux are the size of the action self and the amount of self-appreciation, pride, and self-confidence. These feelings are subject to constant change, but the more they are stabilized, the better off is the individual.

## The Meaning of Life

Perhaps it is fitting at this point to raise the question, What is the purpose of life? Freud says this is an immodest question because nobody knows the answer. And he is right—it is an immodest question. The Constitution of the United States talks about "the pursuit of happiness," a foolproof position. But what is happiness? It seems to me that man considers himself happy when he achieves realization of himself.

Now what is that self that seeks realization? I can evolve only one definition. The self is represented by a set and arrangement of desires. The more an individual fulfills the arrangement of desires that characterize his self, the happier that individual will be. Whether his particular set and arrangement of desires is wise or unwise, nice or not nice, admirable or criminal, is another question. In order to understand any human being, you must think in terms of the set he has of himself, his desires, and his self-image. We might call that the level of activation. The main point is that everybody's life must be measured by the yardstick of his own self.

## The Normal Individual

I think self-reliance in all areas of functioning is the minimal desirable goal for the mentally healthy individual, as opposed to the dependency adaptation. With self-reliance, pride and pleasure in some areas of functioning are necessary for good mental health. Pride is the result of the individual's survival, reproduction, and cultural self-realization, the latter depending on realistic self-appraisal and the values of the environment. In our society, this means the desire to be loved and to love as well as contributing to the community. This yardstick of the normal is, of course, tied up to the society.

# CHAPTER 20

# Disordered Behavior

It is fittting to start this discussion of so-called neurotic and psychotic behavior with a warning. Let me caution you against allowing yourself to think in terms of *the* neurosis and *the* psychosis. There is no such thing. What is meant by the terms *neurosis* and *psychosis* is the change from the ordinary "normal" type of behavior to the one observed. I hope that someday this subject will be viewed as insufficiencies of adaptation. I consider them "insufficiencies" because I view all pathological behavior as the enacting of faulty behavior measures by the organism in an effort to cope with emergency emotions (fear, rage, pain, etc.). This is a brief statement of the emergency dysfunction theory that is a basic principle of adaptational psychodynamics.

As introduction to this difficult subject I would like to state three opinions of mine: (1) Pathological behavior is precipitated when the individual feels that his life or his health are being threatened. (2) Symptomatology develops from the desire of the individual to play it safe. (3) Pathological behavior always shows excessive emergency emotions, loss of self-reliance and self-confidence, and the return to the early adaptive pattern of infantile dependence.

## The Self-Reliant Personality

If we define disturbed behavior in terms of adaptational failure, we should have in mind an assumption about the general emotional behavior of the healthy individual. I view healthy behavior as characterized by the fact that the welfare emotions predominate in the emotional matrix of that individual. The healthy individual is usually in a pleasant state. He is dominated by emotions such as joy, love, sympathy, pride, and the like, which exist on a realistic basis. He is used to feeling good about himself and to seeing life in optimistic terms because his consciousness is usually dominated by the field of pleasurable expectations. By his contact with other healthy people, the individual elicits positive emotional reactions from others which reinforce his own. This process can be called *eliciting the emotional resonance of others*. The ordinary individual has no trouble with the painful tensions arising from time to time in the nonreporting range. They can be readily discharged by spells of fear in the waking state or by fear-ridden dreams. It is difficult to define mental health; the tendency is to define it in terms of what it is not. At a minimum the individual is self-reliant, at his maximum—who knows?

In thinking about disordered behavior, "insufficiencies" of psychodynamic adaptation, the ultimate yardstick derives from the questions: What does the individual do? How does he act? What is his outlook? What does he think about the way he acts? The yardstick is always his relationship to reality, his adaptive life performance. We should compare one individual with another so that we can better understand this wide range of behavior and the way in which "abnormal" behavior differs from "average" behavior. What is the deviation from the "normal" that is causing that individual to make such poor adjustments in social and other areas? These are the questions to keep in mind in making a diagnosis or appraising treatment.

Please do not be misled by so-called insight, which is after all an undefined term. If anything, we should at least think in terms of "effective insight." The amount of insight is not a criterion that should influence us unduly. An individual may understand his motives, but be unable to change his behavior. The main concern of the therapist is the life performance of the patient.

Now what do we know about behavior disorders? I suggest that we think about these "organized" sequences as responses. The so-called neurotic or psychotic is usually making emergency responses in the absence of actual danger or overreacting to actual environmental danger of any degree. These processes are brought into play by a disordered emotional response of the organism. We can usually relate this disordered response to an environmental situation. Frequently, we can trace the behavior to comparable exposures in the past. By psychoanalyzing, we may be able to find the episode in the past history of the individual in which the disordered response made its first appearance. Freud conclusively demonstrates that disordered behavior rarely appears for the first time in adulthood. Its roots and first manifestations are, as a rule, found in childhood and then carried over into adult life.

Severe damage is done to the pleasure functions, as well as the utility pursuits, in all individuals who are caught in the coils of pathological behavior. You must preserve survival before you take care of pleasure and in the struggle for survival, as waged by the pathological personality, the pleasure functions are inevitably damaged. I am sorry to see some psychoanalysts viewing pathological behavior as a matter of preservation of pleasure or ersatz pleasure, although Freud himself revised this early principle.

## The Emergency Function

Before we start to think about repair mechanisms, classes and subclasses of disordered behavior, we should be clear about the emergency function. The basic emergency emotions are pain, fear, rage, and, in a wider sense, guilty fear enhanced by retroflexed rage, and guilty rage. These emotions prompt the organism to emergency moves.

Pain elicits riddance activities aimed at getting rid of its cause. Fear prompts moves of escape or submission to authority. Rage evokes combat or defiance. Guilty fear produces expiatory behavior aimed at recapturing loving care. Guilty rage leads to violence in presumed self-defense. Retroflexed rage or self-reproach is defeated rage turned by the organism against itself. Its self-reproach is usually assimilated with the prevailing pattern of remorse. By preparing the organism to meet emergencies, these emotions play a significant part in biologically effective emergency control.

The key word is *overreaction*. The overproduction of what is normal when functioning properly is too much for the individual. The overreaction leads to the state where the emergency emotions that were designed to warn the organism of possible damage have themselves become a damage to the organism or threaten to damage the organism. In consequence, the organism has to struggle with its own overreactions. This is the state I call *emergency dyscontrol*. I suspect, although I do not know, that proneness to overreaction and dyscontrol develops in childhood, often on a genetic basis, and is carried over into adult life. We do know that the state of emergency dyscontrol occurs when the infantile organism is unable to control the disordered emergency responses by its own psychodynamic means.

The main offending agent in the precipitation of pathological behavior is anxiety, which suppresses the self-assertiveness that is native to the human being and leads to many consequences. The most injurious instrumentality of the organism is excessive rage.

The emergency function breaks down, due to the imperfections and limitations that are inherent in the emergency function itself. We would not have pathological behavior if the emergency function were the ideally perfect biological function. Its efficiency is limited, just as any biological function is limited. For example, if my immunological reaction could do away with any bacterial invader, I would never have an infection. If I had the power of regeneration that is seen in some of the lower species, the replacement of a lost limb would be a matter of simple regeneration. So if man's emergency function were perfect, there would be no neuroses. Every one of the many life-preserving functions of the organism is subject to limitations and imperfections. And just as incomplete and imperfect defense reactions of the organism constitute pathologic somatic behavior, the breakdown in the emergency function opens up avenues for the disordered responses of pathological behavior.

The emergency function mechanisms have at least three fairly serious imperfections. The first imperfection of far-reaching consequence is that the supposedly inborn fear and rage responses are not adjusted to cultural conditions and have to undergo the process of education to become so. The newborn infant starts life with fear responses that are by no means correlated to the dangers of cultural conditions. The infant is likely to respond with anxiety to stimuli that do not indicate the presence of danger in our culture. And he fails to respond to stimuli that do indicate the presence of danger.

I have already discussed the question of fear in the newborn infant and said that it was the opinion of many that the child is born with the fear of loud, sudden noises, for one example. In the jungle, especially at night, a loud noise may well have indicated that danger was approaching. In our culture, noise is no threat to the baby although he may respond to it with great anxiety. From the very beginning the emergency function of the infant has to be modified or conditioned if he is to survive in our culture. The original fear response must be trained to remain quiescent under conditions that do not signify the presence of danger. It must be adapted to the present environment so that it is really and truly indicative of the presence of danger. This conditioning is not always successful. The child may continue to react with anxiety to conditions that are not realistically threatening and vice versa.

The second imperfection of the emergency function is that in some individuals the instrumentalities of emotional control are so powerful that the individual cannot establish supremacy on the thought level. You remember that in the evolutionary process man has reached the point where he can often integrate his behavior on the emotional-thought level by means of angry thought and apprehensive thought. But the severe rage and the intense anxiety that may have dictated survival in the jungle are no longer necessary in our culture. The central nervous system and the autonomic system are not the same in every human being, and it seems likely that the autonomic and somatic sensitivities are greater in some people than in others. Individuals so endowed will tend to generate intense fear and rage in terms of visceral and somatic involvement and will tend to express that emotion outwardly or inwardly, or even in both ways at once. The degree to which emotions can be integrated by the thought processes depends at least in part upon the biological makeup of the individual. Medical literature has invented a number of names in its effort to label this oversensitivity of the autonomic system, this overactive autonomic involvement, that is found in some individuals. If the stress is sufficiently great, strong emotional response may be elicited from anyone. But what I am talking about here is the readiness of the individual who responds to even slight provocation with naked emotional responses.

There is a third inherent weakness of the emergency function. This is that the preparatory signals tend to defeat their purpose—that of alerting the individual to the presence of danger and of energizing the individual to cope with such danger—by easily getting out of control. A flash of anxiety that energizes the organism is a magnificent means of emergency control. But what happens when the anxiety has increased in intensity and in duration so as to become an anxiety attack? It is no longer preparatory. Instead, its energizing effect is overruled by this inhibitory, paralyzing effect. The more severe the panic, the greater is the incapacitation. This beautiful preparatory signal of threatening damage tends to deteriorate into something that itself becomes a damage to the organism.

## Miscarried Prevention and Miscarried Repair

If we accept this assumption that emergency dyscontrol is basic to all forms of disordered behavior, excepting lesional illnesses, then we can proceed to conceptualize disordered behavior as a combination of causative and repair processes. This separation is much easier to do in theory than in treating a patient.

The causative process is the individual's effort to modify his behavior in terms of his inappropriate and excessive fears. In his effort to escape the haunting psychical discomfort, he seeks refuge by refraining from action or by restricting his behavior. He is inhibiting his healthy functioning. There can be only one consequence when the individual is driven to adopt such limitations. He has resorted to his normal range of functions but experiences pain, so now inevitably he incurs losses in adaptive utility, in pleasure, and in healthy pride with the limitation.

When the normal behavior that would have led to some degree of mature life performance and cultural self-realization is inhibited, the individual feels helpless and unable to sustain the demanding adaptive task. Because he feels helpless, he reverts to feeling like the infant he once was and it becomes essential to the distraught individual to get the parental help he received as an infant.

Now what about the repair processes? What is the individual who is faced with emergency dysfunction likely to do? Remember that he is usually a child when the disordered response starts to happen.

For this, I am appropriating the term *miscarried repair*, which is commonly used in general pathology. Organic pathology is full of instances of pathological conditions that result from the miscarried defensive measures that the organism has put into motion. How is an abscess caused? By an overproduction of white blood cells that have been produced by the body as a measure of coping with an infection.

## Four Elementary Mechanisms

I have found it useful to categorize these basic measures of miscarried prevention and miscarried repair into four kinds of elementary mechanisms. So far as I can see, each of these mechanisms appears in all varieties and combinations to form the patterns that dominate in the so-called psychopathological behavior.

The four mechanisms are the phobic mechanism, the coercive mechanism, the riddance mechanism, and the mechanism of self-coercion. Actually, the latter is a morbid derivative of the coercive mechanism.

Turning first to the phobic mechanism, behavior inspired by fear can lead to flight. Once the individual has experienced this fear, he has a tendency from then on to shun the situation that he feels has given rise to the fear. The underlying pattern is the organism's tendency to generalize experience. "Because I have been scared there once, I will probably be scared there again, so I won't go near there." The avoidance of a situation in which we have experienced fear is what we call the *phobic mechanism*. By and large, it appears in two behavior varieties. We avoid going somewhere, or, we avoid doing something. We retreat from participation or we retreat from performance. Whichever it is, the meaning of the phobic mechanism is withdrawal and avoidance. It is an expression of our weakness, of our need for protection, and in childhood we find that protection in the arms of Mama. We take sanctuary.

The second fundamental mechanism, which is prepared for by rage, is coercive in intent. It is primarily calculated to deal with human opponents, but in a broader sense it also includes dealing with the elements. In infantile terms, it means seeking allies, hopefully powerful allies. When the child cannot rely on his own aggressive resources alone, he says, "Papa, John hit me. You hit him back." Since the sanctuary and the ally are always Mama or Papa or both and since the basic activity is that of calling for aid and protection, these two mechanisms can be considered as the infantile mechanisms of invocation.

The third basic emergency mechanism is the riddance mechanism, evoked by pain. As you will remember, riddance is a response that is evoked after the organism suffers the injury or pain, so it is simply the tendency to get rid of what causes pain. I have already suggested that nature endowed the organism with the ability to experience pain so that he may be warned of danger. This is not a one-to-one relationship, but pain is so frequently a warning of danger that we have grounds for assuming that this is what it is supposed to be.

This brings us to the fourth mechanism, that of self-coercion. It is important that a scheme of the emergency function includes guilt and self-punishment or the need for punishment. The individual criticizes himself, and the self-criticism frightens him because he anticipates criticism from without. Guilt is the anticipated criticism from without. This reflects the relationship between the child and the authority figure.

The need for punishment and for self-punishment is another anticipatory move—the individual anticipates punishment from without. Guilt may lead to expiatory behavior, but it always exists in combination with repressed rage. Indeed, because of this, the intensity of the desire for self-punishment may be increased. It is as if we let loose against ourselves the rage that we cannot express against parents and authority figures. Guilt plus suppressed rage intensifies the need for punishment. With the addition of suppressed rage, it has developed beyond anticipation of punishment from without. It has now become a mechanism of discharge for pent-up rage. When this happens, we act like the man in a blind rage who begins to beat himself as if he were expressing his utmost dissatisfaction with himself for not being able to vent his rage on his opponent. He wanted to be a big shot and has proved himself powerless. So the whole fury of his rage is vented on himself.

The need for self-punishment then is not in proportion to the punishment anticipated but in proportion to the pent-up rage. The greater the need for discharge and the greater the pent-up rage in need of discharge, the more severe the self-punishment is likely to be.

Let me say this in another way. Clinical evidence has convinced me that a frustrated coercive tendency is likely to become self-coercive. When my intent to force the authority figure to yield fails, I am likely to use the whole fury of my revolt against myself and force myself to yield—which is the exact opposite of what I wanted to do originally. Probably this occurs as a result of being afraid to be angry at the authority figure, or rage at himself for having such feelings; these lead to guilty fear and expiation.

It is easy to see that it is a dangerous business to allow the organism invariably to be integrated, motivated, activated, controlled by brute emotions. For you can see how easily these emotions become self-destructive. It is indeed understandable why increasing civilization fosters supplanting emotional control by intellectual control.

How does this intellectual control work? Let us use a crude example. Suppose you are faced with a persisting emergency from which you cannot run away and against which you cannot do anything. Suppose you are in the middle of an earthquake or a bad thunderstorm. The most sovereign method of intellectual control would be to become blind to the danger that is on all sides of you and to behave as if the emergency simply did not exist. After all, what is the use of energizing yourself for flight or for combat? Since you cannot do anything anyway, such emotions will only confuse you. By means of scotomization, the individual can remain calm in a crisis. He is not fearful or preoccupied with the danger because he is ignoring it or pretending that there is none. Take another common example: the soldier cannot run away from the line of fire and he cannot make the enemy stop shooting. Since nothing he can do is of any avail, he might just as well ignore the danger and remain calm.

To summarize, behavior disorders are disturbances of psychodynamic integration that significantly affect the organism's adaptive life performance in its attainment of utility and pleasure. The nucleus of disordered behavior is the fact that the individual is experiencing emergency dyscontrol, excessive feelings of fear, rage, pain, and the like. When the organism responds to the stimulus in the environment with an excess of the emergency emotions, he will be unable to handle effectively the exigencies of daily life. These disordered (excessive or inappropriate) emergency responses impede rather than aid the organism in its adaptive task. They elicit processes of miscarried prevention and miscarried repair that produce further disordering effects such as dependency adaptation and lowered self-reliance, which further impairs functioning.

I should like to pause here to say a word about "aggression" and "instinctual danger." Please remember that aggression—the factor that plays such an important role in pathological behavior—is a camouflage for the actual primitive emotions of rage and anger. Every organism reacts to frustration with fight, with defiance, with attempts at self-assertion. It is in the nature of man to put up a struggle to gratify his pleasure desires, his security needs, and his attempts at cultural self-realization. The first injury that occurs to the organism at the onset of all pathological behavior is the restraint of rage by anxiety. If this inner resistance is not broken down, the individual becomes a victim of inhibitions that reduce his handling of the adaptive task. You will see this in patient after patient.

In his remarkable book *Inhibition, Symptom, and Anxiety,* Freud explains that what appears to be an instinctual danger is also a realistic danger because the individual fears the social consequences if he behaves in terms of this instinct. When an instinctual impulse evokes fear, we are not frightened by that instinctual impulse per se. We fear the impulse because we fear the consequences. If we yield to the desire to enact an aggressive impulse, we might have to pay for it in one way or another. This is the reality danger. When the fear of the consequences is overpoweringly strong, we suppress the aggressive impulse and allow ourselves to be dominated by the fears.

There are many ways to approach disordered behavior. First, I have found it useful in my own musing to think in terms of the "diseased phenotype." The phenotype is the outcome of the development of the genotype (the organism at birth); it is what the individual is in appearance, structure, function, and reactivity.

Second, I find it useful to think in terms of adaptive impairment, adaptive incompetence, and transgressive conduct. The term *impairment* indicates the so-called psychoneurosis. *Incompetence* indicates the so-called psychosis. *Transgressive conduct* indicates the so-called psychopathic state.

I have worked out a diagnostic classification system that has been useful to me. It is developed out of my basic assumption that the organism's first survival concern is safety. The important thing is that you see the symptoms and causes and conditions and repair mechanisms and the rest of it as the fluid phenomenon that I have described previously.

I have suggested that behavior disorders fall into seven main classes: (1) Overreactive Disorders, (2) Moodcyclic Disorders, (3) Schizotypal Disorders, (4) Extractive Disorders, (5) Lesional Disorders, (6) Narcotic Disorders, (7) Disorders of War Adaptation.

## TABLE 3 Scheme of Classification of Behavior Disorders

Class I: OVERREACTIVE DISORDERS

A: EMERGENCY DYSCONTROL—A condition that is characterized by the overproduction of emergency emotions, such as fear, rage and guilty fear.

1.) *Emotional outflow.* Symptoms are excessive outbursts of fear or rage. Most minor of neurotic symptoms.
2.) *Riddance through dreams and nightmares.*
3.) *Phobic.* Situational. To prevent fear attacks from an inner threat that is projected outwards, some element in visual memory is avoided as a symbol for the threat, i.e., certain streets, certain animals, high places, etc.

4.) *Inhibitory.* To avoid fear attacks, a motor activity is inhibited, i.e., going out alone, etc.

5.) *Repression.* Repressing of painful emotions or memories by excluding from awareness.

6.) *Hypochondriac.* Recurring bouts of terror are prompted by the patient's belief that he will be destroyed by an illness as punishment.

7.) *Gainful exploitation of illness.*

B: Descending Dyscontrol—Conditions that are usually described as "psychomatic medicine."

C: SEXUAL DISORDERS

1.) *The impairments and failures of standard performance.* Fears of penetration and genital injury leading to frigidity in women, and to potency problems, such as precipitous ejaculation, retarded ejaculation, and impotence in the male.

2.) *Dependence on reparative patterns.*

a.) *Organ replacement and organ avoidance.* This is replacement of the genital organ by some other bodily part—with avoidance of the genitals of the opposite sex. Category includes the exhibitionist and the voyeur.

b.) *Sexual pain dependence.* This is the forced and automated pursuit of advance punishment as the only means by which the individual can attain license to gratify his forbidden desires. See later summary.

c.) *The formation of homogeneous pairs.* Individuals de- deterred by fear and resentments from the opposite sex may find orgastic satisfaction with a mate of the same sex, thus forming homogeneous pairs. See later summary.

d.) *Pattern of solitary gratification.* This category includes fetishism, transvestitism, and self-stimulation. Rado considers self-stimulation a "normal" form of gratification during sexual immaturity.

e.) *Sexual equivalents.* Examples are fire-setting and bed-wetting.

D: SOCIAL OVERDEPENDENCE

1.) *Search for ersatzparent or the lack of self-reliant behavior in adults.* This may occur either because the individual never developed self-reliance (most likely) or because of the over-flow of emergency emotions.

2.) *Forced competition.* In childhood, the individual for various reasons stopped competing for the thing in question and competed for the sake of competing. This can be because of a struggle with a sibling or parent.

3.) *Avoidance of competition.* Here, instead of competing, the individual became frightened at competing with anyone for anything and retreated.

4.) *Self-harming defiance.* Here, the individual has made the false connection between being defiant and being worthwhile and strong. So he has stopped being defiant about issues but defies for the sake of defying, thinking erroneously that it is a good thing.

E: COMMON MALADAPTATION—A combination of sexual disorders with social overdependence.

F: THE EXPRESSIVE PATTERN—Expressive elaboration of common maladaptation. See later discussion.

G: THE OBSESSIVE PATTERN

H: THE PARANOID PATTERN (nondisintegrative type)

Class II: MOODCYCLIC DISORDERS

Class III: SCHIZOPHRENIA

Class IV: EXTRACTIVE DISORDERS—This category is made up of the so-called psychopaths, characterized by the behavior pattern of ingratiative (smile and suck) and extortive (hit and grab). The extractive is described as being both impatient and intolerant of frustrations, rushing to immediate pleasures through shortcuts, which may include parasitic ingratiation and extortion, resorting to physical violence, debauchery, and drugs.

Class V: LESIONAL DISORDERS—These result from specific neurological or biochemical lesions.

Class VI: NARCOTIC DISORDERS—These are patterns of drug dependence.

Class VII: WAR NEUROSES: Disorders of War Adaptation

---

The basis of this scheme is that it somewhat resembles the known patterns in organic chemistry in which we start with a simple compound and derive increasingly complex ones through the rearrangement of the components or addition of new components. With emergency dyscontrol (the first subclass of overreactive disorders) as the simplest common denominator, I have arranged the clinically observed forms of behavior disorders according to the increasing complexity of the psychodynamic mechanisms that are involved.

Please remember that this is a tentative effort. Ideally, the etiological classification of behavior disorders will draw on their genetics and physiology as well as on the psychodynamics. When we know more about these contexts, we will be able to eliminate the apparent inconsistencies of classification that are present. Any psychiatrist who tries to make a classification will find himself handicapped by the current lack of etiological knowledge. In time we should be able to characterize every behavior disorder by "lesions" of the underlying physiologic (biochemic, biophysical) functions. When we have arrived at that point, the handling of lesional disorders as a separate class will have outlived its usefulness.

At present, the best we can do is to experiment with provisional classification based mainly on psychodynamic causes, and to continue the etiological inquiry. We should keep in sight the importance of seeking to disclose the cerebral mechanism of a disordered psychodynamic response, of studying its broader physiologic context, and of searching for its genetic context.

CHAPTER **21**

# Overreactive Disorders:

# Emergency Dyscontrol and

# Descending Dyscontrol

*Emergency Dyscontrol*

IF WE ARE TO UNDERSTAND DISORDERED BEHAVIOR, WE MUST CONSTANTLY keep healthy behavior in mind as a gauge. The healthy organism follows the pattern of its desires and seizes opportunities to attain utility and pleasure.

Emergency dyscontrol interferes with these pursuits, reduces the adaptive value of the patient's life performance, and tends to make him dependent on external help. Failure of the organism to control its overreaction by its own resources results in the adoption of a number of measures, either singly or in combination. I have found it useful to categorize these into seven patterns of emergency dyscontrol, which is a subclass of overreactive disorders: (1) emotional outflow, (2) riddance through dreams, (3) the phobic, (4) the inhibitory, (5) the repressive, (6) the hypochondriac, (7) the gainful exploitation of illness.

### THE PATTERN OF EMOTIONAL OUTFLOW

The simplest form of disordered behavior I have called the *emotional outflow pattern.* Its immediate clinical manifestation is the outward discharge of the excessive emergency emotions in fits of fear or outbursts of rage. It may continue for a while and then disappear without further consequences. This is seen in children. It is a simple mechanism of riddance and discharge.

### RIDDANCE-THROUGH-DREAMS PATTERN

In the riddance-through-dreams pattern, the individual accomplishes the same result—getting rid of the excessive emergency emotions—by means of enraged dreams or terror dreams. Dreaming, as Freud shows, is a mechanism for the prompt disposal of sleep-disturbing tensions.

Now, the organism may seek to stop the overproduction or at least the outflow by its own psychodynamic means. The individual will try to figure out what to do. If conscious thought is of no avail, he will resort to processes of nonreporting thought and fall back on an automatic mechanism of riddance, such as repression. Remember, he is motivated by the principle of hedonic self-regulation, which dictates that he get rid of pain.

### PHOBIC BEHAVIOR

In the psychoanalytic classification of neurotic disturbances, phobias were considered a subdivision of hysteria. This very tentative and early classification is misleading since the criteria of hysteria included the predominance of the sexual motive. Naturally, in a good many phobias sexual content can be involved, but that is not an essential or obligatory part of the phobic mechanism. I believe that the phobic mechanism is one of the basic mechanisms on which morbid behavior is built, much more elementary than hysteria.

The phobic mechanism, the spirit of anxiety, the running away, is fundamental, like the rage or the coercive mechanism, in almost every psychopathological picture. Let me first describe to you briefly the clinical picture of phobias. Almost everything can become the concern of phobia, and there was a time when the phobias were classified and catalogued and given Greek names. There were about one hundred fifty catalogued in this way some twenty-five years ago.

It is in childhood that phobias begin. In former times the most prominent thing was the fear children had for certain animals—a dog, a cow, a horse. These days the objects have changed and I have seen children who were afraid of the fire engine. They develop street phobias, are afraid of crossing the street, or are afraid of seeing a certain type of car. There is no end to choosing situations or objects to which the response is a running away. Among grownups, too, there is the street phobia. Also there is claustrophobia, usually the individual in dread that the walls will close in on him, choke him, and he will be killed, or the closely related phobia of being buried alive, which is a variety of claustrophobia. Then there is the syphillis phobia, the phobia of lightning, and so forth.

The phobic mechanism perpetuates and generalizes the ordinary anxiety reaction to a certain experience. If, in the pursuit of threatened activity or in the midst of a certain situation, under given circumstances, anxiety arises, we consider it most natural that the individual runs from it. This is the basic escape mechanism of anxiety. What makes this mechanism into a phobic mechanism is the generalization and perpetuation of a given experience, and the irresistible force which compels the individual to run from it.

The fact that every phobia begins with an anxiety attack has long been known. Why certain anxiety attacks have these profound consequences, while in so many other instances anxiety attacks are experienced without leaving a trace is not understood. Many children and grownups have anxiety attacks which pass by and leave nothing. But in some instances, the same kind of anxiety attack is suddenly generalized and becomes the norm of behavior for all time to come. That is the problem with phobias. One child is almost bitten by a dog and forgets it and the next day he can overcome the experience and start playing with the dog all over again. The next child is almost bitten by a dog, has an anxiety attack, and from then on the phobia sets in. Once a phobia is established, it is self-perpetuating and readily accumulates new motivations. What I call rationalization of the phobia is a consequence of an effort toward intellectual control of anxiety attacks, finding out things about them so one can avoid them. This starts at a very early age, because the very first intellectual efforts toward controlling anxiety occur at a very immature stage of development.

Anxiety is always an anticipation of threatening injury, of pain from impending injury. The threat of injury gives rise to four searching questions, and there is a typical sequence in which these questions gradually develop in the mind of the growing child. The first question about injury is, How? The second question is, Who? The third question is, Where? And the fourth question is, Why? The How refers to the ways and means of threatening injury and circumstances. It bites, it burns, it cuts—as close as possible to the idea of pain. The second question, Who, comes considerably later; injury threatens from whom —who does it, who is the source of it? The third question, Where, means to which part of the body, what is the threatened site? And the last question, Why, also requires an answer.

Under primitive intellectual conditions, the question, How, often cannot be answered, and the child tries to control the anxiety by linking it up with any given element of the sensory context. This is a crucial point. It happened on such and such a street corner, it happened in such and such a context, a woman was there in a red suit, a man was there carrying a black bag—any part of the sensory context may be connected with the anxiety experience. It is not a rational analysis, only an attempt to link up with another part of the one experience as a whole. The linking of abstract events with the geographical and other elements of the experience is a trait of the human mind. Mozart describes how he got musical ideas, "I remember walking across the bridge on such and such a day, and suddenly it occured to me." The geographical location sticks in his mind years later.

Linking more abstract mental states, such as thoughts or emotional experiences, with the sensory context is a fundamental trend, seen even in the philosophers. It is exclusively so in a child who cannot do anything else about it. Instead of answering the question, How, the child links up the emotional experience with any one impressive element of the sensory context. Only much later comes the next question, Who does all that to me? First there is no Who, but rather What part of me is thereby threatened, such as the integrity of the genitals, and then Why do they do that to me? That is the last line in the analysis, all presupposing higher intellectual development.

My hypothesis about the formation of phobias can be presented as follows: the phobias do not develop out of a blue sky. They do not appear in a happy and healthy child. They develop in children who live under a too great disciplinary pressure, and have developed and constantly maintained a state of diffused anxiety. This is comparable to the diffuse anxiety of a soldier who is in the state of incipient dyscontrol. Something similar exists in a child in whom the disciplinary pressure is too great. We see the development of over-all anxiousness in these children. I can best describe this by saying that the child is afraid of everything.

My hunch is that such children are ready to respond with anxiety to anything that happens. This is described by Freud in grownup neurotics as free-floating anxiety. This state must be painful to the child because it precludes any attempt at intellectual control and the questions of How, Who, Where, and Why cannot be answered. The child can do little, if anything, with his intellectual forces to control that emotional state. Under these circumstances perhaps a crystallization or focalization of this general anxiety state takes place through a chance experience. I do not believe it is necessarily an anxiety attack that brings about such focalization. I am inclined to believe that it is a frightening experience which plays the great role.

By chance the child experiences something frightening, for example, a cat suddenly jumps, and it takes on the value of a traumatic experience. The diffuse anxiety is now focalized. The child suddenly knows what he is afraid of—he is afraid of the cat, or whatever the case may be. Then the child begins to connect his fright with any identifying element of the sensory context, and you have a phobia. The phobic experience acts like an electric condenser, like a biological organizer; it attracts and accumulates all diffuse anxiety, focalizing a diffuse anxiety into a definite and specific one, according to a chance experience of fright. The tremendous gain in the emergency function of the child is that now he has a target, and now he can fight.

A fright or anxiety or scare experienced by a child who is in a state of diffuse anxiety thus becomes the point of departure for a phobic mechanism. We can talk about a critical experience and a critical anxiety. The critical experience which focalizes the diffuse anxiety is apparently always a traumatic one. If this construction is correct, it follows that all phobias are of traumatic origin—they are not hysteric but traumatogenic.

We must also ask why it is that in certain instances anxiety attacks and experiences of fright take place and nothing serious comes of it. The difference, according to my construction, is that if there is a long preparation in the child, reflecting the severity of parental attitudes and their great disciplinary pressure upon the child, there is a chance for the development of the phobia. Once the phobic mechanism is established the phobic content becomes the chief representative of all kinds of behavior and will be connected with all kinds of guilt. Whatever the main conflicts of the child, fear of retaliation, fear of punishment, will be attached to the phobic mechanism. The phobic content will be the punishment for all. In other words, it acquires new motivations and will become part and parcel of new psychological patterns. It proves to be a means of coping with anxiety and will be significant in every situation where anxiety is part of the picture.

The phobic mechanism has the following characteristics: first, it is based on an intellectual effort to control an emotional phenomenon, namely, the outburst of anxiety. But the child who undertakes this intellectual effort is immature, so that his appraisal is faulty. That is why I use the phrase *phobic avoidance*, since phobia is the avoidance mechanism.

The second characteristic of the phobic avoidance mechanism is that it tends to spread, to reinforce one set of precautionary measures by another round of precautionary measures, to reinforce safeguards of the first order by new safeguards of the second order, the third order, and so forth. The more precautionary measures are introduced, the more the conditions of anxiety move along. The phobia itself sets up an anxiety mechanism of its own.

The third characteristic of the phobic mechanism is that it lends itself readily to new explanations. As the child grows and intellectual maturity advances, he begins to invent or find explanations to explain his fear.

If bodily integrity is threatened, the reaction of the child or grownup does not go along rational but along emotional lines. The body organs acquire an emotional evaluation which may or may not coincide with the rational evaluation. The most highly valued organ in the male is his penis, from early childhood the site of the most intense pleasurable sensations. In a system of values that is based on pleasure, it takes on the number one role. Therefore the child's fear of bodily damage is primarily a fear of damage to the genitals. Every kind of bodily fear is usually formulated as a fear of castration. It is in this way that Little Hans in Freud's famous case has his fear of physical damage at some juncture become a fear of damage to his genitals, the most highly valued organ.

This was unintelligible in earlier psychoanalysis which therefore invented the idea of symbolic displacement. I believe that there is no such thing as symbolic displacement. When damage threatens, the person thinks first of his most cherished and highly valued belonging. Any threat to it is experienced as fear for its integrity. In an analogous situation a woman's first fear is of being raped. The anticipation of any kind of damage culminates usually in fear for the integrity of the genital and becomes a "castration fear."

The phobic mechanism is uniquely suited to be utilized as a mechanism of control in a large variety of anxieties. Whenever in later life a situation of diffuse anxiety develops for whatever reason, the individual may resort to a childhood phobia in an attempt to cope with the anxiety. The phobic mechanism thereby becomes a handyman or universal instrument for handling anxiety, with the result that the phobic pictures we encounter have such a remarkably diverse character. Not only have the different types of phobias different psychodynamic structures, but even phobias of the same clinical type, say agoraphobias, may have a different psychological structure from case to case.

The way to treat a phobic mechanism is to neutralize it or, rather, overneutralize or overcompensate it. Something that starts out to be a threat, such as the horse in the case of Little Hans, must be converted into a challenge, and the challenge developed into a triumph. The simplest example of this is the war phobia. Every memory of the war experience elicits a new outburst of anxiety. If that memory can be transformed from a threat into a challenge, and the individual is capable of responding to it with an inflation of his ego, "What a guy I am, I got through all that and here I am," then he will develop the challenge into victory and the inner need for the phobia will disappear.

To repeat what I have already said, phobia is not a disease entity but a symptom, a faulty mechanism of emergency control which can be brought into play for many different reasons.

The most frequent clinical form of phobia is the so-called agoraphobia, or street phobia. Freud made the first clarifying remark about phobias over twenty-five years ago when he said that people who are afraid to go out on the street help themselves by having an escort and feel better and freer with a close relative or friend. From this arrangement one can see that the phobic person behaves like a child, relapsing into childhood. This remark of Freud's is invaluable. It means that the threatening anxiety renders the individual just as helpless as he was when his helplessness was an expression of his immaturity.

In later years Franz Alexander and others have said that if one type of structure can be discovered in a phobia, it can be generalized. I also thought of this as an entity but today I know it is not. The underlying fear in a street phobia was seen as the sexual temptations, and for people who were products of the Victorian period of education it did indeed have this meaning. In the woman it represented what was called in the literature the prostitution fantasy. It was considered that this phobia meant that they were afraid of the temptations of the street—to fall on the street, interpreted by Alexander symbolically as to fall morally. The male was viewed as being afraid of the tempting, illicit, extramarital sexual adventure represented by the street. It was seen to have its climax in a fear of venereal disease. It was sexual temptation, immoral conduct, and fear of venereal infection.

All these mechanisms do exist. But it is important to keep in mind that they are not necessarily components of the picture of street phobia. In a number of cases with agoraphobia, it is a disguised form of sexual phobia. But the sexual damage, of which the sexual phobia is an expression, may have been damage on the anatomic level (such as castration and its derivatives—venereal disease, rape, impregnation) or moral damage (damage to the woman's social standing), in which case, naturally, sexual phobia reflects the cultural standards of the period.

The conception of sexual damage on the social level is to be looked upon from the point of view of the educational background of the individual. Sexual fear on the social level changes its aspect from culture to culture and from period to period. For a woman to have a say in sexual matters or make her own choice is the rule today.

The standard psychoanalytic statement originally was that people who have these sexual fears are impotent or frigid or have some sexual disturbance, which was in turn related to their oedipal fixation. That too has to be established from case to case.

The opposite fear, claustrophobia, was interpreted as having a sexual meaning, that of temptation to masturbate. If street phobia was a temptation to sidestep the marital situation, claustrophobia was a temptation to masturbate, to indulge in something which may prove harmful. There is indeed a subgroup of claustrophobics in which sexual temptation does play a role. But, again, this is not a constant feature of claustrophobia. There is often a combination of mutual conversion of claustrophobia into agoraphobia and vice versa. These phobias may be disguised forms of sexual temptation, an attempt to cope by means of phobic mechanism with the underlying problem of sexual temptation —sexual incapacitation or disablement. Or, the phobia may have no sexual meaning at first and then take on sexual meaning at a time of sexual conflict. Once the sexual meaning disappears from the picture the phobia may even remain.

In claustrophobia, a typical fear is that of being buried alive, to be crushed, choked in some way or another. In typical childhood experiences children were thrown into dark closets and had their first phobic attack there. Bertram Lewin has traced claustrophobia to the primal scene—the child's observation of intercourse between the parents. Here again this is a correct derivation but not essential. In those instances where this derivation exists it is based on a misunderstanding of sexual intercourse as an act of violence. If the woman resists or makes sounds which the child understands as suffering inflicted by the strong and powerful father, the experience is that of being crushed or annihilated. But other experiences without this context have similar consequences. In one study, Phyllis Greenacre describes the relationship between anxiety and early experiences of physical restraint. She throws light on the childhood experience of early restraint becoming a model for being crushed—claustrophobia.

The derivation of claustrophobia from a secret desire to return to the womb or a fear of returning to the womb I would view as erroneous. We know that for a growing child who already has experienced the pleasure of running around, being confined in a small place is terrifying. The womb is a rather terrible abode when looked upon from the point of view of the freedom of a growing child or a grownup. When people express their fear of being locked up in a room or dark closet, they dramatize their fear but do not express the true origin of their phobia. This retrospective fantasy is very common, especially in schizophrenia, and may play a part in the development of claustrophobia.

The motivation of street phobia may be an excessive desire to shine, to attract, to put oneself on display, which once upon a time has been crushed through frustrating experience, so that the individual emerges with a dread of exposure. He interprets every public appearance as an occasion of possible exposure to unfavorable comment, to criticism, to ridicule, and the like. In stage fright this plays a great role.

A few words about another common phobia—height phobia, fear of getting dizzy and falling when looking down from a high mountain, from a high tower, or even from the window of a high apartment. Earlier psychoanalytic explanation was passive sexual fantasies. I myself have historically described it as a masochistic sensation, but now I would specify more correctly that this is a riddance sensation—to put an end to the unbearable tension of anxieties by yielding to the temptation to jump down. It need not, but it may have all kinds of sexual connotations. The mechanism can be brought into play in the presence or absence of sexual conflict.

The term *phobia* is used sometimes in a rather loose fashion. For instance, when people sitting in a theater are afraid they will be tempted to shout and disturb the performers, it is no longer a phobia. This is an obsessive idea, an obsessive thought, an obsessive impulse, against which, on a second or third level of organization, a terrific fight goes on. What the person wants to do is shout, "Stop it, stop it!" He identifies the whole performance with one that put him into a panic during childhood, and the temptation is to shout out.

Otto Rank suggested that being born through the experience of difficult labor brought about phobias and anxiety. He wove a fantastic magic carpet of this idea, stating that life consists of reenacting the trauma of birth. This theory was discredited for a long time but now we are asking, does a natal experience of severe labor predispose toward anxiety? Greenacre stresses that possibly the prenatal and natal experience have been neglected in our literature.

## Little Hans

Freud's famous analysis of a phobic was the case of Little Hans. You will recall that Freud did not analyze the five-year-old boy, but the father analyzed the boy according to Freud's instructions. Freud saw the boy only once and gives us verbatim the reports of the father.

The construction of the case is that the child, after displaying great interest in his own penis and that of others, developed a phobia in which he was afraid of horses and refused to go out on the street. Freud's original interpretation of this anxiety was that the child at that same time had an overly tender and sensual desire for the mother and wanted to be with her all the time. This suppressed and repressed libido, this excessive desire for the mother was transformed into anxiety. In the original paper, Freud says, "Hans admitted that every night before going to sleep he amused himself with playing with his penis. 'Ah' the family doctor will be inclined to say, 'now we have it. The child masturbated: hence its pathological anxiety.'" This is what Freud himself states as the problem twenty years later in his *Problem of Anxiety*—Hans masturbated and is afraid of the consequences.

I feel that the child was afraid not because of the forbidden pleasure but because he was threatened that his penis would be cut off. "Moreover, we may presume that Hans, who was now four and three-quarters, had been indulging in this pleasure every evening for at least a year." In other words, Freud suggests that the anxiety was derived from the suppressed libidinal desire for the mother.

This construction was explicitly retracted in his *Problem of Anxiety*, where Freud says "It is not as I stated before that anxiety develops as a consequence of repression. Here it is anxiety that causes the repression, and not, as I earlier stated, the repression that causes the anxiety."

Freud construed the phobia as follows: The horse is the symbolic representation of the father. Hans is afraid of the father, but at the same time, adores him—what Freud called the conflict of ambivalence. In such a situation it is a great relief to split that same person, the love and hate, into two. One of the objects can then be retained for love and the hate will be deflected to this substitute alter ego. Phobias, in particular the horse phobia of Hans, according to Freud, serve this purpose. Hans can go on now with loving his father because his hatred is deflected to the horse.

It is not the hatred which we see in the phobia, I believe, but the fear of retaliation for the hatred. Freud said, the real phobia is the fear of the father, deflected from the father to the father-substitute, the horse, and, a result of the hostile rebellious intent toward the father, was the fear of retaliation. The hostile intent toward the father is, in turn, a result of the rivalry for the mother's favors. The theoretical formulation of this phobia is the oedipal situation—Little Hans wants the favors of the mother for himself. For this reason he hates the father and has an ambivalent conflict. But the father is stronger and Hans must suppress his hatred and be afraid of retaliation. This fear of the father is deflected to the horse and appears as this horse phobia according to Freud.

I propose that all Freud said about Hans is true, except that it does not explain his phobia. That Little Hans loved his father and hated him at the same time is true; that he wanted the favors of his mother and was jealous of his mother is true; that he had a castration fear is true. This is the anatomy of the infantile situation and can be found over and over again in every nursery. In some instances it does lead to a phobia, and in others it does not.

How did Freud hit upon the idea, which was later generalized and made a fundamental point of explanation, that in the infantile phobias the animal is always a representative of the father? First, he said there is a philogenetic origin, that this is an atavistic relapse, that certain tribes credited certain animals with the honor of having certain characteristics and worshiped those animals. Freud believed that this atavistic thinking revives in a child who develops an animal phobia. The more concrete evidence of Freud was that Hans, when asked why he was afraid to go out on the street and see a horse, answered, "Because the horse will bite me." Freud took that at its face value, and built up an elaborate structure—fear of castration on the oral level, the idea of being eaten up by one's parents. These things which Freud describes do exist—there is a fear in the child of being eaten up by his parents, as exemplified in the Grimms' fairy tale of Hansel and Gretel—but to me it is not an explanation of this phobia.

One day Hans said he was afraid the horse would come into the room. Freud interpreted this to mean, "that would make sense only if the horse is Papa. Papa comes into the room, so the horse comes into the room," indicating here that the horse is Papa. At a certain point of development this horse may have become a substitute for the father, but there is incontestable evidence that this was not the origin of the horse phobia. I believe that in light of our current knowledge we could no longer say that the phobia started out by Hans making the horse an alter ego for the father. Remember that the parents of this child lived on a street where there was a warehouse across from their home, and heavy trucks pulled by horses constantly went by. Hans had often seen these horses collapse. Freud interpreted that it was Hans' wish that his father should collapse. That might have been true at a much later stage of development.

The key to the whole business is revealed in the following statement which suddenly appears in a footnote: "Hans has often been very much terrified when drivers beat their horses and shout 'Gee-up.' In a conversation between father and son, Hans says, 'It doesn't do the horses any harm when they're beaten.' (I said this to him once to mitigate his fear of seeing horses whipped.) 'Once I really did it. Once I had the whip and whipped the horse, and it fell down and made a row with its feet.' "

Hans had seen those coachmen hitting the horses, and as it happened in wintertime when the load was too heavy, the horses were beaten and fell down and were pulled up again and then beaten down again. This is the fear the child had. It is unquestionably a traumatic experience in which the child has identified himself with the horse. The horse identification was not between the father and the horse, but between Hans himself and the horse. Whenever something terrifying happens, the most primitive idea in every observer is, "That could happen to me." When the horse is beaten and collapses on the street, the terror of the child indicates that the child identified himself with this beaten horse. It is not the father who collapses there—it is Little Hans himself.

He says that his mother often threatens to beat him with the carpet beater. So here you have the story. Here is a child who has been threatened with the carpet beater. He goes out on the street and sees the horses being beaten with something which is close enough to a carpet beater to be identified with it (the whip) and is terrified and collapses. To me there is no doubt that the child identifies himself with the horse, because the horse is in a similar situation to that of himself, he has been threatened with a beating with the carpet beater, and now he sees the horse beaten with the whip. From innumerable fantasies you can see that whip and carpet beater are the same for him.

This is the traumatic experience in which the diffuse anxiety of this child focalizes. From now on he is afraid of the horse because the horse reminds him of the terrific beating that can be administered to him. And when Papa so much later asks Hans, "Why are you afraid of the horse?" he is unable to say because the horse was beaten and you could beat me, because that is too painful, and he gives a rationalized answer—because the horse is beaten. This is a secondary elaboration, a rationalization on the part of the child. Every phobic mechanism enriches its own content and later on new elements can be added to the picture. In the Freudian interpretation, the idea of being bitten by the horse has the central and fundamental significance. I view the basic traumatic situation as follows: I am afraid of the horse because the horse reminds me of how terribly I can be beaten myself.

As for the idea that the horse can come into the room, I do not believe it means that the horse is the father; it merely means that this five-year-old child is persecuted by his memory. I do not need to go out into the street, I can still see the horse being beaten.

Freud discovered the principle of how to treat a phobia in 1905. Hans said he would like to beat the horse. There are all sorts of fantasies reproduced—if he takes charge, if he does the beating, then it is sure that he cannot be beaten. He goes over from the passive to the active role, from the victimized to the victimizing role. If he can take pleasure in hitting those horses, then he is no longer terrified by the sight of horses being beaten, because he does the beating. He derives pride and satisfaction from that. He transforms the experience from a frightening one to a gratifying one. He cannot deny that the horses are being beaten, but he does the beating. That is the way to overcome a traumatic experience, namely, from a source of panic, fright, make it into a source of pleasure and gratitude—ego pleasure. That is the meaning of so many of his fantasies. He is trying to take control—if he can handle the whip, then he is safe.

Let me repeat that every phobia is traumatogenic, based upon an experience of fright, panic, or anxiety, due to a background of diffuse anxiety. The trauma focalizes this anxiety to a certain situation and henceforth this situation or event becomes symbolic and representative of all the dangers surrounding the individual, for whatever reason and in whatever form. The cure for that phobic mechanism is the transformation of the specific stimulus pattern from a stimulus that throws the individual into panic, into one that throws him into ego-delight, pleasure, pride, satisfaction, narcissistic gratification.

To return to Little Hans, he is panicky about his masturbation. His mother threatened to cut off his penis if she found him playing with it. Under these circumstances the hitting of the horses became a symbolic representation of this panic, too, and at some point he may have fantasies that the horse is mother and papa, too. All that is highly probable, but it has nothing to do with the basic mechanism of the phobia. This is the natural secondary elaboration. Once a phobic mechanism is formed, it is constantly changing in dramatic content. The mechanism is set up and the man can go through life attempting to handle an emergency on that basis. The phobic mechanism is capable of complicated elaboration, in the sense not only of bringing its content up to date, but of leading to the obsessive mechanism. That which starts out, say, as a fear of castration may disappear and be replaced as a fear of syphillis or fear of venereal disease. All these changes are possible.

Far from being all hysteric in character and structure, the phobias are the simplest neurotic disturbances or insufficiencies of adaptation. Possibly no phobia develops in adulthood in individuals who did not have it in childhood. It may have in the interim receded and is now in adult life revived. Bearing this in mind, we set out to establish the developmental dynamics of the phobic mechanism as follows: on the most elementary and lowest level of dysfunction we find this chain of events: first, environmental stress, which is relative to the individual's makeup, affecting one type of child differently from the way it affects another. What constitutes threat is the pressure relative to the person's makeup. As a result of this environmental threat, a diffuse anxiety develops. It represents the simplest form of insufficiency of adaptation and is called emergency dysfunction. Anxiety, instead of functioning as a signal of emergeny and subsiding when the emergency is over, is here a more or less persistent condition. It has itself become an injury, a harm, a disturbance to the organism. It outlives the situation in which it had justification. The characteristic of this anxiety is that it is diffuse and free-floating, indicating the mildest and simplest form of emergency dysfunction and anxiety outflow.

This simple emergency dysfunction, characterized by anxiety outflow, is the point of departure for a good many kinds of neurotic behavior which are all the result of more and more elaboration. Impending danger elicits in turn defensive measures of control that the organism now undertakes in order to cope with the anxiety. These lead to further elaboration, the results of which are the various clinical types of morbid behavior. The simplest one among them is the phobic behavior. The inhibitory pattern differs from the phobic pattern by the child's memory which remembers something in the motor aspect in the inhibitory pattern, while the memory is in the visual aspect in phobias.

For a moment I would like to revert to street phobia which is often encountered clinically and has been the subject of publications for decades. Much has been made of the many instances where a parent substitute relationship exists between the agoraphobic patient on the one hand and the person whom he favors to escort him in order that he be able to move freely on the street. Also, many have noted that there is a tremendous amount of hostility piled up in the phobic patient, concentrated on the very person on whom he so relies. Helene Deutsch deserves credit for emphasizing this. In the phobic mechanism as it continues there is opportunity for secondary gain. The phobia proves to be a perfect instrument of control in a setting where the patient can count on altruistic feelings, consideration, and regard. If this prerequisite is not fulfilled, the phobia cannot be exploited for such control purposes.

A rather frequently occurring objective in phobias, especially in childhood, is to separate the parents from one another. In many instances, the precipitating factor is that the child sees some sexual contact between the parents, but other factors can give the same picture. The child does this by forcing the mother, for instance, to be with him all the time. Also, the child may cling to the mother because of a hostile relationship between the two—here guilt also is a major emotion. The latter relationship often exists in the "school phobia." The satisfaction of controlling parents or parent substitutes may, of course, be not the primary goal but only a secondary result. The child feels the anxiety, but the meaning and cause are in the nonreporting area.

One more word about the relationship between the phobic mechanism and the self: anxiety is self-discordant. It diminishes self-esteem, reduces the size of the self, and can be a terrific blow to the original estimation of the self. The same applies to the phobias, which are elaborations of anxiety.

In treating phobias, there is an attempt first to neutralize the phobic mechanism itself which is usually infantile in origin and second to trace the underlying particular fears to the conflict from which they came and then remove them.

### THE INHIBITORY PATTERN

Actually, this inhibitory mechanism is often a two-part thing. First, the child attempts to prevent the recurrence of the attack of fear by retreating from and automatically inhibiting the motor activity in which the attack occurred. The second mechanism shows how an even higher degree of foresight is misapplied. To play safe, the organism automatically inhibits not only the activities tabooed by the authorities, or those that the child believes were tabooed by the parents, but on an ever-widening scale he also forbids himself the approaches to those activities. The second happens when the nonreporting responses have become so overwhelmingly strong that the individual is being forced to inhibit activities in a way he cannot understand.

In the adult, strong emotion may block intellectual activity at higher levels. Consequently, his thinking, too, may get stuck in the sensory material of an overwhelming experience. We can see this in patients with acute inhibitions or phobias.

If the parents see early signs of the child's motor dyscontrol, what do they do? Sensing that something is wrong, they link the symptoms to some supposedly dangerous thing that the child has done and forbid him to do it again. They thus teach the child to blame his overreaction on himself. With the automatization of this response, the child develops nonreporting fear of conscience and guilty fear.

### THE REPRESSIVE PATTERN

In the repressive pattern of emergency dyscontrol, the organism, unable to stop the overproduction and overflow of overreactive emergency emotions by other means, may resort to the mechanism of repression. This can be temporarily successful. By means of this mechanism, he excludes an emotionally charged memory or thought or wish from awareness, or he automatically prevents these excessive emotions from rising into consciousness and being outwardly discharged. Resorting to this mechanism is usually, but not necessarily, prompted by non-reporting·fears of conscience. This, however, is an unstable mechanism because it is powerless to halt an eventual overflow of the repressed emotions. This overflow, in turn, is bound to give rise to further dis-ordering consequences. Even when the patient seems to be aware of the emergency emotions he is experiencing, we should keep this mech-anism of repression in mind.

Since fear and rage are antagonistic responses, open fear is often accompanied by repressed rage. I call this dynamic formation *fear over rage*. Similarly, open rage may be accompanied by repressed fear. This I call *rage over fear*. The battle between fear and rage is strongly in-fluenced by the conflict between the organism's desire for security through dependence and its pride in self-realization. Fear over rage shows the victory of the dependency need. The resulting combination of repressed rage and hurt pride is a prolific, though less conspicuous, source of the patient's suffering. The contrary outcome—rage over fear—shows victory of the organism's pride in having its own way. Incomplete repression of fear and rage may produce qualitatively un-differentiated chronic tension states, marked by apprehensiveness or irascibility or both.

### HYPOCHONDRIAC PATTERN

Now just a few comments about the hypochondriac pattern. Let us turn to an adult patient whose life has become miserable because he is now firmly convinced that he has, or is threatened by, a serious physical illness.

This belief may be semidelusional, even delusional at times, in that the patient tends to stick to it whatever the factual evidence may prove to the contrary. In the milder cases, the patient will accept the doctor's reassurance that the disturbing symptoms are nothing and will feel better for a time. But the reassurance wears off fast—how long depends on how severely the patient is suffering these recurring bouts of terror of illness.

If the delusion is firmly rooted because of the nature of the condition, the hypochondriac is driven to rush from doctor to doctor until he finds one that will prescribe the treatment he thinks he needs.

When the hypochondriac is really driven by his need—as in more severe cases—the picture is indeed a sad one. Research studies of surgery on the basis of pathological findings indicate that a high percentage of unnecessary surgery is being performed and that forty to sixty percent of these unnecessary operations were done at the persuasion of the hypochondriacal patient. The surgery lulls his fears for a while, and then he starts all over again.

Take the patient who thinks he has a heart ailment. Though every electrocardiogram and every diagnostic tool prove that his heart is sound, he cannot hold on to this fact. Preoccupied by his belief, he is constantly searching for the telltale signs of the heart ailment he believes he has. He is bound to find something, so the slightest palpitation that the healthy individual would scarcely notice is enough to precipitate a new outburst of fear. Such a hypochrondriac may occasionally be "cured" by having his worst fears realized. If he has a severe coronary, he may at last be free from the fear that has dogged his life. But the cost of that kind of "cure" is high.

The main defense of the hypochondriac is to behave like the helpless child in his reaching out for one doctor after another. He may put some faith temporarily in health fads and regimens that are supposed to preserve his good health. But just let him "discover" his symptom and all his faith vanishes.

The behavior of the hypochondriac is very much like that of the phobic. The phobic is faced with imagined dangers threatening from the environment. He masters them by the phobic mechanism of avoidance, which is essentially flight. But against the imagined danger that threatens from within the organism, the patient is helpless. The recourse of flight that activates the phobic is not available to the hypochondriac. Hence, the hypochondriac runs to the doctor and literally cries for help.

Clinical analysis illustrates that the essential mechanism of hypochondria is always the same. The delusional idea stems from the patient's nonreporting belief that such illness is the long-overdue punishment that is now catching up with him. This guilty fear may be at the root of the fear of some specific illness that most people occasionally experience.

Hypochondria is a good example of the animistic thinking of inescapable punishment, the kind that is natural to the child or to an individual belonging to a preliterate tribe. This reigns triumphant in the hypochondriac. To primitive man, the cause of death is never a natural one. Death is punishment, death is the doing of an evil spirit, death is a machination of some kind of magic thing, and so forth. The hypochondriac's attitude toward his supposed illness is an example of this type of animistic thinking.

For a period psychoanalytic literature propounded the theory that the tenacious fear of illness experienced by the hypochondriac had its root in the "master guilt of the child"—the fear of castration as a result of self-stimulation, or wanting the castration he feared. I suggest rather that the hypochondriac can fear punishment for any number of real or imagined "sins."

However, it is true that most fears have an infantile root and that orgastic self-stimulation or masturbation is an activity too often shrouded in guilty fear. Many hypochondriacal patients expect the punishment of illness to smite them for exactly this very reason. But it is a mistake to generalize this to the exclusion of other motives.

Why the fear of the hypochondriac is riveted on illness is something about which I cannot even speculate. David M. Levy believes that many hypochondriacs have had a series of illnesses in childhood and have become used to the idea of being sick as a way of life. But too many hypochondriacs who had healthy childhoods also accept this idea.

Hypochondria, like the phobic disorders, may occur in the individual as the only disease entity, or more likely it may be one syndrome in a more complicated illness. In the paranoid syndrome, for instance, it plays an important part.

I will wind up these few comments on hypochondria by reminding you that the hypochondriac has developed his syndrome in his effort to cope with his excessive production of fear and rage.

Emergency dyscontrol interferes with the healthy individual's functioning and self-satisfaction. It reduces the adaptive value of the individual's life performance and tends to make him dependent on external help. If his life situation, his family and friends, permits, he capitalizes on his illness. He vents his repressed rage and recaptures his pride by exploiting the privileges of the sick child. The same infantile and vindictive exploitation of relatives and friends may occur in every form of disordered behavior or, for that matter, in every illness. Emergency dyscontrol enters as a basic etiological factor into the emotional dynamics of almost all behavior disorders.


## Descending Dyscontrol

The discharge via the autonomic nervous system of the repressed yet overflowing emergency emotions into the various component systems (respiratory, circulatory, alimentary, endocrine, etc.) of the whole organism may precipitate disease processes in the peripheral systems affected. I suggest that we call the disordering effects that this phenomena produces in the physiology (and anatomy) of these systems *descending dyscontrol*.

The cerebral system becomes aware of the peripheral disease thus precipitated and responds to this internal event just as it responds to events in the environment. The same circular operation of responses occurs when a peripheral disease of purely peripheral origin elicits emergency overreaction with autonomic overdischarge.

As you can see, the significance of emergency dyscontrol extends far beyond the psychodynamic realm of behavior disorders. By means of the mechanism of repression, it is part of this circuit of peripheral disease.

Clearly, the clinical manifestations of descending dyscontrol and purely peripheral physiology are interpendent and inseparable components of the same organismic context. When the discoveries of psychodynamics are incorporated in its body of theory, purely physiological medicine may advance to a more comprehensive medicine.

# CHAPTER 22

# Common Maladaptation:

# Sexual and Social Disorders

COMMON MALADJUSTMENT IS A COMBINATION OF VARYING QUANTITIES of sexual disorder and social overdependence. The vast number of patients that you will be treating will suffer from it. In this entire area, the basic factor is overreactive dyscontrol in childhood, perpetuated in later life. The seed of the disordered behavior is the same emergency dyscontrol that I have been talking about.

## A Summary of Common Maladaptation

Why are so many disorders primarily located in the sexual and social areas? First, think of the highly prohibitive attitudes our culture fosters. Prohibitions fence in sex on every side and make it especially forbidden to children. What is perhaps less obvious is that the child is also forbidden to assert himself. He is supposed to forego his genital pleasure and give up his rage at the prohibitive parent and be a nice little boy about the whole thing. The average child is highly endowed with sexual drive and the need to assert himself. When he is raised in a culture that forbids him to gratify these two needs, the makings of a neurosis are there. Abnormal behavior may or may not develop, according to the amount of the endowment, the repressiveness of the environment, the kinds of other qualities he develops, and so forth. But it is important to remember that this conflict between child and parent in these areas is a cultural phenomenon.

The great minds of our time have had some awareness of the danger of overinhibiting the child. John Dewey based a philosophy on the idea of allowing the child self-expression. His idea was that society was to lessen the amount of prohibition to which it was exposing the child and permit him to vent his defiance. I do not know that this is better for the child than old-fashioned rearing. It is possible that the child who cannot revolt against discipline, because there is none to revolt against, may be cut off from a necessary bodily expression.

## Social Overdependence

Social overdependence is the common garden variety of disordered behavior. Such an individual has no faith in himself and does not know what the goals of life are or what to work for. In general, the individual who suffers from this condition does not know how to be a family member or how to live in the community or how to earn a living. Frequently, he is unable to handle responsibility, dependence relationships, or close emotional ties. He can be characterized as being less self-reliant and more dependent than other individuals in his age group. This is the person who will not let you pass him on the highway today, but will let himself be taken advantage of at work tomorrow.

The crucial point is that the overreaction to danger which this individual suffers has led him to the development of inhibitions. Because the inhibitions prevent him from developing his own resources, he feels helpless. Sooner or later, such an individual looks for an ersatz parent who is expected to take care of him as his parents once did. The patient believes the parentified person will do for him what he cannot do for himself, provided he can obtain the parentified person's affection. Of course, he is courting failure. The parentified person cannot take care of the dependent individual in so comprehensive a way, even if he is willing to assume the role of the dependency figure. The individual, because of his need for a parent, must inhibit all his defiance and sexuality as he did as a child.

When orgastic desire invades the child's dependency relationship with the parents or substitute parents, fears result. Freud designated this relationship as the Oedipus complex and felt the superego was formed by the repression of the Oedipus complex. I feel that repression occurs as a result of the child's fear of the parents and the omnipotence he has delegated to them.

An example of how sexual feelings are dealt with in a dependent adult is as follows: A male patient who was dependent on a female psychiatrist felt that he could not have any sexual feelings toward her because when he was a child such feelings toward his mother were forbidden him. Just as he had to repress the incest desires when he was a child, out of obedience and fear because it was demanded by his real parents whom he actually needed, the dependent patient will feel that he must suppress them now to please the parent substitute, whom he feels he needs.

The difficulty here is said to be caused by regression to an earlier adaptation. Actually, regression, along with the emergency dyscontrol and the inhibition, are part of the repair pattern which is supposed to bring the parent back to help the individual in his helplessness. If the repair pattern goes beyond the attempt to get a substitute parent, the maladjustment may take on any of the more elaborate forms—expressional, obsessive, paranoid. Or the maladjustment may express itself in irrational actions, such as shoplifting.

Because he feels inadequate and helpless and because he is not self-reliant, he searches for the ersatz parent, or the dependency figure on whom he can lean and depend. In other words, analysis reveals that the essential fact of his malaise is that he is in a childhood state of dependence and can get along only by relying on a parental figure.

Such an individual cannot get along in social life or make his way in the business world because he tends to handle domination or competition in either of two unfortunate ways. One way is to avoid competition, and the socially overdependent person may do everything possible to stay far away from the frightening competition. Unable to be normally self-assertive and normally aggressive, he is timid and shy and indiscriminately submissive. He does this because he must repress his anger to keep his dependency relationship. This lowers his self-esteem and makes him feel unable to compete.

It is also likely that in childhood, the individual became frightened about competing with anybody for anything, and so retreated. This means that he has exchanged the gratifications that usually reward normal self-assertiveness for the emotional security he gets from non-competition.

The other way is to live a life dominated by forced competition, in which the individual is unable to handle his need to be indiscriminately aggressive or competitive. The pity of this is that the individual is competing for the sake of competing. At some point in his childhood

he gave up competing for the thing in question and settled on competition itself as his motivation. The cause of this switch may have
been a power struggle with a sibling or parent. As an adult, he wastes
endless time competing with people he sees as siblings because he is
still involved in a childhood level of acting and feeling. Over and over,
he interprets events and people in terms of the family constellation he
grew up in, instead of seeing them as they are. Sometimes, the socially
overdependent individual develops the self-harming pattern of defiance
for the sake of defiance, giving him a point of departure around which
he can act out the old patterns of domination and rebellion. Even
when he is aware that his rebellious behavior is inappropriate, self-
destructive, or futile, he cannot relinquish his behavior.

What has happened is that in his childhood he made the erroneous
connection between being worthwhile and strong and acting defiantly.
Unconsciously, he still harbors this false notion and controls his behavior by the fallacy that defiance is a good thing. You may feel pretty
good when you tell off the boss, but you will pay a price for it. You will
not feel so good about yourself when the rent is due and you have no
job. The person who is not caught in such self-defeating patterns will
line up a job before he tells off the boss. He might then even forgo
that pleasure if he wants to be able to turn to the boss for recommenda-
tions in the future. The other side of the coin is that the socially overdependent individual feels worthless and self-contemptuous when he
does what he is told to do even if the matter is trivial, and even if he
knows how unimportant it is.

This common disorder causes much misery and frustration. Because
he is living as a dependent child, he is forced to react like a child to
keep in the good graces of the parent substitute. Whatever his chrono-
logical age, he must enact the pattern of expiation—atonement, guilt,
ingratiation—that is required of the child in the sanctuary. Because
of his need for the ersatz parent and his dependence adaptation, he
must do these things even when he is old enough to be a free agent,
and frequently he wants to be free to do as he sees fit.

These people talk about "being tied down" and "being held back"
and "not being a free agent." The sad truth is that these complaints
are a self-deceiving cover-up, because the person is not self-reliant
enough to be master of his own destiny. No individual is ever "given"
his freedom; he must fight for it and be strong enough to hold onto it.
This is what self-determinism means.

Let me remind you of one other point about the socially overdependent person. When he turns to a parent substitute of the same sex,

he may seem to be the homosexual that he is not. The clue to the correct diagnosis lies in the motivation of the relationship. Upon examination, you may find that the basis is of the nature of child-parent dependence rather than of sexual needs.

## Sexual Disorders

Before we proceed to our discussion of sexual modifications, please bear in mind my suggestion that the utilitarian aspect of the sexual function as opposed to the reproductive function is to discharge the organism's tension. There is no evidence to show that the minimum orgastic requirements of a given organism at a given time, whatever they may be, can be adequately met by means other than the climactic release of sexual tension. It is probably correct to say that the adult requires the pleasure of orgasm in itself.

Although our society is a great deal freer than it was in Freud's day, we still see sexual pathology. Let me remind you of what we called the fears of genital degradation. These are the emotional preoccupations with the threatened mutilating consequences that the child fears will be his punishment for all kinds of "forbidden" sexual activity. The child, the adolescent, the troubled adult, have extended this view of the dangerous nature of sexual self-stimulation so that it may include any and all kinds of sexual activity as potentially dangerous.

Another deterrent aspect is the development of the fear of penetration in both sexes. The girl is taught that the male's sexual approach is an assault and that such contact will destroy her anatomic and emotional integrity and social standing. The boy is told that he will inflict fateful damage on the girl, which will lead to merciless retaliation.

This indoctrination is reinforced by experiences such as the primal scene, so that boy and girl both inevitably arrive at the violence misconception of sexual intercourse. The boy comes to believe that the female organ is an open wound, resulting from the violent removal of the missing penis. The girl comes to believe that the male organ is a destructive weapon. Naturally, each is also influenced by the other's misconceptions.

Fortunately, in the process of becoming self-reliant adults, these sexual fears and guilty sexual fears are most often outgrown. But everybody is not so fortunate and in some adults these fears persist throughout life. We do not know why. It may be that in a particular child the innate predisposition to fear may have been too strong. Or it may have been that the environmental experience was too severe. Also, an adult who is still dependent will tend to act as if he were still a child and sex is forbidden to him.

To an individual filled with such persistent fears sexual activity is not a promise of pleasure, it is a threat. He is predisposed not to sexual fulfillment but to sexual failure and frustration, which in turn increase his plight. By inhibiting any or all of its phases, these fears and repressed yet overflowing rages and resentments may inflict lasting damage upon his sexual organization.

Let me insert a word of caution here, that symbols must be interpreted in the emotional context of the patient's life. When you are treating patients you will be handling material that abounds in sexual terms. The patient may indeed be worrying about his sexual prowess, sexual inadequacy, fears, whatever. But sexual symbols appear in competitive and dependent contexts and the interpretation of the symbol must be decided within the context. The man who talks about having a small penis may fear that his co-worker has the jump on him for the next promotion.

### IMPAIRMENTS OF STANDARD SEXUAL PERFORMANCE

Many individuals who suffer in this way adhere faithfully to standard heterosexual performance and try to get what they can out of it despite their handicaps. When I speak of standard heterosexual performance I am talking about the penis in the vagina. Hence the many so-called potency and frigidity problems. The frightened boy sees in the little girl a victim of the threatened genital mutilation. The persistence of this dreadful feeling may cause him to avoid the "wound-like" female organ ever after. If he salvages some capacity for penetration, he will be forced to perform as if in a hurry to get out of that dangerous place. This is seen in praecox ejaculatio.

Precipitous ejaculation may turn into a retarded one. The male is then capable of performing with full erection for a lengthy period of time—at the cost of losing all sexual sensation. The return of sensation at once precipitates release. It is a mechanism of miscarried repair because orgasm cannot be achieved.

Freud described the plight of the male in whom desire and love are mutually exclusive. Such a male is forced to shower his love upon a woman who appears to him dignified and to seek physical satisfaction with another woman who he feels is not dignified. These men fear that a woman worthy of being loved would be degraded by physical contact and would avenge herself for the indignity. Denis De Rougemont, in the perceptive *Love in the Western World*, makes some interesting comments on the Tristan syndrome, the romantic lover who prefers not to consummate his relationship with the medieval "mistress" he yearns to idealize.

The frightened female does not always act as if she is intimidated by the male organ. The so-called phallic female who is motived by "penis envy" tries to torture the male, exploits him financially, and undermines his potency. She is trying to get the power position of the male. But I now view the meaning of the symptoms of penis envy as quite different from the original meaning of the term *penis envy*. The significant aspect here is that such a woman is operating out of fear of sexual damage. Because she is still harboring the violence misconception of sex, she is trying to minimize the effect of the threatening encounter in self-defense. Also important is the fact that she is driven to try to dominate the situation because she is afraid of being dominated, not just in a sexual way but possibly in every area of her life.

The intimidated girl recognizes in the male organ that dangerous weapon which is to damage her by penetration, causing her to lose her bodily, personal, and social integrity. She may dream about snakes and daggers and firearms, which may be symbols of that feared male organ.

Years later, such a woman is slated to undergo sexual intercourse in a state of vaginal anesthesia and emotional nonparticipation. Fortunately for her, the clitoris, and possibly the urinary meatus, often escape the incapacitating action of her penetration fear. The orgasm reflex may then be elicited by stimulation of these areas.

If the inhibition, however, is severe enough because of sexual fears and repressed yet overflowing rages to incapacitate the individual for standard heterosexual performance, he suffers a serious loss of function, which endangers his health and happiness and depresses his pride. The human being gets pride, which is essential for a healthy life performance, from his ability to produce pleasure for himself.

### THE MODIFIED PATTERN OF SEXUAL ACTIVITY

Let us focus our attention on what we will call the *modified pattern* of social activity, as opposed to the standard pattern of heterosexual performance. What is common to all these modified patterns? Essentially, no penetration of the male organ into the female organ occurs. Orgastic peristalsis of genital structures is elicited by non-penis-vagina kinds of stimulation, which may be applied either to the genital itself or to some other part of the body near or far, or to the mind alone.

The characteristic of the modified pattern is that the dreaded and resented genital organ of the opposite sex is either replaced by other body parts or, by means of still other arrangements, avoided altogether. The extreme form of avoidance is replacement of the human mate. The individual often evolves these patterns by reverting to a mode of arousal discovered and successfully used during the early period of growth. The organism's innate sensory susceptibilities to sexual arousal have a spectacular compass. Depending upon the circumstances, almost any person, animal, object, or activity may come into play as an effective stimulant. Because of anatomic variations, a body part may have a richer nerve supply. Because of this, its stronger pleasure response to stimulation may then establish a site of preference. Belles lettres, mythology, folklore—all attest to the many strange passions men have succumbed to.

We also know that a specific variety of sexual motor activity may ensue from a variety of motivations and mechanisms. The motor behavior that I might consider morbid, a disease condition which requires treatment, in the case history of one patient is not necessarily what I would consider morbid in another person. We have to consider the specific kind of motor activity in the context of opportunity, the individual's own psychodynamic structure, and other factors.

The situation the individual is in, the actual circumstances of his life, may well be the most important factor in determining his sexual behavior, regardless of his preference. Lack of opportunity, segregation by sexes, and other circumstances may force the healthiest individual to seek orgastic satisfaction by adopting a modified pattern for the time being. Because these expedients are the products of conscious deliberation, rather than methods devised on the nonreporting levels, the individual tends to drop them as soon as he finds himself in a situation in which he has access to means of standard heterosexual performance.

Even under ordinary circumstances, the healthy individual may yield to the desire for variation in performance. In some cultures, such experimenting, surplus activity is part of the sexual mores. In other cultures, it is sheer individual enterprise.

Generally, it is not characteristic of the modified pattern that the motor activities are flexible and show a marked tendency toward combination. Motor behavior that comes from environment or whim has nothing to do with the realm of sexual pathology, which is our present interest.

To my mind, the primary fact about sexual pathology is that the individual has resorted to deviations from the standard heterosexual performance as a means of repair. If the sexual fears and repressed rages are strong enough, the individual in such a state of emergency dyscontrol will be too inhibited to undertake standard heterosexual performance. Such a serious loss of function as an impairment of the essential sexual activity leads to unfortunate consequences, among them the depressing of the individual's pride. However, his salvation may lie in this very loss of inner stature. His desire and need to regain his lost stature, on which his general life performance hinges, may elicit in him processes of repair on a nonreporting basis that mobilizes all his psychodynamic resources. As a consequence of this activity on the nonreporting level, the individual who cannot achieve orgasm through standard heterosexual performance may discover that he can achieve it through some modified form.

These sexual modifications are essentially repair processes because they attempt to recapture his losses in function, pride, and social usefulness. It is better for the individual and for society, usually, that the inhibited individual engage in the sexual activity that will give him the orgastic gratification he needs. This has to be taken with qualifications, and here we are assuming that consent of a willing partner of due age is secured, that no harm is to be inflicted, and that the reservations of a broadminded man in a civilized society are being observed.

The need of the individual for his own kind of sexual pattern is a medical fact. Western civilization is far from recognizing this. Too many of our legal codes are like the laws of medieval times in that they prohibit these modifications. We ask the sexual deviant to pay the price of guilty fear, if not legal punishment, for something that is beneficial to him and possibly to society. On the contrary, these penal laws create an opportunity for true and serious crimes, such as blackmail. We need to work toward creating a sexual climate in which reasonableness prevails.

It was Freud's epochal achievement to awaken society to the importance of the sexual function as a pleasure function and to the responsibility of improving the indoctrination of the young. We have as yet no answers to the problems that arise from the fact that the various opportunities for orgastic, reproductive, and social and economic security are each attained at a different time.

This category includes the various contacts of mouth-genital, genital-anus, petting, and the like, in which one or both mates uses a physical organ other than the genital in the sexual function. The individual avoids the genital organ of the mate because of his persistent genital fears and resentments. The selection of the substitute organ usually follows pleasure preferences that the individual acquired in childhood. It is even possible that the selection stems from some inherent factor— the individual may have been endowed with an unusual abundance of nerve supply in an area. We do not know. What the individual ignores in practicing this pattern is that in his effort to avoid imaginary dangers, he may be ignoring real ones.

This category also includes the individual who avoids tactile contact with the partner, but who achieves orgasm because of the very presence of the partner whom he does not want to touch. These are the two factors that contribute to the orgastic pleasure of the exhibitionist and the voyeur, the self-exposure activity and the Peeping-Tom activity. I think of both disorders in terms of *contact avoidance* because the essential factor is that neither wants to touch, though one wants to be looked at by a partner, and the other wants to look at a partner; I am using the word *partner* in a broad sense. The partner may not even know what is going on, or is probably not consenting, contrary to what the word *partner* usually means. The repair mechanism hardly goes beyond perpetuating an arousal pattern established in childhood and the genital development of these people is highly arrested.

The exhibitionist is incapacitated for standard heterosexual performance through persistence of his genital degradation fears. He brings about orgasm by the abrupt exposure and manipulation of his genital organ in the presence of a strange and preferably juvenile female. This is an act of vengeance and triumph. When he was a boy, self-exposure was part of his attempt to seduce his mother to give him orgastic stimulation. But she disappointed his ardent hopes. Now, out of vindictiveness, he forces any unknown woman to witness that he can achieve orgasm by himself. Now in triumph he shows them that his penis is still there. Jean Jacques Rousseau "confesses" to this in his autobiographical account. Man has been known to "confess" to what he has done in fantasy, so I have some reservations about its authenticity. But this does not detract from its psychological import.

The voyeur advances himself to orgasm by spying on a woman's privacy. He tries to get her when she is undressing or bathing or involved in some such activity. Often enough, he is sexually still the frightened little boy dependent for arousal on peeping into the bedroom of his parents. In one version of this pattern, the male gets sexually aroused when he watches a woman go through the motions of urinating.

SEXUAL PAIN DEPENDENCE

Let me impress upon you one simple fact about sexual pain dependence, the so-called masochism and sadism of classical psychoanalysis. Here we are speaking of people who depend on pain as a sexual stimulus to achieve orgasm. These pain-dependent individuals are not seeking death or pleasure-coated self-damage, as is frequently assigned to them but are seeking pleasure just as much as the rest of us. But standard heterosexual performance is inhibited by the individual's feeling that he has to pay an inescapable price for it. He pays in advance, takes the humiliating and dreaded punishment he thinks is necessary, and achieves the pleasurable orgasm that he wants to experience.

He might pay the price in an inverse form—by vicariously atoning by means of his partner's pain, which he himself inflicted in a burst of rage. Having repented in advance, he too can now enjoy his orgasm. To state it more formally, let me say that pain dependence is the forced and automatized pursuit of advance punishment so that the individual can permit himself to take pleasure in the forbidden activities.

Sexual pain dependence is only one form of the pain dependence that can be seen in every area of behavior. Pain dependence develops in early life in response to disciplinary stress. The stage is set when the child is asked to forgo his pleasure by prohibitive parents. If the upbringing is restrictive enough to defeat the child's defiant rage, his pursuit of forbidden pleasure may take the roundabout way of pain dependence. The child develops a pattern in which pain is overruled in its function as a hedonic regulation. The child does not act to get away from pain as he was born to do. In the development of this pattern, he suffers the pain willingly because he feels that he cannot have the pleasure without paying the price, but his goal is to get pleasure. Through this feeling that he has to pay the price, pain becomes enhanced as a contrast to and a paradoxical stimulus for pleasure.

Essentially, it is one mechanism of the many repair mechanisms that the organism resorts to in order to recapture lost pleasure and lost pride. But it may involve self-damage. It is certainly a deficient adaptation.

The two contrasting forms of sexual pain dependence—what we shall call the active and the passive forms—were first described clinically by Krafft-Ebing. He named them masochism and sadism. Many psychoanalysts have been misled because these conditions appear to be so different, and they think of them as two conditions. I found that concentrating on the term pain dependence enabled me to stress the basic element of suffering that is the common ingredient of the two faces of what is one disease entity.

In the frightened, submissive form of sexual pain dependence, the individual achieves orgasm by accepting the required painful stimulation from the mate. This is the passive "masochistic" form. In such an individual, the old guilty fear of the disciplinary authority is stronger than the defiant rage. The individual, his rage depleted by his fear, cannot help pursuing the necessary punishment in open submission. Some individuals act out these fantasies by securing the cooperation of a partner who is ready to play the assigned part. In other individuals, these conditions are fulfilled in imagination only. They indulge in fantasies to this effect and reach orgasm either by way of a spontaneous ejaculation or through self-stimulation that climaxes erotic fantasies of suffering pain.

In the angry, defiant form, the individual achieves orgasm by venting his repressed yet overflowing rage upon the mate and making the mate suffer pain. This is the active "sadistic" form. The same forced pursuit of punishment prevails, but the rage is stronger than the fear. The individual, still enraged against the disciplinary authority who caused him to become dependent upon this pursuit, defiantly conceals his pain dependency by shifting the brunt of its burden upon the mate. But this sense of triumph masks the true source of orgastic pleasure for him—which is his own vicarious suffering. He needs a partner who permits himself to be whipped, humiliated, debased. Here again there are two kinds of sadists. One performs these deeds only in imagination, the other actually carries them out. The two forms usually have a mixture of both types.

For the sake of convenience, there are three kinds of sexual pain dependence: dramatized, criminal, and hidden. The dramatized form is the kind that everybody thinks of when they hear the words *masochism* and *sadism*. These forms first came to public attention through the literary output of the Marquis de Sade (1740–1814) and von Sacher-Masoch (1838–1895). In these forms two consenting mates enact, short of severe pain and serious physical injury, a dramatized version of the violence misconception of sexual intercourse. Both forms, the fear-ridden and the enraged, are staged performances.

The form that poses a grave menace to society is the criminal form of sexual pain dependence. In the criminal forms, pain dependence precipitates what amounts to a savage enacting of the violence misconception of sexual intercourse. Lust murderers, some twenty of them, examined for the German courts by the late Johannes Lange, were without exception incapable of standard sexual performance and could reach orgasm only after committing the act of violence. The prototype of the criminal form of sexual pain dependence is rape.

In milder cases, the forced pursuit of pain may remain a hidden phase of the coital pattern. It may even be unsuspected by both partners who, for example, experience bitter quarreling as a prelude to a truly happy embrace, quite a common situation. Other common clinical manifestations are: surprise orgasm elicited by latent or open fear in the absence of sexual desire; lack of sensation or orgasm during genital activity due to an unconscious dread of rape; and use of the self-torture of irrational jealousy as an aphrodisiac.

One can distinguish four degrees of sexual pain dependence: (1) The pain aspect is inflicted or experienced only in the imagination and leads to spontaneous ejaculation. (2) The pain aspect is experienced only in the imagination, and the orgasm is brought about by manipulation, as in self-stimulation. The daydreams attendant upon pain-dependent genital self-stimulation often draw their material from literary sources. (3) The pain aspect is actually acted upon and orgasm is reached. (4) The pain aspect is acted upon as a preliminary, a certain amount of excitement and readiness for intercourse is reached, and the activity culminates in some sort of intercourse, distorted or conventional.

In the female, pain dependence frequently appears in the guise of the old familiar hidden desire to be raped. This derives from the violence misconception of sexual intercourse. The hidden desire for rape is then bound to elicit an open dread of rape or intensify this dread if it already exists on other grounds. In a state of pain dependence, the male too may develop a hidden desire to be raped by a female, and then will have an open dread of such rape. Here rape is meant in a social rather than physical sense, referring to loss of male stature, public sexual humiliation, and the like. In individuals of paranoid predisposition, this dread of being raped by an individual of the opposite sex may give rise to sexual delusions of persecution and reference.

Pain dependence is also the clue to the problem of sexual jealousy. This complex emotional response is elicited by the real or imagined danger of losing the beloved mate to a successful rival, with all the damaging consequences to the individual's own pride, prestige, and security. Fearful of the threat of this loss, the individual is enraged against both the supposedly successful rival and the supposedly disloyal mate. At the same time, he secretly envies the successful rival for his presumed sexual superiority. Beneath this envy lies his own desire for sexual adventures, which is held in check by his fears of sexual inferiority.

While in the grip of these humiliating emotions, he visualizes the successful rival enjoying intimacies with the disloyal mate. These fantasies throw him into a state of sexual excitement. He is now again, as he once was as a child, witnessing the primal scene in the bedroom of his parents, the sexually aroused but excluded third party. Jealousy is a pain-dependent aphrodisiac.

What chance does an individual have of overcoming sexual pain dependence? A combination of factors may give him respite from his burdensome sexual pain dependence or perhaps mitigate it. First, the individual must learn how to release defiant rage and face the consequences of it. Periodic release of repressed yet overflowing rage is a prime prerequisite. If this is combined with abundant gratification of the person's desire for love, affection, warmth, appreciation, and respect, the individual will experience a sharp rise of inner stature and self-respect. If this can happen, the individual can then feel that he has the right to a particular kind of pleasure without paying the prepunishment for it. This has an especially good chance of happening when the pain-dependent person is female. In favorable circumstances the combination of the aforementioned factors may even enable her to overcome her vaginal anesthesia.

### HOMOGENEOUS PAIRS

I know of nothing that indicates that there is any such thing as innate orgastic desire for a partner of the same sex. We know that the homosexual male often cherishes and emphasizes fond memories of childhood homosexual experiences in order to hide his fear and resentment of women from himself and to persuade himself and others that he was "born that way." This should not distract us from the facts. The homosexual male often clings to the myth that he belongs to a third sex, superior to the rest of mankind. This would seem to be the effort of an individual who lives in constant dread of detection and punishment, which is the milieu of the society that prohibits homogeneous mating, to restore his shaky equilibrium. This is another of the many fallacies about homosexuality. Equally fallacious in my opinion is the whole theory of bisexuality. To me the significant fact of homogeneous pairing is that it is based on the male-female design, even though this does not always appear so on the surface.

The sexual is only one of the elements involved. Generally, in the in-love state of homogeneous pairs, three kinds of love compete for dominance. One is the orgastic love which is not inevitably the most important factor. Sometimes the relationship is dominated by magical love, which strives to reinstate the alimentary child-parent design. This is the familiar infantile dependence pattern, which affords the dependent mate the illusion of the alimentary security that I have talked so much about. As Helene Deutsch pointed out, the homogeneous relationship between females may be a reenactment of the mother-child relationship. Between males it might be a father-son reenactment.

Or, again it might be the mutual dependency that is characteristic of heterosexual fall-in-love, in which each partner derives emotional security from his unfounded belief that he has found the all-giving parent who will take care of him. A third kind of love hinges upon the economic security factor. Here, too, one of the mates may achieve a reflected sense of security by assuming the role of the parent and providing for the other. Obviously, these factors also form the basis of heterogeneous relationships.

What evidence enables me to assume that every homosexual act or homogeneous relationship is a statement of the male-female design? If male desires male, why does he seek out a male who pretends to be a female? Why does a male affect femininity if he wants to express a male's desire for a male? Why does a female turn to a masculine-acting female if she is expressing the desire of a female for a female? How else can the crucial fact be explained that in male pairs one male impersonates a female, and in female pairs one female impersonates a male? Sometimes evidence for the male-female pattern is deeply repressed, but I think it can be found with a thorough search. They are pretending to be a male-female pair.

The male-female sexual pattern is dictated by anatomy. Almost as fundamental is the fact that by means of the institution of marriage, the male-female sexual pattern is culturally ingrained and perpetuated in every individual from earliest childhood. Homogeneous pairs satisfy their repudiated yet irresistible male-female desire by means of shared illusions and actual approximations; such is the hold on the individual of a cultural institution based on biological foundations. This mechanism is often deeply buried in the individual's mind under a welter of rationalizations calculated to justify his actual avoidance of the opposite sex.

The male's sexual desire for a male—and the female's for a female—are blinds that enable them to represent their sexual defeat as a triumph of sexual self-realization. If the male-female desire is driven underground, it achieves imaginary fulfillment through homogeneous pairs, despite the fact that such pairs are formed in forced avoidance of the opposite sex. Such "return of the repressed," by way of the very bulwark erected against it, is one of the best-known Freudian mechanisms.

Here again one sees the true significance of Freud's momentous discovery that in childhood these individuals were closely attached to persons of the opposite sex and had strong sexual desires for them. I believe that had Freud not accepted bisexuality as a proved biologic tenet, he would have traced the activities of these homosexual pairs to an original male-female desire and to have recognized homosexuality as the continuation of the male-female pattern. It was unfortunate, in many ways, that he adopted the bisexual interpretation that the formation of homogeneous pairs is prompted by a genuine "homosexual desire."

Why is the so-called homosexual forced to escape from the male-female pair into a homogeneous pair? This brings us back to the familiar campaign of deterrence that parents wage to prohibit the sexual activity of the child. The campaign causes the female to view the male organ as a destructive weapon. Therefore the female partners are reassured by the absence in both of them of the male organ. The campaign causes the male to see in the mutilated female organ a reminder of inescapable punishment. When the never-recognized fear and resentment of the opposite organ becomes insurmountable, the individual may escape into homosexuality. The male partners are re-assured by the presence in both of them of the male organ. Homosex-uality is a deficient adaptation evolved by the organism in response to its own emergency overreaction and dyscontrol.

Other factors in the background of the homosexual exert some influ-ence. The male homosexual often remains in a strong but expurgated attachment to his mother. The attachment is purely alimentary be-cause he lost orgastic desire for her the instant he discovered her mutilated state. The female homosexual usually harbors bitter resent-ment against her father or mother or both because she was denied parental affection and because a son was preferred to her.

The male homosexual may include in his childhood history sexual contacts with other boys, fantasies of being a female, and other experi-ences that foreshadow his subsequent retreat into homosexuality. How-ever, such infantile experiences have no such consequences in plenty of men. Upon maturation, such men find their way to women and get full pleasure from the standard heterosexual performance of the male-female pair. Obviously, the biologic and social forces of the male-female design overrule the conditioning power of juvenile homosexual experiences. Only men incapacitated for the love of women become dependent for orgastic gratification upon the homosexual patterns that they evolved in childhood.

In terms of the male-female design, the homosexual motor activity should be thought about carefully. In the male pair, in which one male plays the part of a male and the other assumes the role of a female, the characteristic activity is anal mount. This male pair is in an openly simulated male-female position. Their sexual activity ap-proximates standard heterosexual performance as closely as the anatomy available to them permits.

In the female pair, the same male-female pattern prevails. In fright-ened fascination with the threat of penetration, the female who pre-tends to play the male role develops an illusory penis, and pretends herself to be the lucky penetrator. In actual performance she must content herself with anatomy that is ill-suited to serve as a male genital organ or resort to artificial substitutes. In turn, her female mate accepts stimulation from the harmless female, which she would be afraid to accept from the dangerous male.

The simulation of penetration is one of the modified patterns homo-sexual mates have recourse to. They also engage in manual stimulation or mouth-genital contact, which is reminiscent of sucking at the mother's breast. The patterns of motor activity may include voyeurism, cross-dressing, and any one of a number of things. Of course, the male-female design is less obvious when these kinds of motor activity are practiced. Fading of the male-female design may also result from the integrative deterioration of the sexual organization. This is notably the case in schizophrenia. The schizophrenic disorganization is the only factor that can break the strength of the male-female design and desire, I believe.

The development of the male who assumes the active role is usually quite different from the development of the male who takes the passive role. The one playing the male part tends demonstratively to over-emphasize his masculinity. He may be domineering, demanding, and somewhat irascible. In sexual contexts, he may be given to flurries of anger that reveal a degree of hidden sexual pain dependence. Because of this pain dependence (of which he may be unaware), he may be prone to inflict painful humiliation upon his mate. He is unaware of the fact that he really longs for a female with a penis, and that he finds her in the sexually effeminate male.

The sexually effeminate male is incapacitated for standard hetero-sexual performance because his sexual fears and resentments have destroyed his power of penetration. But he knows how to elicit pleasur-able orgastic peristalsis of his genital structures through stimulation from the anus, which, by variational richness of innervation, may have been anatomically predisposed to this vicarious function. Consequently, he has assumed the less demanding role of the female by vaginalizing his anus and deriving pleasure from penetration.

The psychodynamics underlying the behavior of the homosexual has many patterns. In the male patient, decline or loss of the capacity for standard heterosexual performance may precipitate a diffuse panic that derives from the patient's unrecognized dread of anal rape. This panic means that he is afraid he is a homosexual, not that he wants to be a homosexual. The term *homosexual* has been stretched to the point of being meaningless; any relationship between individuals of the same sex is called homosexual, even the girl infant toward her mother. The basic dynamic of the individual who wants a sexual relationship with a member of the same sex is fear of the genitals of the opposite sex. Domination, submission, competitive struggle, dependence, or friendly cooperation have been interpreted as manifestations of "unconscious homosexuality" regardless of whether or not they have any conscious or unconscious bearing on the patient's sexual life. Sexual symbols must only be interpreted in the context in which they occur. In actual homosexual sexual relationships there can be a number of different motivations besides sex, just as there are in heterosexual ties. The basic motivation can then be dominance or dependence as well as sexual. I have had several cases in which men were in a homosexual relationship because they felt guilt which resulted in feelings of worthless inferiority or homosexuality, in a way similar to the hypochondriacal pattern. A man in our society, when he feels inferior, will often think of himself as a homosexual.

Let us take a look at the theory of constitutional bisexuality that, I feel, stands in the way of understanding the homogeneous pair. The term *homogeneous pair* should be limited to the human species, for in animals only motor behavior can be ascertained. As soon as one interprets the animal's motives, he is applying *human* psychodynamics. In order to derive full benefit from comparative studies, we should bear in mind, first, that experimental animals are less encephalized than man and, second, that the differentiation into male and female still permits many shared characteristics that have nothing to do with genitals.

Research seems to indicate that in experimental animals a relative overflow of sexual excitation may be vicariously discharged through homosexual as well as heterosexual channels. However, since man is more encephalized than these animals, in the formation of homogeneous pairs these responses can hardly play more than a minor role. Not a trace of evidence has been presented to show that any of these fragments of bisexuality play any part in the causation of the pattern. Different types of homogeneous pairs have different developmental histories. On psychodynamic grounds, we rather suspect that if innate factors are involved in certain of these developmental processes, they do not fall within the classification of bisexuality.

There are many fallacies in the theory of bisexuality. The fear that the patient so often voices that his genetic constitution includes a "homosexual component" as part of his bisexual constitution has no foundation in fact. The theory of constitutional bisexuality was evolved by Krafft-Ebing, and Freud uses it in his assumption that every human being has some innate sexual desire for a member of his own sex. However, this theory fails to explain the most conspicuous facts of observation. In about the middle of the nineteenth century, it was discovered that the urogenital systems of the two sexes derive from a common embryonic origin. The question of whether this *Anlage* should be considered neutral or hermaphroditic was at first a subject of debate. When it was found to contain cellular material of both gonads it was definitely labeled hermaphroditic. This opened the door to indiscriminate speculations on man's bisexuality. These speculations, resting on generalizations drawn from biologic findings in lower animals, seemed to offer a scientific basis for the explanation of homosexuality, and it was because of medical interest in this subject that the concept of bisexuality found its way into psychiatry.

The fact that the urogenital system of the two sexes have a common embryonic organ and that the zygote has the potential to develop into a male or female does not mean that the potential that exists in the developing embryo still remains in the mature individual. I believe sex can only be determined by the reproductive system as a whole—which in the adult is either male or female. We see that sex in its entirety refers to the differentiation in individuals as regards their contrarelated systems of reproduction. Taking these considerations in reverse order, we start from the fact that insofar as the reproductive system is concerned individuals are of two contrarelated types. It is precisely this difference that constitutes the character of the sexes. Each of the two systems may be dissected into a multitude of structures, substances, and functions. The sex aspect of every one of these constituent parts is derived from its participation in the system as a whole.

At this point there arises the question of the extragenital pleasure functions, discovered and explored by psychoanalysis: oral, anal, tactile, and the like. These are rooted not in the reproductive system but in the alimentary or some other basic biological behavior area. They interact and combine with one another and with the genital pleasure function to make up the individual's entire pleasure organization. This pleasure organization, which is obviously neither sexual nor nonsexual, is an entity of a new order. It undergoes typical changes during the life cycle and is characterized at every stage by a measure of functional flexibility, working in the service of one and then another of the underlying biological systems. If it is pathologically disturbed, it hampers rather than benefits the utility function of the behavior area involved. I use the phrase *pleasure organization* for want of a better name —one that would reflect its biological nature and avoid confusion between the superior entity and its component parts. The identification of pleasure and sex made by classical psychoanalysis I feel is biologically untenable.

Essentially, the procedure of psychoanalysis in the past has been as follows. Certain types of behavior or attitudes or even fantasies have been interpreted in the male as "feminine," and in the female as "masculine," and were presumed to be manifestations of the individual's "negative Oedipus complex" or "homosexual component." Such a component has been assumed, on the basis of the concept of bisexuality, to be present in every individual. So far as I can see, a closer scrutiny reveals no less than six major flaws in this procedure.

1. The words *masculine* and *feminine* can be used only in terms of the small group of fantasies that are concerned with possession of the male or female genitalia, or to impregnation, pregnancy, or childbirth. Where no possession or reproductive use of genital equipment is implied, as is the case in numerous fantasies, attitudes, and types of behavior, such a designation, though perpetuated by convention and routine, has rested on purely arbitrary grounds. Freud was always aware of this stumbling block, and in 1905 he suggested as the psychological definition of male or female the pursuit of active or passive goals, although by 1933 he was forced to admit the futility of such an attempt.

2. In diagnosing psychic manifestations as masculine or feminine, no distinction has been made between the adult and the very young child, in total disregard of the differences in information and intellectual maturity. A fantasy whose content is unquestionably male or female in an adult, might in a child reflect nothing but complete ignorance.

3. Equally unwarranted is the idea that these so-called masculine and feminine manifestations are the direct expression of an opposite-sex constitutional component. It is well known that fantasies draw their content from experience and therefore to a large extent reflect environmental influences, but this has been lost sight of in the field of sex. A fantasy, even though influential in attitude or behavior, may or may not be the expression of a particular constitutional component. Inspired by birds, man has dreamed for millennia of flying under his own power, but no one has ever suggested that this implied a flying component or predisposition in his makeup.

4. The constitutional component itself has been a subject of further ambiguity and error. In general theoretical formulations it is indiscriminately referred to either as a homosexual component or as the female component in the male and the male component in the female.

5. The term *homosexual* has been stretched as to become almost meaningless. Any relationships between two individuals of the same sex—domination, submission, competitive struggle, or friendly coopera-

tion—have readily been interpreted as manifestations of "unconscious homosexuality," regardless of whether or not they have any conscious or unconscious bearing on the patient's sexual life. The word homosexuality has been more broadly misapplied than the word sex in psychoanalytic usage.

6. The assumption of a "homosexual" or "opposite sex" component in the constitution has not served as a challenge to discover what such a component might actually consist of, and in what specific ways if at all it influences man's sexual behavior. On the contrary, it has been relied upon as if it were the outcome of research.

In general, the vague notion of biological bisexuality, and the unfortunately loose manner in which it has been used in psychoanalysis, have had deplorable consequences. It has acted like a will-o'-the-wisp, always and everywhere luring our attention, so that it was impossible to see where the real problem lay. And it has gravely detracted from the benefits to be derived from the method of research possessed by psychoanalysis. This could not but have the effect of lowering our therapeutic efficiency.

In conclusion it is imperative to supplant the deceptive concept of bisexuality with a psychological theory based on firmer biological foundations. The functional pattern of the sexually mature human individual bears no significant causal relation to the zygote's bipotentiality of embryologic differentiation. A human being is either a male or a female or, due to a failure of embryonic differentiation, is anatomically deformed. It is common knowledge that these malformed individuals are possessed by the desire to be of but one sex.

## Patterns of Solitary Gratification

The essential feature of this pattern is that the individual achieves orgasm without a mate. I find it useful to subdivide this pattern into the following five kinds of activities: (1) the fetishistic pattern, (2) orgastic self-stimulation in cross-dressing, (3) orgastic self-stimulation in the illusory twosome of a daydream or a dream, (4) blank orgastic self-stimulation in the waking state, (5) surprise orgasm (in the waking state or in sleep) and the paradoxical orgasm (in the waking state).

The fetishist elevates some characteristic possession of the beloved female to the function of being his exclusive sexual stimulus. According to Freud, such a sexual fetish is a symbol for the penis attributed to the female by the fetishist in order to allay his dread of the "mutilated" female organ. As a boy, looking furtively at his mother in sexual excitement, he stopped short of her genital region by fastening his view to some other point that subsequently became his fetish.

The sexually significant wearing of clothes of the opposite sex, which was first called "transvestitism" by Magnus Hirschfeld, was later named "cross-dressing" by Havelock Ellis. The female may do this for certain social purposes as well as for sexual reasons. As for my direct experience, I have observed cross-dressing only in the male. The male who does this is impersonating to himself as well as to others, that eternally sexually unattainable female, the mother, to whom he remains inseparably attached by ties of alimentary affection. Consequently, he becomes resentful when a male mistakes his cross-dressing for an invitation and makes advances to him. The orgastic desire of the so-called transvestite is enfeebled, and the mechanism is schizophrenic.

Orgastic self-stimulation in the illusory twosome of a daydream or a dream may be looked upon as the "normal" form of gratification during the entire period of sexual immaturity in our culture. In the healthy adult, it may be a situational expedient. In the sexually inhibited adult, it may be a truly reparative pattern in that it may be the only way the individual can achieve orgasm.

In early life, blank orgastic self-stimulation in the waking state is a chance development. In later years, it may be a repair mechanism or it may be a product of schizophrenic disintegration.

Surprise orgasm, awake or asleep, is released by an automatic mechanism that is operating on the nonreporting levels. It may be a true repair mechanism, that is, the only way in which the individual can achieve orgasm. Otherwise, the surprise orgasm acts as a safety valve for repressed sexual tension.

Paradoxical orgasm, the most significant version of surprise orgasm, is elicited by the rising tension of fear. I interpret this as a mechanism of pleasurable riddance. There is ample clinical evidence that it is often the developmental forerunner of pain dependence. Sometimes, it is a repair mechanism.

In a certain psychodynamic organization, fire setting, shoplifting, and the like may become sexual equivalents.

# CHAPTER 23

# Expressive and Paranoid

# Behavior

*The Expressive Pattern*

THE EXPRESSIVE PATTERN WHICH IS SIMILAR TO THE SO-CALLED HYSTERIA of classical psychoanalytic literature is an elaboration of common maladaptation. The disturbances occur in the sexual and social areas and are more common among women than men. The explanation lies in our cultural set-up. Because they have not been able to free themselves from their inhibitions, individuals fall back on expressional behavior to recover what they have lost through sexual inhibitions and social limitations.

The most common symptom of the expressional type of disorder can be summarized as pretense in lieu of performance. The individual believes he deserves recognition and acts as if he were a prominent person. At times these people may be hard to tell from genuinely creative people. But, unlike the actor who disappears as a person when he is playing a part, the disordered individual never completely disappears when he is playing a part. The egocentricity of this expressional type is a telltale clue.

Another symptom of expressional disturbances is the interlude syndrome or dreamlike episodes, such as the twilight states, amnesias, and so forth. The content of such states are wishful fantasies acted out with outbursts of fear, rage, and guilty fear. Because of his excessive fear and rage, the expressional type can only free himself from these emotions by precipitating such states. By this technique he declines social responsibility. Since this motivation is now generally understood, today the symptom has tended to disappear.

Another symptom of the expressive pattern is conversion hysteria, or rudimentary fantasmic symptoms. This is described by Freud and Breuer and means the conversion of psychic into somatic phenomena. The conversion is only a change in the frame of reference by the observer. All the movements in this syndrome are abortive motor phenomena. As rudimentary expressions of the expressional individual's fantasies, they are comparable to gestures. Most of the time, the rudimentary expressions are pantomimes. If they can be properly interpreted, the whole story becomes apparent. One of the commonly known symptoms of the expressional is the copying of disease, in which the individual "copies" an organic illness. He also tends to exploit his symptoms, although this is a secondary gain. One factor that was not pointed out is the overemphasis that the expressional places on love and affection over physical stimulus. Overemphasis on love results from the attempt of the woman to counteract the severe childhood limitations on physical sexual experience. She had to do this so as not to feel like a prostitute. This is not quite as harmless as it seems, since love should not be used as a medicine that is supposed to cure fear of penetration. In an extreme form, this overemphasis is a repair pattern. The individual has overemphasized the affectional aspect of sex, which compensates for the incapacity for successful performance.

All the fantasies of expressional patients are full of sex. Historically, this is very important because it led Freud to the idea that all pathological conditions are rooted in sex. Freud also discovered that the fantasies of these patients were mainly concerned with sexual perversions. Because these women were incapable of standard heterosexual performance, they managed to escape in their fantasies the most dreaded idea of being penetrated. My observation is that fear has motivated these women to replace standard heterosexual performance by less threatening patterns.

One characteristic that is always present is grave immaturity. The expressional shows this immaturity invariably in his relationships with people. Sometimes this is revealed in the way he retains certain adolescent-type aspirations, such as an insatiable desire for recognition and social prominence, with immature criteria of what this prominence is. Or, his insistence that he get fulfillment by magic and in his faith in emotional thought.

## The Paranoid Pattern

First, let me make one distinction clear. In my classification, the paranoid pattern is the label only for those who are suffering from a nondisintegrative elaboration of common maladaptation. The dividing line between the paranoid as so-called neurotic and the paranoid as so-called psychotic is the irrationality and illogical reasoning; when the whole disintegrative process of the schizophrenic sets in, the diagnosis is schizophrenia, with paranoia as a qualifier.

In its common garden variety, paranoia is the extension of sexual disturbances and social overdependence. Like common maladaptation, something in childhood triggered the pattern of sexual and social inhibitions and a sense of overwhelming insecurity. What distinguishes it from other emotional illnesses, however, is its kind of repair.

To compensate for the fears, the paranoid usually formulates an expansive system, the cardinal characteristics of which are an exaggerated sense of justice, self-righteousness, and sexual pain dependence. All these are given strength by absorbing the defeated rage of the child who was forced to submit to the powerful parent.

But these do not enable him to handle the outbursts of guilt. When one of these is too strong or occurs too often for him to handle, he resorts to another mechanism. In this, he presents himself as a victim and claims he has been accused of infamous acts. He also presents himself as a victim of threats, and acts out these threats on a sensory level. He dramatizes his shortcomings and acts as if the threats were real. This explains his proneness to violence and apparent rationality. The rationalization is that his enemies want to degrade him by depriving him of social and sexual integrity. Underlying this rationalization are his fears and dreads that this will happen. In the paranoid pattern, as is true of all pain-dependent behavior, the true core is always fear.

The clue to the paranoid pattern is the patient's conception of sex as an act of physical violence or social degradation. Because in our society the male is usually the more powerful and dominant, the supposed aggressor in the imagination of the patient is usually male regardless of the sex of the patient. The female fears being raped by a man, the male fears being abused by another man. This is especially true when the fear is that of physical violence. If the patient fears sexual degradation in the form of a social injury and believes it can be inflicted by cunning, the supposed aggressor is usually a woman. The significant fact here is the concern with violent sex rather than with the element of homosexuality. In the nonschizophrenic paranoid, none of this comes out in the open.

The most perfect example in psychoanalytic literature is the Schreber case. Freud never saw the man but analyzed the case on the basis of Schreber's autobiography and other data he was able to obtain. Schreber was undoubtedly schizophrenic and proclaimed his delusions publicly. But the process of the disease that occurred in Schreber may also occur in the nonschizophrenic.

I would like to point out here the work of the French psychiatrist Magnan in the 1890s who gave a brilliant description of the evolving stages of paranoia. Unfortunately, his work, which could have been so valuable to psychiatrists, was completely overlooked. Relatively few paranoids, it is true, go through the whole Magnan development. The Magnan sequence is always precipitated as a consequence of frustration or a fear of failure. Schreber, for instance, was unable to father a child.

I have slightly revised Magnan's outline into a series of four developmental phases: hypochondriac, referential, persecutory, and grandiose.

Briefly, the case history of Schreber is that he had his first attack of nervous disorder when his condition was labeled *hypochondria*. He was treated in a clinic for fifteen months and was returned to normal life. When he was discharged, he was in a normal mental state with one exception—he retained certain fixed delusions. Years later he had another, more severe breakdown and was institutionalized for six years.

In the second hospitalization phase, the illness fell into two rather distinct states. In the first phase, Schreber suffered from the delusion that he was the victim of bestial homosexual assaults, which were being performed by his former psychiatrist. Before long, the psychiatrist was being helped in these atrocities by God himself. In the second phase, Schreber had surrendered to his destiny of being a sexual object for God's disposal. He had also developed various religious and megalomanic ideas, one of which was that he would become a female savior of the world and would breed a new and superior race of human beings.

Freud analyzed the Schreber case into five stages: initial withdrawal of libido, regression to narcissism, reparative advance from narcissism, advance to homosexual object choice, and the warding off by projection. I suggest that Schreber went through the following four stages, following the Magnan syndrome: hypochondriac phase, phase dominated by referential and persecutory ideas, development of delusions of the end of the world, and development of delusions of grandeur.

During the hypochondriac phase, which was the diagnosis for the first episode, the patient had the nonreporting belief that long-overdue punishments were catching up with him. He took his failure to sire a child as proof of his inadequacy. By the time of the second psychotic episode, this fear had moved from his body to the social sphere, and he began to believe that the whole world was punishing him. The area in which he was to be disgraced was sexual, and he became afraid he would be unmanned and abused like a female. This is a climax of a dread that clearly must stem from childhood ideas that as an unmasculine man or as a female he would be raped. The crucial paranoid point in the development of this disease was the one at which he asked, "How can a man of my integrity be exposed to such injustice?"

Now comes Schreber's use of logic. He said, "If such a thing could happen to me, there is no law and order in the world. Therefore since it is without law and order, the world will go to pieces."

In the reparative process, there is additional logical consistency: "If the world is coming to an end, why am I the only one to know?" There has to be some divine purpose. "God wants to turn me into a woman and beget on me a new race." When Schreber was frightened, God as the sexual aggressor looked threatening to him, but when he managed to patch it up, the once-dreaded sodomy became an act of divine grace. In the Schreber case, God the male figure is the aggressor feared by the male patient, but many women have the same fantasy or delusion.

# CHAPTER 24

# Obsessive Behavior

~~~~~~~~~~~~~~~~~~~~~~~~~~~~~~~~~~~~~~~~~~~~~~~~~~~~~~~~~~~~~~~~~~~~~~~~~~~~~~~~~~~~~~

THE FIRST PSYCHIATRIC OBSERVATIONS ON OBSESSIVE BEHAVIOR DATE FROM the 1860s, but it was not until after the turn of the century that Freud opened the way to a deeper understanding of this disorder and its recognition as a well-defined clinical entity.

## The Clinical Picture

The designation *obsessive behavior* will be applied to patients who have obsessive attacks and obsessive traits. For convenience, I shall subdivide the attacks into spells of doubting and brooding, bouts of ritual making, and fits of horrific temptation. The form of attacks may shift from one to the other; they may be mild or severe, last half an hour or longer, may be quiescent for a while or occur many times a day. Obsessive traits, however, once evolved, do not change significantly.

Spells of doubting and brooding may be described as a swinging back and forth without being able to reach a decision. Doubt may invade a belief, observation, or recollection, and the patient can trust neither his memory nor the testimony of his own eyes. Upon leaving home, he may feel forced to rush back to make sure that he turned off the light or locked a certain door, or, upon sealing an envelope, he may have to open it over and over again to reassure himself that he has signed the enclosed check.

In his bouts of ritual making, the patient repetitively executes a sequence of motor acts. Most often these sequences are ceremonial and distortive elaborations of some routine of daily life, such as going to bed, getting up, taking a bath, dressing and undressing, getting down to work, or finishing work. Also included may be apparently nonsensical motor acts. Repetition tends to be continued until the patient is exhausted.

There may be obsessive hand washing, washing or cleansing pieces of wearing apparel or other objects as if they were soiled or somehow contaminated. The obsession to count (for example, the number of parked cars), to touch (for example, every lamppost on the street), or to avoid touching certain objects (for example, doorknobs), or to step on or avoid certain spots (for example, the pavement cracks), and the like.

In his "fits of horrific temptation" the patient, suddenly beset by the idea to kill someone (usually a close relative), shrinks back in horror from a thought so alien to his entire being.

Turning to the obsessive traits, we observe that the patient is over-conscientious in his own particular way. What he is mostly concerned about are the minutiae, the inconsequential details, the meticulous observance of minor rules and petty formalities. Specializing in trifles, he is always in danger of missing the essentials. His orderliness tends to be excessive and inappropriate, costing time and effort. In his life, the clock is a menace.

A scientist, though never noticing when his shoelaces were untied, was so meticulous in his literary documentation that his colleagues dubbed him a footnote fetishist. Another patient had his secretary keep several indexes to his private files—a regular index, an ever-growing series of cross indexes, and an index of the indexes. Whenever he consulted the files himself, he had to take time out to see whether the item concerned was indexed to perfection.

A rough sketch of the obsessive patient would depict him as highly opinionated and proud of his superior intelligence, avowed rationality, and "unswerving integrity." He may indeed be an honest man, but he may also turn out to be a sanctimonious hypocrite. He is the ultimate perfectionist. While very sensitive to his own hurt, he may be destructively critical, spiteful, and given to bearing grudges in trivial matters. Or, he may be overcautious, bent on avoiding any possibility of conflict. His "common sense" militates against what he views as fancies of the imagination. He is a "man of facts," not of fancies. He smiles condescendingly at people who are fascinated by mysticism, including "the unconscious" and dreams. But let him undergo some psychoanalytic treatment, and he will attribute oracular significance to slips of the tongue or the pen. His interest in fine arts is slight or pretended. He rarely has artistic gifts and conspicuously lacks genuine charm and grace. His amatory interests are laden with ulterior motivations and pretense. His envy of a successful rival—in work, for example —may carry him to dangerous lengths. If the opportunity arises, he may subtly cut the man's throat, as a token of his admiration and respect. This sort of thing is usually termed *ambivalence*. Finally, the obsessive patient is almost never completely free from tension and irritability, though in general the degree of these characteristics fluctuates from slight to severe.

## The Dynamics of Obsessive Behavior

Overreactive disorders arise from the organism's inability to handle danger situations. Instead of acting as signals, the emergency emotions themselves inflict damage. In Freud's view, all obsessive behavior originates in childhood from conflicts between the child and parents. Though the conflict and its consequences become repressed, they may nonetheless distort the patient's development and produce neurosis. These findings, now widely recognized, are embodied in adaptational psychodynamics.

As regards the specific etiology of obsessive neurosis, Freud held that the patient's development was to some extent arrested and thrown back to an earlier stage. The patient's "genital level" was weakened by "fixation" at the previous levels. His regression to that level at which the child's life was dominated by "anal erotic and sado-masochistic impulse" was considered the key to his obsessive neurosis.

Freud's theory calls attention to the processes of bowel training. The child must be helped to bring evacuation under voluntary control. However, bowel control presupposes maturation of the requisite neuromuscular apparatus. If the mother is overambitious, demanding, and impatient, and if the child is marked by a particular combination of characteristics, then the stage is set for the battle of the chamber pot.

Irritated by the mother's interference with his bowel clock, the child responds to her entreaties with enraged defiance, to her punishments and threats of punishments with fearful obedience. The battle is seesaw, and the mother, to fortify her position, makes the disobedient child feel guilty, undergo deserved punishment, and ask forgiveness. This indoctrination transforms the child's fear into guilty fear, and impresses upon him the reparative procedure of expiatory behavior.

The mother/child conflict provokes in the child a struggle between his own guilty fear and his own defiant rage. It is characteristic of this type of child that his guilty fear is always stronger; sooner or later the fear represses the rage and the child acquires a crucial predisposing factor towards obsessive behavior.

Freud's theory of obsessional neurosis features a "sadistic super ego" and a "masochistic ego," a dramatization unquestionably inspired by observations similar to the ones from which our interpretation derived. Thus, our interpretation is a development of Freud's early insight. On the other hand, his emphasis on the destinies of evacuative pleasure, their significance in the causation of obsessive behavior, is refuted by clinical experience. He assumed that bowel obedience forces the child to relinquish evacuative pleasure by "sublimating" the desire for it or by stemming its tide by "reaction formation." These developments were then reflected in the shaping of obsessive symptoms. Bowel defiance, he thought, increases the child's evacuative pleasure. The fact is, however, that children forced into bowel obedience enjoy the evacuative act just as heartily as other children, whereas bowel defiance is often enough strengthened by the intent to avoid an act rendered painful by constipation or anal fissure. With her insistence on bowel regularity the mother hurts not the child's evacuative pleasure, but his pride in having his own way. This struggle of obedience vs. defiance can also originate in other behavior areas.

An abnormal power struggle between parents and child leads to difficulties in conscience formation. Conscience is the main mechanism used by the parents to obtain obedience, and, of course, the conscience develops in response to the parent's demands. The pathological development of conscience is directly traceable to the usual strength of two presumably inherited traits, hopelessly at variance with each other. One is the child's craving for autonomous self-realization, a derivative of his primordial belief in his own omnipotence that drives him to reshape the world about him in his own image. The other trait is his rationalism, his realistic foresight which forces him to take no chances when it comes to preserving the parent's loving care. In adult life this trait is manifested as a strong desire to be treated by one's social environment as an admiring mother treats a favorite child. Since, however, the parents insist on obedience, and, later, society an adherence to its laws and mores, the organism so constituted will eventually do its utmost to conform.

That a child is born to stubborn and tenacious self-assertion may be surmised from the inordinate strength of his rage. This provokes the parents into severe retaliatory measures which, in turn, elicit his defiant rage and even stronger fears. The child is thus forced to move with undue haste from ordinary fear of punishment to fear of conscience, that is, fear of inescapable punishment, and then to guilty fear and the reparative pattern of expiatory self-punishment.

Automatization at such an early age makes these mechanisms over-strong as well as rigid. Healthy conscience, as previously noted, fulfills its adaptive function smoothly; it has little need for guilty fear and the reparative work of repentance. But with early automatization, conscience grows into an organization dominated by the morbid mechanisms of expiatory self-punishment. The patient does not initiate automatized operations, nor is he aware of their meaning. A conscience so constituted will diminish rather than increase the organism's capacity for happiness.

Endangered by its rage and forced to control it, the organism does not rely on merely repressing it. To forestall explosive discharge, the organism turns the larger part of its repressed rage against itself. Fear of conscience and guilty fear rest on the belief in inescapable punishment. The belief is basically a dread of the omnipotence which has been delegated to the parents, and now the organism is terrified to discover that the parents can turn his own omnipotence against him. We must assume that stronger-than-average residues of primordial omnipotence are a factor in the predisposition to obsessive behavior.

In the healthy individual the supreme pleasure of genital orgasm gives rise to a host of affectionate desires, which act to soften rage. In the obsessive patient in whom the pleasure of genital orgasm is seen to be comparatively weak, these derivative motivations are enfeebled. One must assume that a shortage of sexual love is genetically determined. In any case, we consider this deficiency a factor in the predisposition to obsessive behavior.

One must qualify the oft-repeated statements that the obsessive patient is overconscientious; he is that chiefly, if not only in areas of infantile discipline. His silly excesses in cleanliness, orderliness, regularity, and punctuality show that his conscience still operates mostly in the world of the nursery.

In a temper tantrum the discharge of rage is explosive. In an obsessive attack we see the organism struggling with the imperative task of ridding itself of its morbid tensions. Here the discharge of rage, continuously interrupted by counterdischarges of guilty fear, is extremely slow and always incomplete. Humiliated by its guilty fear, the organism soon represses its guilty fear as well. The outcome is a tripartite motivating system—restored pride over repressed guilty fear over more strongly repressed defiant rage.

We call this restored pride *domesticated* or *moral pride*. Now proud of its virtuous conduct, the organism does not choose to remember that it has been forced into morality by its guilty fear of inescapable punishment. These repressions do not, however, sufficiently control the patient's emergency emotions. The overflowing tensions of the patient's fear and rage penetrate his consciousness. Though the degree of his tension fluctuates, he feels tense most of the time, complains about it, and recognizes it when it is brought to his attention.

Our next task is to trace the multifarious influences that contribute to the shaping of obsessive attacks and traits. The rage that filters through in an obsessive attack is the characteristic reaction to frustration. Some of the patient's present resentments repeat the ones he experienced in childhood when his parents denied him fulfillment of his desires. His rage then as now was his instrument for making them give in or go away. He wished they were dead. Of course, he took it for granted that when needed they would promptly return and behave. The child's death wishes are not really murderous; they are only coercive as are so many other expressions of his rage. The child uses rage to force satisfaction of a particular prohibited desire. Later, he wishes to keep the parents under permanent control; they should let him have his own way and still love him. The desire to dominate becomes a goal in itself.

Next the child wishes to eliminate, or at least dominate, his siblings; they must not be allowed to compete with him for position of the favorite child. This motive produces the clinical pictures of "sibling rivalry." The obsessive patient is the child who has retained these attitudes for life. His ritual making and brooding perpetuate the struggle for dominance, drawing the original dramatic contents from the repressed conflict situations of his early years. The remarkable fact shows that its repressed rage glues the organism to humiliating experiences of its past. Its thirst for wiping out those humiliations takes precedence over its desire to repeat routine gratification: triumph is a stronger self-reward than routine pride.

The child with sexual desires where sex has been prohibited is caught in the clash between two groups of forces of almost equal strength: defiant rage versus fear of conscience plus guilty fear. This is a precarious situation—to touch or not to touch is now the question. He or she may find a mode of orgastic arousal that does not depend for its success upon touching the genital organ. He outsmarts the parents by sticking to their words. Later, he will try to circumvent, in the same manner, other prohibitions. It is almost unbelievable to what extent the obsessive ritual may draw its basic conflicts from the now-repressed tragedies of the past. This is particularly true of the struggle, begun in childhood and resumed at puberty, to achieve the genital abstinence demanded of him.

The child may advance his forced precautionary moves to an earlier target point. His parents' intimacies, which he witnessed by chance if not surreptitiously, aroused him. Were it not for his parents' example, he would not have to struggle with his temptation. His effort to keep the parents sexually apart may continue under the guise of an obsessive ritual.

It should be noted that motives of this kind may produce socially valuable results. A brilliant electrical engineer, in his middle twenties, had more than a dozen patents to his credit. Until his treatment, he never realized that his success each time hinged upon preventing the formation of an electric spark. He was an only child who as an adolescent had managed to break up his parents' marriage. His infantile obsession to prevent them from having another child eventually invaded his scientific imagination.

The organs the obsessive patient most often uses in his ritual making are the four extremities. Their psychodynamic significance dates from the corresponding stages of neuromuscular maturation and derives from the sequence of illusions which the child develops about his newly won powers. Gorged with his success in coordination, he overestimates the might of his hands and feet, in particular, of his trampling feet. This illusion persists in the patient's ritual making.

Earlier, the child believes that his mouth, in particular the biting teeth, is his most powerful weapon. He will have fear-ridden dreams as does the adult in which he loses his teeth; this means that he loses the magic power of his coercive rage to secure domination for him and the magic power of his sexual organ to give him orgastic satisfaction. Attempts to control the dangerous power of teeth may eventuate in compulsive grinding in sleep. The charm may spread to saliva (compulsive spitting) and to speech. Verbal attack knows no limits when words have magic power. This is seen in the obsessive patient's resort to magic words and in the ordinary citizen's use of cursing. The magic of words is also a significant component in the dynamics of stammering.

To spit, void, or defecate upon someone are the expressions used in the vernacular to signify contempt. This language usage derives from the annihilating magical effect attributed by the child to his excretions and evacuative acts. But in the opposite emotional context of yearning for help, the same excretions are relied upon to produce a healing effect. The puzzle of their antithetical meaning and significance is solved by the simple fact that they are utilized as tools by love and hate alike.

The fact that magic thought appears in the shaping of obsessive behavior was discovered at an early date by Freud and Ferenczi. We have shown that magic's deepest root is the infant's belief in his own omnipotence. From this source derive the obsessive patient's superstitions which he is reluctant to admit even to himself.

Magic is universal. In our culture its most common manifestations are our wishful or fear-ridden dreams and daydreams, the creative arts, the performing arts, the born leader's charisma. In emotional thought—be it lovebound, ragebound, or fearbound—the power of the wish corrects reality. To a degree, all emotional thought is magic thought. In pathology, however, the purpose for which magic is used depends upon the nature of the disorder. The obsessive disorder specializes in coercive magic; the expressional, in the performance magic of illusory fulfillment. In the former, unknown to himself, the patient seeks to break his prohibitive parent, turn him into a first-class slave; in the latter, likewise unknown to himself, he materializes his adolescent dreams of drama, romance, and glory.

As to the patient's fits of horrific temptation, though hardly more than a signal of rage below, they shake the patient's proud morality. His reaction of horror amounts to a voluminous discharge of guilty fear; it may take him hours to regain his composure. His groping for safeguards tends to disrupt the pattern of his routine activities; he is distracted, makes mistakes, loses himself in aimless repetitions, and does not know where to turn.

It would be a serious mistake to surmise that the patient is bursting with repressed rage. On the contrary, closer examination shows that his outward-bound rage has been almost completely retroflexed, turned upon himself; all he can do with it now is to torture himself. To be able to vent it upon the environment would be his salvation.

Extreme retroflexion of rage may be precipitated by opposing errors in education. Too harsh discipline is bound to break the child; oversolicitousness is likely to disarm him: "My parents are so nice to me, I cannot allow myself to get angry at them even when I should." A patient who suffered from the horrific temptation to kill the grandchild she loved most had been overindulged all her life.

Horrific temptation may take the form of obsessive confession, a mechanism first described by Theodor Reik. Learning about a crime from the newspapers, the patient may at once be convinced that he did it. Nonreporting guilty fears may accumulate from an endless series of nonreporting temptations. To relieve such insupportable guilty fears, to secure deserved punishment and eventual forgiveness, the patient may confess to a crime he never committed. Feodor Dostoevski, our best pathologist of conscience so far, described memorable examples of this obsession. Police chronicles abound with such cases.

If the patient develops a severe depression, his morbid self-accusations not infrequently refer to a beloved person whose actual wrongdoings he blames on himself.

From the model of the patient's obsessive attacks, we can readily understand his obsessive traits, for, in one way or another, most of these permanent marks derive from the same motivating system—perpetuation of the infantile conflict between the child's overstrong tendency to self-assertive domination versus his still stronger clinging to the security of being loved and cared for.

Special mention must be made of the attitude the obsessive patient displays toward the competitive aspects of life. He may be prudent enough to limit his fierce competitive efforts to his major areas of aspiration. He often professes the doctrine of fair play which calls for competitive cooperation, victory through superior performance. At the same time, not always unwittingly, he may quietly employ all the tricks of sibling rivalry, seeking to discourage if not to disqualify his most dangerous competitors from staying in the race, then rush to offer assistance to his victims. When in a slightly elated state, he may be seen competing indiscriminately for almost anything.

In the obsessive patient the manifold and widespread motivations ordinarily sustained by affection and sexual love are diminished in both strength and scope. It must not be confused with the patient's capacity for sexual performance, which may be unimpaired. Unwittingly, the patient is prone to make up for his romantic impoverishment by pedantic execution of the act. He is not exactly a lover, but he is a dependable ritual maker.

A few words should be added about the obsessive patient's "ambivalence." Bleuler, who coined the term in his work on schizophrenia, distinguished between intellectual, emotional, and volitional ambivalence. We trace these manifestations uniformly to the severity of the underlying obedience-defiance conflict. Bleuler stressed the fact that the schizophrenic patient, like the child, tolerates the coexistence of conflicting thoughts or feelings or impulses in his consciousness. The opposite is true of the obsessive patient. While the schizophrenic patient is, or appears to be, unaware of such conflicts in him, the obsessive patient is, more often than not, only too keenly aware of them. He ponders unendingly: Must he give in, or could he gain the upper hand without giving offense? Since the two tendencies concerned are almost equally overstrong, he will always believe that he made the wrong decision. He is aware that his indecision is both widespread and chronic. Facing the same question, the ordinary citizen makes a decision and sticks to it.

Stammering is a speech disorder closely related to obsessive behavior. They have two dynamic features in common—motivating system and interference pattern of discharge. The person gets stuck at the start— in the first letter or syllable—and repeats it until he is able to complete the word. As previously stated, in stammering the organism acts upon the early illusion that its most powerful weapon is the mouth; its rage is channeled into speech.

When I was a young psychoanalyst, a mentor of mine referred a severe stammerer to me for treatment, explaining the nature of this disorder as follows: "Stammering is a conflict between the urethral-erotic tendency to expulsion and the anal-erotic tendency to retention, displaced upward to the mouth." In this explanation my friend's romantic enthusiasm for the libido theory, which in its literal form had a very strong influence at that time, eclipsed his native brilliance.

Like all chronic disorders, obsessive behavior imposes unfavorable modifications upon the organism's pattern of interaction with its social environment. It forces the patient to live on an ever-rising obsessive note of tension, lowering his adaptive efficiency, capacity for enjoyment, and active achievement in life.

The onset and further course of the disorder, as well as the measure of its severity, vary widely. In evaluating the degree, we have to consider three pathological factors: the first is the degree to which the self-punitive mechanisms of conscience have become automatized; the second is the degree of the patient's pleasure deficiency, which is indirectly responsible for his severity of conscience; the third, closely linked with the first, is the presence and degree of pain dependence.

Clinically, we can readily appraise degrees of automatization and residual flexibility by watching the influence that stress, absence of stress, and other factors have upon an established response. But about the organization of these highly significant processes we are completely in the dark and will probably remain there until behavior physiology comes to our aid. Unfortunately, as far as mechanisms of conscience are concerned, little help can be expected from animal studies.

Pain dependence is a chronic disturbance imposed upon the organism chiefly by its own retroflexed rage, which, in turn, is an outcome of restrictive upbringing. Its various forms may be observed in the pathological context of any disorder. In the obsessive patient, the form called moral pain dependence is most frequent.

No man can stay alive without satisfying his minimal hedonic requirements, and so the patient is forced to find solace and high moral gratification in the fact that he is a "fine man." He discovers more and more opportunities to "fulfill his duty," imposing upon himself burdens and sacrifices which often enough do no good either to him or to anyone else. He becomes a self-styled martyr—without a cause. In moral pain dependence, under the supremacy of retroflexed rage, conscience defeats its purpose.

As a healthy source of pleasure, genital orgasm is unrivaled. The obsessive patient may also suffer from sexual pain dependence. If the parents interfere, the organism puts up a hard fight. We have already seen that the child may circumvent the parental prohibition by indirect modes of stimulation. Defeated as a child by deterrence, the adolescent may find himself incapacitated for standard sexual performance. By chance he then discovers that his submission to humiliation or other abuse has a disinhibitory effect upon his performance. Analysis reveals the reason: he has taken the inescapable punishment beforehand; now he is entitled to prove that he deserved it. He develops the practice of inviting abuse (short of serious injury) from the mate, thereby restoring his capacity for performance. We call this practice the fear-ridden or submissive version of sexual pain dependence.

Another patient may discover that coercive rage takes care of his trouble. Assuming the role of the authority, he inflicts the dreaded punishment upon the mate, enjoying vicariously the mate's suffering. The triumph unfreezes and strengthens his sexual potency even more. This practice is called the enraged or triumphant version of sexual pain dependence. The two versions of this disturbance are far less self-destructive than is moral pain dependence.

I shall now sum up the etiologically significant results of this analysis. Obsessive behavior is based on a predisposition which is acquired in childhood and includes five clearly discernible factors: (1) overstrong rage; (2) guilty fear made stronger by retroflexion of the larger part of repressed rage; (3) stronger-than-average residues of primordial omnipotence that make rage strong and its paradoxical retroflexion possible; (4) relative pleasure deficiency in the area of genital orgasm, with its consequent enfeeblement of genital love and affection—a deficiency that makes it imperative to control repressed rage by retroflexion; (5) intelligent foresight leading to realistic fears. Presumably, the acquired predisposition to obsessive behavior is based on a genetic predisposition in which the overstrength of rage may be linked with the pleasure deficiency of sexual orgasm.

## Differential Diagnosis

A sprinkling of obsessive mechanisms may be found in any person. The diagnosis of obsessive behavior must rest on the evaluation of the total picture. On the other hand, as will presently be shown, obsessive behavior may be complicated by mechanisms known to be characteristic of other disorders; this fact calls for differential diagnosis.

Phobic avoidance, the mechanism of the so-called phobias, is frequently seen in obsessive behavior, but there is no difficulty in telling the two disorders apart. We speak of phobia when the clinical picture is dominated by the avoidance mechanism but other signs of obsessive behavior are absent. Analogous considerations apply to the differential diagnosis between nonschizophrenic paranoid behavior and obsessive behavior.

The presence of sexual pain dependence does not by any means point to obsessive behavior. As mentioned before, this disturbance may occur in a variety of behavior disorders or may constitute one by itself. I have never seen a true expressional pattern combined with true obsessive behavior in the same patient. In early psychoanalytic literature, statements to the effect that obsessional neurosis always has a "hysteric nucleus" are explained by the fact that Freud calls the phobias *fear hysterias* (Angsthysterien). We classify them as phobic forms of emergency dyscontrol; psychodynamically, they are unrelated to the syndromes of expressional behavior.

Obsessive behavior may appear during the intervals between two phases of moodcyclic behavior. This fact is revealed by the patient's history.

Though these questions may claim theoretical interest, their practical value is nil. In contradistinction, the diagnostic separation of genuinely obsessive behavior from certain forms of schizophrenia is a task of serious theoretical as well as practical significance. In retrospect, there can be no doubt that Josef Breuer's famous patient suffered not, as he and Freud believed, from hysteria but from schizophrenia. Freud suspected that his famous "Wolfman" was schizophrenic. With our increasing knowledge of schizophrenia, we are now sure of it. The analysis of this case became a classic in the psychoanalytic literature of the psychoneuroses. The patient from whose observation Ferenczi abstracted his concept of "pathoneurosis" was subsequently treated by myself in a mental hospital where he spent month after month in a catatonic stupor. One cannot escape the impression that the number of schizophrenic patients erroneously diagnosed and treated as "obsessive-compulsive neurosis," "conversion hysteria," "anxiety hysteria," "mixed psychoneurosis," and so forth has been and continues to be very high.

The clinical pictures of schizotypal disintegration can hardly be mistaken for obsessive behavior, but there is a large margin for diagnostic error in pseudoneurotic schizophrenia. Here the clinical picture may include a variety of pseudo-obsessive, pseudophobic, pseudo-expressional, and still other mechanisms, all deriving from the obedience-defiance conflict, which, in my view, is the predominant motivating system in schizoadaptive behavior. The differential diagnosis rests on the presence or absence of minute schizophrenic traits and on the experienced psychiatrist's ability to use his own emotional resonance as an exploratory tool. Verification of his findings by subsequent developments may teach him to spot the schizotype "by feel."

# CHAPTER 25

# Moodcyclic Behavior

MOODCYCLIC BEHAVIOR DESCRIBES PERIODS OF DEPRESSION AND REPARATIVE elation as well as the pattern of alternating cycles. These disorders can occur in a variety of forms which differ greatly from one another in severity, complexity, duration, frequency, and biocultural context.

The emotional matrix of healthy life performance is dominated by welfare emotions, such as pleasurable desire, joy, love, and pride on a realistic basis. By his contact with other healthy people the individual elicits positive emotional reactions from others which reinforce his own. The ordinary individual has no trouble with the painful tensions arising from time to time in the nonreporting range. They can be readily discharged by spells of fear in the waking state or by fear-ridden dreams. The mild depressive spell of guilty conscience, lasting a few hours or days, is experienced by a multitude of healthy individuals. In our culture it belongs to the emotional repertoire of daily life.

More severe depressive cycles may be engendered and develop in the course of almost any psychiatric disturbance. They are frequently seen in the patient suffering from schizotypal, overreactive, or narcotic disorders, or brain damage of aging. In clinical psychiatry these forms are described as symptomatic manifestations or complications of the given primary disorder.

In still other forms of depressive cycle, the severe mood swing itself appears to be the primary disturbance. These forms are usually classified under headings such as reactive depression, endogenous depression, cyclothymia, and manic-depressive psychosis.

The feature common to all clinical forms of depression is the patient's depressive behavior. Assuming that the difference in symptomatology will prove traceable to those differences of the biocultural context which produce them, we may focus our attention on the common core and examine the depressive behavior itself.

First, I shall draw the clinical picture of a depressive spell. The patient is sad and in painful tension. He is intolerant of his condition, thereby increasing his distress. His self-esteem is abased, his self-confidence shattered. Retardation of his initiative, thinking, and motor actions makes him incapable of sustained effort. His behavior indicates open or underlying fears and guilty fears (self-reproach). He is demonstratively preoccupied with his alleged failings, shortcomings, and unworthiness; yet he also harbors a deep resentment that life does not give him a fair deal.

He usually has suicidal ideas and often suicidal impulses. His sleep is poor; his appetite and sexual desire are enfeebled. He takes little or no interest in his work and ordinary affairs and shies away from affectionate as well as competitive relationships. He has lost his capacity to enjoy life and is drawn into a world of his own imagination, a world dedicated to the pursuit of suffering rather than the pursuit of happiness.

The onset may be sudden or gradual, the duration from a few days or weeks to many months. The severity ranges from mildly neurotic to fully psychotic. Often in neurotic and almost always in the psychotic cases there are conspicuous physical symptoms, such as loss of weight and constipation. In some patients spells of depression alternate with spells of elation, while in others no spells of elation occur.

The depressive spell is precipitated by a loss, real or imaginary, which may be of a person, object, position, or status. It is characteristic of the depressive to react to this actual or presumed emergency with an overwhelming emotion of fear and rage that threatens to destroy his capacity for adaptive control. Because of the loss to his emotional security, his action self shrinks and he experiences diminished self-reliance, self-esteem, and self-confidence. He is overwhelmed by agonizing inner pressure that keeps him preoccupied with himself and blurs his realistic outlook and judgment. He cannot even begin to evaluate his remaining resources. How does the self-reliant person of comparable background and position act when he suffers loss or other misfortune? His circumstances would prompt him to recover sufficiently from his acute distress and ask himself how he could rearrange his life or what he could do about the predicament. To a self-reliant person adversity is a challenge because he is confident of his own resiliency.

But the depression-prone person does not meet adversity in a self-reliant way. The conflicting waves of emotion make him feel so inadequate that he tries to get loving care like a frightened and helpless child. In this sense the resulting depression is an adaptive maneuver, a cry to be taken care of. Actually, he suffers regression to dependence, which means automatic reactivation of a childish behavior pattern, demanding again that he be the obedient child. This adversely affects his entire relationship to himself and the world about him. Hence the regression and dependency adaptation are miscarried repair. The dependency adaptation, overflow of emergency emotions, and loss of self-reliance are the framework in which all disordered behavior including depression must be viewed.

To understand the pattern of the infantile dependency we have to go back to the power struggle between child and parents. As you remember, the child wants to have his way and still be loved and cared for. This, however, he cannot have because he must be obedient to keep the parents' love and care. Slowly, he learns to anticipate the parents' responses. Through endless repetitions, the anticipatory mechanisms of conscience become automatized, which helps make him obedient to his parents' wishes. Since he is necessarily dependent on them, this is the price he has to pay. Prompted by his guilty fear (self-reproach), he learns when he is defiant the prescribed expiatory procedure which in time may also become completely automatized. An automatic act of self-punishment can be forced upon the individual by his nonreporting brain which functions here as his nonreporting conscience.

To tame the child's defiant rage is the pivotal task of education, but this is hard to do as rage is the fighting emotion of the organism. The conscious system's capacity to hold rage under repression is narrowly limited. When the individual cannot vent his rage on the one who provokes it or on a scapegoat, because of fear, he vents his rage on himself. In the child this occurs first at the motor level with his extremities and later in the adult by violent self-criticism. Retroflexed rage helps fear of conscience keep temptation in check.

With this review in mind, let us see what happens to the depressed person who has regressed in the nonreporting process to infantile dependency. The patient is afraid of the future. How can he maintain his emotional (if not also material) security? This fear elicits rage against the parent or parent substitute. Why was he not taken care of better (for instance, why did he suffer this loss)? At this point, fear of conscience enters to prevent defiance and leads to retroflexed rage, guilty fear which in turn leads to expiatory behavior and self-punishment. The patient does not have the remotest inkling of any of this. Clinically, the patient is only aware of depression, self-reproaches, and self-punishment. He may execute the self-punishment automatically without conscious intent or recognition.

The guilty fear splits his defeated coercive rage into two parts that follow different courses. The smaller part, the stubborn core, is forced underground or into the nonreporting range. There it remains what it is, coercive rage against the parent, no longer in conflict with the guilty fear because it is repressed. The larger part of defeated rage, defeated because of fear, is now turned against the patient himself and travels the path I have outlined.

Though such self-punishment from retroflexed rage is excruciatingly painful, this remorse is often but a façade. Beneath this façade at the nonreporting level, the patient is furious at the parent for not taking better care of him and at himself for not coercing the parent to do so. Bitter with wounded pride, he thus punishes himself, not in contrition but for his failure to gain his coercive ends. This deeply hidden meaning of his feeling toward the parent and toward himself makes mockery of the patient's conscious remorse and reveals the true root of his sense of unworthiness. His violently self-belittling repentance is clearly the action of his twofold guilty fears: (1) for getting angry at the parent and jeopardizing his relationship with the parent; (2) for not coercing the parent to do what the patient wanted.

When the parent does not help him, he attempts to win back the presumably offended mother or parents as he did as a child by expiation. In order to do this, he attempts to increase the severity of his expiatory self-punishment. Thus, it is by means of punishing himself that he hopes to repair the mother's loving care and above all her feeding breast. These maneuvers are all in the nonreporting process and are apparent from dreams and through the psychoanalytic method of contextual inference.

There are minor variations in this pattern, depending on what the patient has lost or failed at. At times, of course, the loss may be a parent or parent substitute. Depressive behavior is a pathological form of atonement rendered unrecognizable by the automatization of its motivating system. It may also be described as a pathologic manifestation of the patient's nonreporting conscience.

Hopeless fear and rage are common human experiences, and so is the counsel of despair. Accordingly, the resort to the automatized repair pattern of guilty fear is by no means limited to the depressive spell. But there is one characteristic that sets aside true depression from the various forms of unrecognized atonement. This feature is the patient's nonreporting fear of starvation, voiced usually as a fear of impoverishment. This fear can be traced to the two momentous experiences of the infant—his hunger and the intoxicating pleasure of satisfaction when he gorges at his mother's breast (the alimentary orgasm). Consequently, feeding at the mother's breast remains forever the mode of magical fulfillment of man's wishes in life.

The patient develops true depression when, in his nonreporting imagination, he begins to dramatize his "emergency" as a threat of starvation. The patient loses his appetite, he loses weight, and, paradoxically, he even punishes himself by fasting. But these manifestations merely rationalize and augment his mortal fear. Though this fear is based on an oversensitivity to the threat of alimentary deprivation developed in early life, its onset may be precipitated by current influences from lower physiologic levels. The patient may be subject to an actual metabolic disturbance that spoils his appetite and scares him in still other ways. Dependent for his well-being on the pleasure of satiation, he then blows up his scare to a fear of starvation.

One clinical trait appears to contradict the interpretation that fear of starvation is one of the earliest discernible factors in the developmental psychodynamics of depressive behavior. How is it possible that the patient, while dreading starvation, refuses to eat, loses appetite and, as a rule, body weight? The answer is that, unbeknown to himself, he fasts. To avert the threatening punishment of starvation, fasting is the appropriate form of expiatory self-punishment. "You need not punish me, I am doing it myself." Through the ages, fasting has been (and still is) a universal form of religious atonement. In its secularized form— the hunger strike—its coercive intent has become obvious. Under the influence of rage, the fasting of atonement may be replaced by defiant overeating. Instead of losing weight, the patient thus gains weight, pocketing beforehand the reward expected for repentence. Connecting causally the visible facts, the German vernacular refers to weight increase of this type as *Kummerspeck* (fat of grief).

A significant feature must be added to the characterization of the depressed patient's coercive rage. This rage proposes to use the teeth as coercive weapons. The infant's teeth enhances his alimentary delight, but rage remembers the destructive power of biting and chewing. In the nonreporting reaches of his mind, the enraged patient is set to devour the frustrating mother herself as a substitute for food. In dire need, prehistoric tribesmen may have devoured their chieftain (later their totem animal) with similar ideas in mind. Sometimes this cannibalistic feature is clearly revealed in the depressed patient's dreams.

## Enraged Atonement

The atonement pattern may absorb additional motivations and mechanisms. In one class of cases, a significant part of the patient's rage escapes retroflexion and must be repressed in its original, environment-directed form (rage against the parent). Ordinarily, continuously replenished rage at some point breaks through the repression and forces its way to explosive discharge. But in depression this does not happen because the prevailing atonement pattern clamps down on the discharge process midway. It forestalls an open outburst by dispersing the environment-directed rage upon its arrival in consciousness. His dispersed rage keeps the patient highly irritable, tense, and restless. He presents the clinical picture of agitated depression.

A measure of environment-directed rage may slip through and find satisfaction when it appears to serve the self-denigrating purpose of retroflexed rage. This happens when the patient, at the height of atonement, blames the parents' failings on himself. Neither he nor the environment suspects the hidden ironic intent of such self-accusation. Irony is the most refined expression of environment-directed rage.

## Mourning, Grief, and Depression

Mourning is an institution of prehistoric origin for the ritualized expression of grief over the death of an esteemed (loved, respected) person. The essential motivating system is expiatory self-punishment. It seems likely that in tribal times the survivors lived in dread that the departed would return and avenge himself for his death. The practicing psychoanalyst is familiar with these primitive sentiments because they are faithfully reproduced today. For example, the individual routinely represses occasional flare-ups of anger and resentment occurring in his friendly relationship to a certain relative. The relative dies, and the individual grieves for him. Analytic exploration of the patient's grief may be summed up in one sentence. His repressed feelings—angry, coercive, vindictive—have elicited in him a reaction of guilty fear, which has in turn ushered in a process of expiatory self-punishment.

In its reaction to death, the nonreporting mind singles out the hostile feelings present in every human relationship and sees them as evidence of a "death wish," which has come true. The dead "victim" must be propitiated at once in order to forestall his vengeance. The nonreporting mind reacts just this way even when the conscious mind shies away from the prescribed ritual of mourning. Grief is a refined emotional response evolved in the course of cultural history from the primitive tribal ritual of mourning, which must be recognized as the archaic prototype of depressive behavior.

## Failure of Hedonic Control in Depressive Behavior

In depressive behavior the patient's consciousness succumbs to the self-damaging torrent of the emergency emotions arriving from his nonreporting mind. In the framework of adaptational psychodynamics, I view this pathologic fact as a failure of the organism's hedonic self-regulation. I can explain this failure only by means of the pain barrier. This is the combined effect of hedonic control mechanisms (intentional suppression, selective attention, and, above all, automatic repression) that operates within limits to protect consciousness against the danger of being inundated with painful feelings and thoughts. In depressive behavior the excessive nonreporting tension breaks or extensively punctures the pain barrier and thus produces the illness. Along with the invasion of the emergency emotions, the consciousness is afflicted by the change of the field of pleasurable expectations (combined with self-reliance) into a field of painful expectations (combined with a sense of helplessness). At this point a vicious circle is established between the nonreporting mind and the range of awareness.

The repressive mechanism is no more successful in the control of retroflexed rage than it is in the control of environment-directed rage. While under repression, retroflexed rage, like environment-directed rage, may rise to a strength that provokes automatic discharge. To relieve the pressure of its inner tension, the organism produces an attack of retroflexed rage. Unaware of the true nature of his behavior, the patient may then carry out entire sequences of expiatory self-punishment.

The extreme form of expiatory self-punishment is suicide. As seen in patients who survived an attempted suicide, its motivation springs from the illusory expectation that by giving his life the patient will break his mother's heart, be at long last forgiven, and live happily ever after. Suicidal attempts so arranged that the patient will be discovered and saved have a realistically coercive intent.

## Two Modes of Validation: Clinical Observation and Psychophysiologic Correlation

My theory about depressive behavior derives from clinical observation. Hopefully, it will some day be applied in a large number of cases in which the observation is extended over every phase of the depressed patient. Without the guidance of psychodynamic theory based on communicated deep introspection, psychiatry can hardly hope to disclose the true meaning and value of the clinical "facts" it collects. As the example of the physical and biochemical sciences shows, penetrating theory is the most creative component of the investigation process. In contradistinction to speculations which dominated and obstructed the development of psychoanalytic theory for quite some time, truly scientific theories must in the first place satisfy the criteria of testability and in the course of time prove their fruitfulness. In addition to seeking validation of all theories by introspectional means, we must look forward to psychophysiologic correlations.

I have suggested that the automatic motivating system of depressive behavior derives from the pattern of expiatory behavior taught the child by the parents and others entrusted with his education. The child can of course understand and absorb the ideas involved only after he has acquired the requisite language. Presumably, this process takes several years. It comes therefore as a surprise that babies less than one year old develop a depression—that is, display outward signs of a depression. I assume that at this early age, when the atonement pattern does not yet exist, depressive behavior may come about by the rage-retroflexing mechanism, which begins to function some time during the preverbal or early verbal period of life. In the course of postnatal growth and development, it takes its place as the core of the highly complex atonement pattern. In the sense of our hypothesis, infantile depression has to be interpreted as a prolonged attack of retroflexed rage. We may further assume that the rage-retroflexing mechanism forms part of the innate brain organization of the infant. It is not newly created but brought into play and developed by frustrating experiences that form part of the organism's interaction with an unfit human environment. These are problems for the behavioral physiologist, embryologist, and geneticist. Taking retroflexion of rage as a point of departure, it is possible that inspectional inquiry may disclose the biological roots of conscience and, with it, of depressive behavior.

In the developmental history of depressive atonement, the psychodynamic event of outstanding significance is the infant's overreaction to hunger in terms of rage. At times of extreme hunger and rage, he would like to bite off his mother's nipple or perhaps her whole breast. In some form, these fantasies are carried on to an age when the child becomes capable of responding to his wish to inflict violence with guilty fear. This combines with the desire to propitiate the offended mother by fasting as an expiatory method. By temporarily suspending the use of his teeth for biting and chewing, the child tries to discourage his temptation to violence. The strength of the hungry infant's rage reaction may be due to physiologic causes.

It has long been suspected, though for different reasons, that the etiology of depression includes a metabolic disturbance, but so far none has been found. Analyzing infantile depression in the conceptual framework of adaptational psychodynamics would, I think, prepare the ground for a renewed physiologic investigation of the problem of depression. It is my hope that my suggestions about the psychodynamic mechanisms involved in depression will give added impetus to the physiologic (biochemical, genetic) exploration of depressive behavior. Only through transoperational correlation can adaptational psychodynamics achieve its goal of transforming the introspectional artistry of Freud's later years into a science for which, in his early work, he himself had laid the lasting foundation.

## Differential Dynamics

The depressive spell is composed of three primary constituents: the alteration of mood to one of sustained gloomy repentance; the regressive yearning for the alimentary security of the infant; the struggle between the excessive emergency emotions, in which submissive fear defeats coercive rage. The first two of these three constituents are altogether peculiar to the depressive spell, but the third is not. A similarly grave conflict between excessive emergency emotions is a primary constituent also in the obsessional and the paranoid patterns. However, in these contexts the relative strength of the contending forces is different and so is their disordering effect.

In the nonreporting foundations of the obsessional pattern the coercive use of the teeth is eclipsed in actual effectiveness by the coercive use of the hands and of the trampling feet. In certain circumstances, the infant may also resort to the coercive use of defecation. In the infant's experience, the hands could be used both ways, to fondle or to beat; and the control of reputedly poisonous feces too could be used either to obey and accommodate or to have fun and defy. The coercive use of the extremities (which includes the infant's "murderous" impulses as well) was the enraged infant's response to maternal discipline in general. Enraged bowel defiance was his reaction to the mother's particular effort to impose bowel "regularity" upon him. With the progressing biologic maturation of the infant, the struggle for power between him and the mother is thus extended and intensified. In the obsessional the combined forces of straight rage and prohibited desire are about as strong as the combined forces of guilty fear and retroflexed rage. This makes the struggle between obedient submission and defiant coercion interminable. "Must I let Mama have her way? Or can I force Mama to let me have my way and still love me?" Although the emotions concerned are repressed to an astonishing extent, their conflicting tensions penetrate into the range of awareness and raise havoc with the patient's doubts, doings and undoings, sidetracked precautions and sidetracked temptations, token transgressions and token self-punishments. The function of these symptoms is to insure discharge. The formation of interference patterns explains the puzzling fact that the discharge, though forced, is nonetheless slow and tortuous. Whereever the desire or demand is irrespressible or inescapable, such as in the areas of evacuation, sex, and work, the patient may obtain satisfaction through pain-dependent pleasure behavior. The patterns of pain dependence are interference patterns of discharge composed of two antagonistic sets of tension: guilty fear and retroflexed rage on the one hand and defiant rage and inhibited desire on the other. Each of these patterns derives its special characteristics from the particular pleasure organizations involved. The inhibition of desire is automatized, varies in severity, and results from parental prohibition in early life. In summary, the obsessive patient experiences less emotional turmoil, but he tends to become pain dependent and is forced to squander his finest resources on a hopeless and unending task. In the paranoid pattern, straight environment-directed rage rises to dominance. Hence, the patient's proneness to violence. This may help to explain the clinical observation stressed by Karl Abraham, that, during the intervals between depressive spells, the behavior of moodcyclic patients often shows an obsessive pattern. I have observed that the intervals between depressive spells may occasionally reveal a paranoid pattern. These patterns tend to disappear during the depressive spells, but the patient's pain dependence persists.

## Elation

We cannot predict how long a wave of depressive behavior will last. But we do know that it always subsides, though we are unable to give a detailed psychodynamic account of the processes that bring about its recession. Clinical experience shows, however, that the patient's resumption of a healthy life performance presupposes a period of *gradual* recovery. From some turning point onward, the torrent of emergency emotions slowly loses its momentum—we do not know how and why. At the same time, just as slowly, desire, initiative, and enterprise reappear and grow. The patient begins to recapture his adult self-reliance and regains his capacity for the healthy enjoyment of his activities. Correspondingly, he experiences the rise of his downcast mood to a normal level. This ideal course of events is, however, none too frequently seen.

In many cases the patient overreaches himself. Impatiently, he skips or unduly shortens the requisite period of gradual recovery. Instead he rather abruptly swings over to a cycle of slightly or severely elated behavior. The inhibition of depression is now succeeded by overfacilitation, the lack of self-confidence by overconfidence, the agony of depression by a strange quality of pleasure that must be recognized as morbid. It does not, as does healthy pleasure, issue from activities that benefit the organism. Instead, it interferes with a realistic life performance and produces further self-damaging consequences, which is why I call it antiadaptive pleasure.

Elation is for the organism a calamitous way of cutting short the agony of depression. We attribute it to an automatic process of miscarried repair work. Antidepressive elation resembles narcotic elation, except that the underlying pleasure is not pharmacogenic. Old time psychiatrists must have sensed the self-healing intent of elation, for in my own medical school days it was an established practice to treat depression with opiates. The fact that the organism uses elation as an antidepressant is to me further proof of the adaptational psychodynamic analysis of the motivating system of depressive behavior. Beneath the patient's guilt and self-punishment we found his shrunken self (more precisely his shrunken action self) smarting from deeply hurt pride. Truly remedial action would seek to build up the self again by realistically successful effort and performance. But elation, seeking a shortcut to the same end, produces merely an inflation of the self with all the dangers such a condition entails. The duration of an elated cycle is just as unpredictable as that of a depressive cycle. About the psychodynamic mechanisms involved in its recession, we know even less.

Recovery, spontaneous or therapeutic, sets in when the patient begins to recapture his lost capacity for pleasure, for the enjoyment of life. But this statement must be qualified. We already talked about the two kinds of pleasure. One is true, the other is spurious. True pleasure is the earned reward of successful effort. It stems from the transformation of stored organismic potentials into adaptive control. Spurious pleasure on the other hand is obtained by little or no effort. It springs from the mere illusion of control. The action self responds to true pleasure with due pride; to spurious pleasure, its reaction is exalted. This effortless pleasure appears to it as an actual proof of its magic powers. It responds with triumph and may even lift the organism to a state of intoxication or elation. As we now see, the patient is on the road to recovery only when he begins to achieve true pleasure.

### The Predisposition to Moodcyclic Disorder

I have explained why I believe that the depressed and elated cycles of mood are directly traceable to impairments of the hedonic control of the organism. An overwhelming emergency response to a real or imagined loss culminating in the fear of starvation punctures the pain barrier. This damage brings forth the depressive cycle. In order to end the depressive cycle or to prevent its threatening onslaught, faulty self-regulation turns to producing spurious pleasure and thus manipulates the gauge of hedonic control. This damage brings forth the elated cycle.

In this light, proneness of moodcyclic disorder must include the following three phenotypic traits:

1. Proneness to emergency overreaction and dyscontrol.

2. Critical significance of alimentary security in the hedonic pattern of the organism. This implies a high susceptibility to the threat of alimentary deprivation.

3. Intolerance of pain, marked by an acute fear of pain that increases pain in a vicious circle. Moreover, intolerance of pain may be a direct expression of an underlying vulnerability of the pain barrier and, therefore, of the entire machinery of hedonic control.

In people prone to moodcyclic disorders, the development of these traits may be based on the congenital presence of predisposing factors. Actualization of these presumably inherited factors would then be the outcome of their interaction with the sequence of environments to which the organism is exposed. In this respect, most significant of course are the environments encountered during the early years of growth. Loss of the alimentary security of loving maternal care may be the earliest environmental influence capable of starting the actualization of an inherited moodcyclic predisposition.

# CHAPTER 26

# Schizotypal Behavior

~~~~~~~~~~~~~~~~~~~~~~~~~~~~~~~~~~~~~~~~~~~~~~~~~~~~~~~~~~~~~~~~

SCHIZOPHRENIA ORIGINATES WITH THE PRESENCE OF CERTAIN MUTATED genes in the fertilized egg from which the patient developed. Although the nature of these mutated genes is not yet known, their existence is established to my satisfaction. Therefore, borrowing a genetic term, I call an individual so determined a *schizophrenic phenotype* or, briefly, a *schizotype*. The interrelation of the pathologic traits peculiar to this type I have termed *schizotypal organization;* the manifestations of such traits, *schizotypal behavior*.

Some of these traits are accessible to inspection, other to introspection. The use of physiologic methods discloses the traits accessible to inspection, the range of inquiry extending from biochemical genetics through biochemistry to brain physiology. For the disclosure of the traits accessible to introspection, we must use the psychoanalytic technique of communicated deep introspection.

Because physiologic knowledge of our subject is still in the early stages of accumulation, the theory of schizotypal organization and behavior is founded on data drawn from the two sciences of genetics and adaptational psychodynamics. It also has posed problems for physiologic investigation.

The immediate causes of schizotypal "differentness" reside in two fundamental forms of damage of the integrative apparatus of the psychodynamic cerebral system: (1) The capacity for pleasure is diminished; pleasure's usually strong motivating action is enfeebled. This damage is designated as integrative pleasure deficiency. Its neurochemical basis is unknown. (2) The individual's awareness of his own body is, or tends to become, distorted. This clinical fact is interpreted as damage of the action self, precipitated by what we provisionally call a proprioceptive (kinesthetic) diathesis. The physiologic nature of this disturbance is still unexplored.

This fundamental damage of the organism's psychodynamic organization suggests correspondingly fundamental damage of its biochemical organization. My own expectation is that eventually the latter will be shown to originate with, as Linus Pauling puts it, "molecular disease," directly traceable to the individual's mutated genes.

Capacity for pleasure develops within the limits of the inherited pleasure potential coded in the infant's genes. Under favorable environmental influences, ontogenetic development will release in full the infant's genetic pleasure potential; and the organism's established capacity for pleasure will remain unimpaired as long as it continues to operate in a state of good health.

Pleasure deficiency may be defined as a significant lowering of the organism's capacity for pleasure. It may be caused by one or two or all three of the forms of damage we designate as genetic, developmental, and operational. Let me say a few words about each of them: (1) *Genetic*. From the observations accumulated by psychiatric geneticists we must conclude that gene mutation may significantly reduce the organism's inherited pleasure potential. (2) *Developmental*. In the absence of adequate contact with a loving mother (notably in the first year of life) ontogenetic development falls short of releasing in full the inherited pleasure potential regardless of the latter's size. (3) *Operational*. Conflict and repression may inactivate the organism's established capacity for pleasure to a significant extent. Operational pleasure deficiency is seen to be accessible to psychotherapy; genetic pleasure deficiency may prove to be accessible to biochemical therapy some day. In the pleasure deficiency of the schizotype, the genetic damage is the crucial factor.

Pleasure deficiency alters every operation of the integrative apparatus. No phase of life, no area of behavior remains unaffected. The two kinds of emotion we have learned to classify, the welfare emotions and the emergency emotions, undergo contrasting changes: the welfare emotions contract; the emergency emotions expand. This is a consequence of their contrasting relation to pleasure and pain. The welfare emotions —such as pleasurable desire, joy, affection, love, self-respect, pride—are experienced as pleasure or the expectation of pleasure; and the emergency emotions—such as fear, rage, guilty fear, guilty rage—as pain or the expectation of pain. Pleasure deficiency vitiates welfare emotions in quality as well as intensity, thus causing a deficiency in the entire gamut of affectionate feelings. Ordinarily, these pleasurable feelings help to subdue the emergency emotions; here, this counterbalancing effect is enfeebled or gone. Consequently, fear, rage, and their derivatives may grow to inordinate strength.

Pleasurable desire, like the greasing of an engine, facilitates performance; lack of pleasurable desire makes performance more difficult and reduces the patient's zest for life. The absence of adequate pleasure and love impoverishes the patient's human relationships and makes healthy development of the sexual function impossible.

The action self is basically dependent on proprioceptive information. Its significance is paramount, for it is the organism's highest integrative unit. In the schizotype, the cohesion of this unit is endangered by pleasure's diminished binding power and, perhaps even more significantly, by the proprioceptive diathesis. The fact that the patient's action self is subject to fragmentation is revealed to the observer by direct manifestations or by circumstantial evidence. Brittleness of his action self may be the deepest source of his sense of inferiority, of his haunting uneasiness, and excessive fear of dying. It may also be the factor predisposing him to spells of depersonalization or to fears of being dismembered.

While anhedonia has been repeatedly listed by many writers as one of the "symptoms" of schizophrenia, Eugene Bleuler, to my knowledge, was the first to notice the frequent occurrence of proprioceptive disturbances in this disorder. The organism responds to such genetic damage with highly promising repair work. It creates a compensatory system of adaptation, composed of extreme overdependence, operational replacement in the integrative apparatus, and a scarcity economy of pleasure. This, however, is not the whole story. The organism makes yet another attempt at compensation which miscarries badly. Its essence is a vast increase in the patient's craving for magic. This compensatory craving, so difficult to control, defeats adaptation. The patient not only finds solace in magic, he tends to rely upon it. We recognize this phase of miscarried repair work as the prime mechanism of compensatory maladaptation; its extreme product is delusion.

Let me now describe briefly the compensatory system of adaptation. The schizotype's extreme overdependence is a response to his profound lack of self-reliance. Open or camouflaged, this attitude has, however, been complicated since childhood by a strong obedience-defiance conflict. The patient bitterly resents his craving for and dependence on loving care. This is the motivational basis of the trait which Bleuler termed *emotional ambivalence*. The schizotype rebels above all against the parental figure without whom he cannot live.

The healthy individual, in choosing his words and making certain responses, spontaneously relies on his friendly and affectionate feelings. The schizotype, when such responses are called for, tries to "figure out" what he is expected to say or do. Lacking the guidance of warm emotions, he presses his cold intelligence into service. This operational replacement shapes his entire conception of the world. His outlook and some of his observations may strike the ordinary person as "funny" or "sophisticated" or "bizarre." Forced into a scarcity economy of pleasure, he may experience the loss of any routine satisfaction as a severe blow. His favored pursuit, if he has one, may absorb his entire capacity for pleasure.

Success in the compensatory system of adaptation depends largely upon the total balance between the schizotype's liabilities and his resources. From patient to patient the grade of genetic damage varies from low to high; intelligence, from borderline to genius; creative talent, from nil to unique; socioeconomic status and opportunity, from one extreme of the scale to the other. If the total balance between his liabilities and resources becomes unfavorable, the degree of inner tension may tax the patient's adaptive powers and precipitate untoward developments.

## Development Stages

Schizotypal behavior may be divided into four development stages: compensated, decompensated, disintegrated, and deteriorated. Compensated schizotypal behavior means that in favorable circumstances the schizotype may go through life without a breakdown. Paul Hoch and Philip Polatin designated this form of schizotypal disorder *pseudoneurotic schizophrenia*.

In decompensated schizotypal behavior, "emergency dyscontrol" is marked by the production of inappropriate or excessive fears and rages. An attack of emergency dyscontrol is bound to break the compensatory system of adaptation and thus precipitate decompensation, characterized by what appears to be a scramble of phobic, obsessive, depressive, and still other overreactive mechanisms. The psychodynamics of decompensated schizotypal behavior is dominated by the patient's extreme overdependence, the severity of his obedience-defiance conflict, and his overt reliance on magic. He may remain in this stage for a long time or recover spontaneously or go into a disintegrative breakdown.

The stage of disintegrated schizotypal behavior is known as overt schizophrenic psychosis. Disorganization of his action self has reduced the patient to adaptive incompetence, the disintegrative process resulting in thought disorder, activity disorder, and the like. The clinical pictures have been variously classified. We understand best the psychodynamics of a paranoid subtype: a phase dominated by guilty fear (hypochondriasis, delusion of reference) is followed by one where, in presumed self-defense, the patient releases his guilty rage (delusion of persecution). Eventually he may find peace in a delusion of grandeur—the work of miscarried repair. The process of schizotypal disintegration may go on for an indefinite period of time. There is, however, a chance of spontaneous remission, as well as a threat of progressive deterioration. Deteriorated schizotypal behavior is marked by a progressive cessation of function, a nearly complete withdrawal from the adaptive task.

The schizotypal lives under an infantile dependency system, seeking to lean on a parent or ersatz parent. The system is undermined from the outset by the severity of the obedience-defiance conflict which reflects the excessive strength of guilty fear and defiant rage. The patient is self-willed. He wants to have his own way and still be loved, as most children do. Prompted by either latent fear or latent rage, he finds it difficult to compromise. He is visibly angry and resentful, regardless of the benefits that may be showered upon him. His accumulated bitterness may become too painful to endure. If there is no one to turn to, his growing tension may precipitate emergency dyscontrol which wipes out the gains derived from overdependence. With this pillar of security now threatening to collapse, the patient resorts to magical thought. His awareness of reality becomes blurred and his behavior decompensated.

On deeper scrutiny one discerns that the apparently unrelated clinical manifestations stem from a common root, formed by a relatively simple motivating system. In one way or another, all symptoms are addressed to the parent or ersatz parent. All are brought into play either by guilty fear or defiant rage or by a combination of the two. When dominance shifts from one emergency emotion to another, the symptom picture undergoes corresponding, often abrupt, changes.

Some of the symptoms demonstrate fear. Others are thinly veiled if not open outbursts of uncontrollable rage, coercive or vindictive. Still

other symptoms show a negativistic attitude. The patient's self-harming
defiance elicits automatic acts of self-punishment—tacit expiatory moves
aimed at reconciling the offended parent or ersatz parent. Transient
manifestations of phobic avoidance of certain situations or activities as
well as the sudden yet passing inhibition of one or another phase of
routine performance are intended to say to the parent or ersatz parent:
"Look what you have done to me." By means of a single act the patient expresses both his self-harming vengeance and his need for help.
The excessive fears and rages disorder the patient's sexual life to an even
greater extent than before. Both sexes, but especially the female, may
alternate between phases of severe inhibition (guilty fear) and reckless
indulgence (defiant rage). In schizotypes of paranoid predisposition,
guilty fear and defiant rage are exacerbated by the patient's suspicion
and distrust.

The motivations are, as a rule, hidden from the patient's awareness.
In addition, decompensation involves an ominous slackening of secondary elaboration—of the tendency to bring even a semblance of consistency and coherence into his performance. Instead, magical thought
comes to the fore. Signs of thought disorder and fragmentation of the
action self foreshadow disintegrative developments. The patient goes
off to the realm of unreality, where magic prevails and the adaptive
concerns of daily life can be abandoned.

The healthy individual knows approximately what he is and what
he would like to be, which I call the tested self or the desired self.
Both are closely interrelated functions of the action self. But in the
decompensated schizotype, this unit is much too brittle to withstand
the onslaught of retroflexed rage. The patient cannot have, and does
not have, self-confidence in the realistic sense. With his unbridled
rage turned against himself, he comes to feel that he is a hideous,
monstrous, destructive creature. When a beautiful woman can say in
deadly earnest, "I am a column of feces," one sees that the patient's
tested self is degraded to a detested self. This degraded self-image is,
however, surrounded by an overcompensatory halo, an illusory (delusional) self, created by wishfully anticipating the actual existence of
the desired self.

The two distorted aspects of the self alternate in holding sway. At
one time the patient is his detested self, at another, his illusory self.
In the former state, his rage is directed against himself; in the latter,
against the environment. Nevertheless, his pathology differs from the
swings of mood seen in other types. The decompensated schizotype's

experience of being his detested self is far more torturous than depression, for here the latent hope inherent in depression is greatly diminished if not destroyed. And the experience of being his illusory self lacks the sustained euphoria of elation. We attribute these differences in mood quality to the pleasure deficiency.

The pathologic development of a split producing a detested self and an illusory self is but one indication of the fact that the patient's action self lacks cohesion and is prone to become disordered. In the power to split and disrupt, proprioceptive disturbances far exceed retroflexed rage. The naked human body is a favorite form of art; if the schizotype happens to be a gifted sculptor, his distorted awareness of bodily self may be stunningly reproduced in his creative work. If he is a poet, his imagery and language may reveal the kinesthetic impairment of his self-experience. The Gestalt organization of perception as shown by Wolfgang Koehler mirrors the Gestalt organization of the action self, including its fragmentation and faulty reconstitution.

Psychotherapeutic intervention has three tasks: to prevent disintegration, to return the patient to the compensated stage, and to forestall future episodes of decompensation. We look forward to the day when reduction of the excessive emergency emotions will be aided by appropriate drugs, and pleasure deficiency become manageable by biochemical replacement therapy. The patient's distorted awareness of his bodily self enters the domain of motivational dynamics as a given fact; its control is presumably a neurochemical problem.

# CHAPTER 27

# *Extractive and Lesional Behavior*

*Extractive Disorders*

I SUGGEST THE TERM EXTRACTIVE DISORDER TO DESCRIBE THE BEHAVIOR pattern of the individual who is sometimes called the constitutional psychopath, later retermed sociopath. The essential facet of extractive behavior is its antisocial quality. The extractive is guilty of transgressive conduct. He is out for gain, seeking to achieve his own ends at the expense of other people and his environment.

The extractive depends on the two basic techniques of ingratiating and extorting, both of which are parasitic and coercive. It is all smile and suck, hit and grab: this is all the extractive knows and wants to know. As you remember, ingratiation is one of the weapons of the sanctuary. As a technique, it is acceptable for the child who has to get along as best he can because of his helplessness. But only the extractive adult tries to get along in life by these means.

One characteristic of the extractive, as opposed to the individual suffering from schizotypic and moodcyclic disorders, is the extent to which he lacks the capacity for delayed response. He is at the mercy of his strong pleasure drives. The extractive is not alone in losing, under duress, the restraining mechanism of conscience. Even the healthy individual can be so dominated by his biological needs that the restraining mechanism of the conscience is overwhelmed. But the extractive's conscience is overwhelmed at the slightest whim. Guilt and expiation do come in but they are to no avail. The extractive cannot learn from experience unless he can learn self-control. He spends his life going from whim to whim, and trusting to his good luck. When the past threatens to catch up with him he tries to avoid disaster by enacting another round of transgressive behavior. He indulges in much magic thinking, essential to his way of life. His emotional security depends on social approval. Just as his malfunctioning conscience cannot prevent him from engaging in extractive behavior, it is equally unfit for the task of rewarding himself with self-approval, which is the function of the healthy conscience.

Paradoxically enough, the extractive has a conscience that makes very high demands on other people, but he never makes these demands on himself when they are most needed to control pleasure desire. Another characteristic of the extractive is that his sexual activities are often sustained by pain dependence. As for his intelligence, he may be a moron or a genius, or anything in between. His transgressive conduct is usually precipitated by competition or frustration. It has been observed that when the extractive is maintained in an indulgent environment, he is relatively quiescent because he does not meet with the frustrations that precipitate his usual mode of behavior.

Now I cannot defend the stress on the antisocial quality of the extractive as a very good distinction, because schizophrenia, for instance, also leads to antisocial behavior, and also, all neurotic and psychotic behavior is a burden to the environment to some degree. But generally speaking the individual suffering from adaptive impairment or adaptive incompetence engages in behavior that results in consequences that are primarily damaging to that individual himself. The repair mechanism adopted is to effect one imaginary gain or another. A characteristic of every so-called neurosis and psychosis other than the extractive is the loss of pride, pleasure, self-reliance that every person so afflicted suffers.

We do not have anything better at the moment than this distinction of the antisocial quality of the extractive. But I caution you never to try to diagnose this disorder on the basis of examination of the patient. If you have reason to suspect that the patient is extractive, you will have to do some investigation and get your hands on outside facts. This is also true of the drug-dependent person.

Not all extractive behavior can be traced to childhood experiences, oedipal conflicts, or anything that we know now. I suspect that the extractive phenotype has developed because of some inherited defect. The defect may be some impairment of the hedonic control, like the deficiency that seems to me to be possibly innate in the schizotype and in the moodcyclic individuals.

The syndrome of extractive behavior was first described by Pritchard in 1835. He organized such behavior under the label *morally insane* with its connotation of moral condemnation. For the next sixty years nobody tried to define it. Kraepelin, Berbaum, and Monroe Meyer did some analysis of this behavior and decided that extractive people were to be considered as a group that was distinct and different from the neurotic and the psychotic groups. In World War II, the military reduced all extractive behavior to one classification—antisocial behavior.

Franz Alexander developed the syndrome and called his delineation of the psychopath a characteristic neurotic type. A few years later, Wilhelm Reich said this personality was instinct ridden. A. Eichhorn, in his book *Wayward Youth*, showed more insight into the nature of the disorder, as did Phyllis Greenacre, in "The Conscience in the Psychopath."

The misunderstanding of this disorder by psychoanalysts revolved around the use of the psychoanalytic term *acting out*. Let me emphasize that acting out means one thing—the using of infantile patterns by a neurotic adult who has relapsed into dependence. But psychoanalysis extended this term to describe all kinds of behavior, such as cheating. The legend of the extractive is that his illness burns itself out. It may burn out or it may not, just as the ordinary citizen may or may not recover from an emotional crisis. No treatment method is available at present. The best we can do is to experiment with educational techniques.

## Lesional Disorders

What can we say about those individuals who suffer adaptive incompetence and adaptive repair because of intoxication, high fever, syphillis and tuberculosis, senility, congenital defects? What can we say about the behavior disorders that derive from demonstrable, anatomical, physiological, and biological irregularities? You will perhaps understand better why I have elected to group all these as one class after I have pointed out what I think are the salient principles.

I should like to make one qualification. I have suggested to you the assumption basic to adaptational psychodynamics that emergency emotions (the excessive quantity that is produced, the handling thereof, and the like), lie at the core of every behavioral disorder. This is my only exception to that assumption and it may or may not occur in individuals suffering from lesional disorders.

Let us start with the basic principle of systemic self-readjustment. It is a principle that goes far beyond the range of lesional disorders.

If I were to speculate, I would say that this may well be one of the central activities of the whole organism. When the organism incurs damage, it immediately attempts to make automatic adjustments in terms of the injury. It tries to arrange for that function to be taken over by some other organ or for that function to be performed in some other way. Its effectiveness is determined by various limitations, such as the quantity of the pathways that were severed. The principle of self-adjustment to damage is well demonstrated.

The fundamental attitude that the psychiatrist has to keep in mind is that the nature of systemic self-readjustment depends (1) on the nature and site of the lesion, (2) on the effect of the lesion on a particular characteristic of the organism, and (3) on the response of the psychodynamic cerebral system to that injury.

A basic principle is that every organism has a highly individual way of reacting to damage. The stunning clinical fact that is beginning to emerge is that the reactions to cerebral lesions are more characteristic of the psychodynamic makeup of the organism than they are of the offending agent. Senile changes, for example, that are of a similar type change the vascularity and the metabolism in a similar way. But the different and dynamic psychological consequences that are produced vary highly from one individual to another. The first thing to be done is to find the lesion, which is not always easy to do. The systemic self-readjustment frequently tends to obscure the exact nature of the lesion and frequently has achieved something on its own. Therefore, the element of time must figure in the physician's calculations. Also, the range of behavior disorder is subject to change because it will depend on the state of the lesion.

When I went to medical school, neurology was dominated by the concept of local lesions. It was assumed that there was a one-to-one correspondence between the physiological lesion and the symptom. Many textbooks still try to explain all symptoms as caused by focal lesions.

Of course, in many instances of physiological damage there is a one-to-one correspondence; for example, between an injury to the optic nerve and a seeing malfunction. Accordingly, medicine came up with the conclusion that the psychodynamic cerebral system responds with over-all systemic reaction to lesion in the central nervous system, and this tends to cover up the one-to-one correspondence. I believe that we should forget about this alleged correspondence between cause and result. The clue lies in the nature of the systemic self-readjustment rather than in the nature of the lesion.

# CHAPTER 28

# Narcotic Drugs and

# Narcotic Bondage

THE LARGE NUMBER OF NARCOTIC DRUGS THAT CAN THROW THE PATIENT into narcotic bondage produces a correspondingly sizable variety of clinical pictures, each with certain fundamental characteristics common to them all. As the severity of the disorder increases, the conspicuous differences traceable to the chemical individuality of each drug tend to recede, and the clinical picture comes to be uniformly dominated by the same essential pathology. This fact suggests that we need first a general theory of narcotic bondage, which will in turn lead to the construction of a special theory for each drug or group of drugs. Also we must be aware of the difference between the individual drug addict and the individual who takes drugs in a group setting. Obviously in the latter the situation is more complex.

In 1933 I attempted to evolve a general theory of the dependence on narcotic drugs, using the libido theory as my conceptual framework. I am here reexamining the subject from the point of view of adaptational psychodynamics. Dependence on narcotic drugs is regarded as a malignant form of miscarried repair, artificially induced by the patient himself. Since our chief investigative concern is motivation, let us first find out what the patient believes the drug does for him. He gives us the following invaluable information: "It puts an end to my despair. It makes me feel happy. It restores my self-confidence. And it does all this in a moment, without any effort on my part. The drug is a miracle. I can't live without it."

In the past, we found that at the time the patient first took the drug he was often in a state of depression and felt unable to make a go of it. He blamed himself and others, sometimes even the one he loved most. Embittered, he longed for miraculous help. This prodromal depression is a precipitating etiological factor, because it sensitizes the patient to the psychodynamic action of the narcotic drug.

By removing pain, relaxing inhibitory tensions, inducing pleasure, and facilitating performance, narcotic drugs produce a narcotic pleasure effect. Conversely, every drug which produces this effect must be classified as narcotic. The average patient, upon therapeutic administration of the drug, responds to its pleasure effect with a sense of relief and satisfaction. But the patient who is about to develop drug dependence behaves differently, presumably because he has a special predisposition which may be twofold, biochemical as well as psychodynamic. In any case, he has a long previous history showing marked intolerance and fear of pain, and strong, though often overcompensated, dependency needs indicative of a lack of emotional maturity and security. He sees in the narcotic pleasure effect fulfillment of his longing for miraculous help and responds to it with a sense of personal triumph, a surge of overconfidence. He gets drunk with success. We call this exalted reaction narcotic intoxication or narcotic elation.

The grown organism lives under a more or less realistic system of self-government presided over by an adjusted though lovingly retouched self-image, the tested self. This image derives from and inherits the organizing functions of the primordial self, which now has become the hidden core of the organism's desired self, the secret aim image of its most deeply repressed aspirations.

If in the adaptive struggle for existence self-government fails, the organism may seek to strengthen its tested self with regressively revived features of its primordial self. However, such repair work is bound to miscarry, since the resulting aggrandized self-image can only undermine realistic self-government.

This also applies to the intoxicated patient. The sudden change from pain to pleasure, from inhibition to facilitation has proved to him by the full weight of an actual experience that, after all, he is the omnipotent giant he had always fundamentally thought he was, an illusion bound to collapse as soon as the wave of elation subsides.

Narcotic elation is followed by sleep and in turn by the morning after. The patient's depression returns, deepened by fresh guilty fears and made more painful by the contrast. His situation is worse than before, he feels he must recapture yesterday's grandeur by taking another dose. Thus his craving for elation develops. Augmented by concomitant physiological changes, it builds up in him ever-increasing tensions which can be discharged only by means of a fresh elation. Henceforth, every phase of elation leads to a phase of narcotic craving for elation, thence to taking the drug, which brings forth another phase of elation, and so forth in a cyclic course. A narcotic system of self-government, founded on dependence on the intoxicating drug, is established.

The interdependent phenomena of elation and craving for elation show that the patient's grandiose idea operates with delusional strength. Failure of the pleasure effect forces him to combat his rising physiological tolerance to the drug by increasing the dose to quantities which he may find hard to obtain. He may be visited by illness after illness resulting from the drug's toxic side effects. The intoxicating pleasure effect of the drug diminishes his appetite for food and often destroys his capacity for standard sexual union. His relatives and friends implore him to stop and save himself from certain ruin. While aware of these facts, he nonetheless insists on taking the drug. In an unguarded moment he gives away his secret: "Nothing can happen to me." Though his powers of reasoning and judgment appear to be otherwise unimpaired, he believes unshakably in his personal invulnerability and immortality. The patient's image of himself as an omnipotent and indestructible giant must be clinically described as a thinly veiled narcotic delusion of grandeur rooted in the drug, which has produced the intoxicating pleasure effect for him.

Paradoxically, even conscience tightens the patient's grip on his drug. His guilty fears and self-reproaches, strengthened by his defeated rages turned against himself, elicit automatic acts of expiatory self-punishment. To placate his conscience, his unconscious mind thus drives him to self-destruction by means of the drug; his conscious mind does not object because it believes that nothing can happen to him. Under the sway of its primordial self, the organism can unconcernedly behold its own march to death.

The "magic" of narcotic drugs lies in their direct biochemical action on the brain, in their bypassing the prerequisite adaptive effort and performance. Through this shortcut they surpass nature's ordinary rewards and, whenever desired, lift the organism from pain to a pleasure intensified still further by the contrast. As a sort of super pleasure, the drug's effect makes an irresistible appeal to the organism's hedonic control, displacing more and more the ordinary pursuits and rewards of healthy life. As we have seen, this substitution involves three mechanisms: one of superpleasure, silencing the warning signals of danger; another of intoxication, ushering in a delusion which, uprooting the patient's reason, foresight, and judgment, sanctions his craving; and a third, of conscience, paradoxically promoting the patient's narcotic self-destruction. And yet, viewed in the context of hedonic control, it is only a supporting part that these mechanisms play. The essential factor in the pathology of narcotic bondage is corruption of the organism's hedonic control by the super pleasure of narcotic drugs. By wiping out the adult's enlightened responses, the absolute priority of super pleasure reduces self-regulation to the precultural hedonic responses of the infant, aimed at immediate reward. In other words, corrupted hedonic self-regulation inevitably dehumanizes the patient's behavior. It is on this ground that we consider narcotic bondage a malignant disorder.

I would like to quote a few brief passages from two earlier papers of mine. The first was published in 1926: "When a person adopts the practice of pharmacotoxic gratification, momentous consequences ensue to his whole psychic and somatic condition. The phenomena presented to the clinical observer in cases of morbid craving are so multifarious that in this brief survey we must confine ourselves to stressing certain fundamental characteristics. The changes are enacted principally, of course, in the abode of the libido, for erotic gratification by means of drugs is a violent attack on our biological sexual organization, a bold forward movement of our 'alloplastic' civilization. Let us confine ourselves to morphinism and to the most 'fashionable' method of administering the poison by means of the Pravaz syringe. To put the matter in a nutshell, the whole peripheral sexual apparatus is left on one side as in a 'short circuit' and the exciting stimuli are enabled to operate directly on the central organ. I propose to term this phenomenon, which deserves to be distinguished by a special name, 'metaerotism.' With the advance of organic chemistry the manufacture of the most refined substances for producing sexual gratification is assuredly only a matter of time, and it is easy to prophesy that in the future of our race this mode of gratification will play a part as yet uncalculable."

In 1933 I wrote: "What is immediately evident is the fact that the pharmacogenic attainment of pleasure initiates an artificial sexual organization. . . . The pharmacogenic pleasure instigates a rich fantasy life; this feature seems especially characteristic of opiumpharmacothymia. . . . The crux of the matter is that it is the pharmacogenic pleasure effect which discharges the libidinal tension associated with these fantasies. . . . The genital apparatus with its extensive auxiliary ramifications in the erotogenic zones falls into desuetude and is overtaken by a sort of mental atrophy of disuse. The fire of life is gradually extinguished at that point where it should glow most intensely according to nature and is kindled at a site contrary to nature."

Now, we must remember that in the libido theory such terms as *libido, sexual,* and *erotic* were used in a wider sense denoting desire for and love of pleasure, which might be nonsexual as well as sexual. Accordingly, I now view *sexual organization* as *pleasure organization, peripheral sexual apparatus* as *peripheral pleasure apparatus,* and the like. The appropriate name for the phenomenon I called "metaerotism" is *metahedonism.* My early formulations firmly established the intoxicating pleasure effect as the key to the psychodynamic action of narcotic drugs and, in the long view, as a threat to the future of our species.

We may look forward to a physiology of the narcotic pleasure effect. By viewing the narcotic super pleasure as a developmental derivative of alimentary orgasm, psychodynamics may even offer a clue to the search for its biochemical mechanism. I believe it is possible that eventually biochemists will discover a method for the immunization of the organism against the narcotic pleasure effect.

To achieve clarity, in our general theory we have separated the pathology of drug dependence from the pathology of the underlying disorder. In this light, drug dependence is seen to be a self-inflicted process of miscarried repair. It transforms realistic self-government into narcotic self-government. Utilizing our previously suggested concepts of narcotic pleasure effect, narcotic elation, and narcotic craving for elation, both elation and craving for elation are interdependent manifestations of a thinly veiled narcotic delusion of grandeur, elicited by and rooted in the intoxicating pleasure effect of the drug. This chain of pathological events is traced to corruption of the organism's hedonic self-regulation by the effortless and instantaneous super pleasure of narcotic drugs.

Trapped by the subversive super pleasure, the patient abandons his enlightened hedonic responses based on delayed reward and reverts to the precultural responses of the infant, aimed at immediate reward. It is this dehumanizing consequence of a corrupted hedonic control that makes drug dependence a malignant disorder.

# CHAPTER 29

# Overreactive War Behavior

OVERREACTIVE BEHAVIOR IN WAR DOES NOT MEAN THE SAME THING AS overreactive behavior in civilian life. The first step of psychodynamic analysis shows what was clearly stated by Freud in World War I—that the war situation is fundamentally different. We are not used to living in an environment in which we are constantly exposed to the danger of death. This transformation of the citizen requires two things: (1) that he lift himself out of his civilian life (its conveniences and pursuits and love and happiness and family) in order to constantly expose himself to the danger of death, and (2) that he carry on the killing of other people. This change is a momentous one, and we cannot begin to understand the neuroses of war before we have a full comprehension of what the terms war *adaptation* and *combat adaptation* mean.

To simplify matters, I have condensed the whole proposition of war adaptation to the proposition: desire to serve. This desire to serve proves to be in conflict with the desire to live. The desire to serve involves all these dangerous activities, as a consequence of which one can die at any moment. To quote from a previous article of mine, "In facing the novelties and dangers of military life, the soldier is provided with various psychic resources, notably his sense of duty, which is backed by his desire for self-respect and the regard of his fellow soldiers, superior officers, and home relations, and heightened by fear of punishment and disgrace."

That shows the positive and the negative side. Complying with the demands of conscience brings a sense of stature and social security. This moral force, originating as it does in the situation of the helpless child, dependent for its very survival upon the love of its parents, may

be so powerful as to increase vastly the soldier's strength and endurance. His capacity may be further stimulated by an ambition rooted
in early sibling rivalry to be distinguished and thereby achieve still
further stature. In some cases a powerful factor is the escape from the
failures and frustrations, neurotic or otherwise, of civilian life. Feeling himself transposed, as if by magic, into another life, the individual
may become intoxicated with the determination to make good this
time. The soldier is also fortified by the satisfaction contingent on his
new life—the pleasures of comradeship, mass action, freedom from
the usual responsibilities, etc.

Now these are the positive resources that enable a soldier to carry
out his desire to serve as against the elementary desire in him to stay
alive. Freud, in 1920, looking back upon experiences of World War I,
described this desire to serve tentatively as a parasitic idea. It was so
dangerous to the ego that the ego may go to pieces, may get killed,
led on by this parasitic idea. This parasitic idea—a combination of public sentiment and pressure on the soldier—threatens to kill the ego by
its adventuresomeness.

The next step is that the victory of the desire to serve manifests itself in achieving a pattern of successful adaptation to war conditions in
general, to combat conditions in particular. So the next step in our
analysis is to ask, What does a successful adaptation to combat conditions look like? The ideal adaptation would be to scotomize almost
completely the danger of combat, not to allow our minds to think all
the time, "The next one will be me," and the like. The ideal adaptation would be to ignore that situation and distract ourselves from this
basic situation of danger and occupy ourselves with the technical tasks
of service and doing the right things.

The word scotomization is not very good, perhaps a better word
would be filtration. You have to filter your sense perception and your
thinking, in the physical sense of that word. The more perfect the
filtration, the more ideal is the adaptation. Where the filtration is
imperfect and anxiety and rage responses arise and have to be suppressed, the next best thing is to develop the pattern of successful
combat adaptation.

Such a phase of exposure to combat conditions produces anxiety
and accumulation of latent rage. During the phase of subsequent rest
period which is introduced, anxiety and rage subside. The man is then
rested, has neither anxiety nor latent rage. He comes into his next

exposure where again anxiety and latent rage accumulate. He goes into his next period of rest, where anxiety and rage subside. So there is an alteration of a period of exposure and a period of rest. The man is fresh again. This is in my view the best actually achievable adaptation to combat conditions as far as the emergency function is concerned, and the emergency function is a key function on which everything depends. Neurotic behavior in war, then, means a failure to achieve this ideal adaptation. Civilian neurosis is a failure of civilian adaptation; war neurosis a failure of war adaptation.

How does failure come about? There are two changeable regions. One is the insufficiency of filtration—the man cannot keep his mind off death completely. He becomes preoccupied with danger instead of doing his work mechanically. Two, he belongs to that group of human beings whose autonomic sensitivity is comparatively high. In other words, the generation of the affects of anxiety and rage goes on more intensely in his body than in that of others.

A combination of these two factors, insufficient filtration and higher autonomic sensitivity, will lead to the accumulation of a greater volume of anxiety and latent rage in this man during the same period of exposure with the result that when he withdraws from combat and goes into the period of rest, he is incapable of getting back into his previous normal condition. By the time his next exposure comes, he is still in anxiety and latent rage, carrying it over from the period before. Then he is in the danger zone, because he starts his next period of exposure not with his full capacity but carrying an anxiety load.

Latent rage is synonymous with irritability. Irritability means one's proneness to explode. Irritability means latent rage. In the development of war neuroses, failures of combat adaptation, insufficient filtration plus high autonomic sensitivity result in emergency dysfunction. Anxiety and latent rage, that is, irritability, persist over the period of rest, so that when the new period of service comes the man is still anxious. This condition is indicative of his impending breakdown. The next step is acute dyscontrol.

From now on anxiety and latent rage not only persist all the time, regardless of whether the man is exposed or not, but there sets in a spontaneous discharge in the form of attacks of anxiety. The man has attacks of anxiety and terror dreams, nightmares, displaying the tremendous irritability, latent rage, and readiness to discharge that latent rage. This constitutes the first form of acute dyscontrol which I call the outflow type, meaning outward discharge of anxiety, actually of rage. This is the condition which was diagnosed inaccurately as anxiety hysteria or anxiety neurosis.

Insufficient filtration plus high autonomic sensitivity result in emergency dysfunction. The desire to live is very strong underneath. The moment the man sees himself being victimized by attacks of anxiety a way out is there, "I am sick," "I am entitled to go home." The door is open to an honorable retreat from responsibility. If the man says this to himself consciously, he is considered a malingerer. But his unconscious mind, a lower behavior pattern prompted by the desire to live, will do the thinking for him for the purpose of getting home.

This is the crucial point of overreactive war behavior. The ordinary dyscontrol in itself is almost a physiological mechanism. It is almost inevitable that for everybody there should come a point where his combat adaptation fails, where he accumulates more anxiety and latent rage than he can dissolve in rest or in properly organized rest. But his desire to live sets in motion the unconscious exploitation of dyscontrol to serve as a legitimate pretext to take him home.

This unconscious intention of the soldier is seen particularly in the second group of acute dyscontrol which, for want of a better term I call *inflow type*. This group, erroneously diagnosed as hysteria, has little if anything to do with conversion hysteria. These are the dramatic cases with sharp tremors, inability to stand and walk, inability to speak, inability to hear, and all sorts of paralyses, the apparently hysterical symptomatology. If you analyze it, you see that every one of these symptoms represents a fragment of symbolic behavior, symbolic of the soldier's incapacitation.

The choice of the symbol shows a large variety of mechanisms. The tremor is the simplest to understand. It is simply the perpetuation of a component phenomenon of the ordinary expression of anxiety. In a severe panic or anxiety state, the man begins to tremble, and that picture of a trembling individual is perpetuated and coldly reproduced. It becomes a symbol type of condition when the somatic expression of panic goes on in a cold fashion. The man no longer has any anxiety attacks. He is calm, he does not think of being afraid, you do not find any other signs of fear, but this part of the motor expression is retained, perpetuated, and continued. That is why I term it *behavior fragment of value*.

Not to be able to talk, to walk, is also a partial phenomenon of strong fear. There are anxiety dreams in which we want to shout and our voice fails. Not to want to hear, a deafness, an attempt not to hear the oncoming airplane—this is all part of the emergency situation and response.

Other symptoms perpetuate the particular conditions of exposure. The man had to stand for hours in water, and when he comes out he has a paralysis of the legs. The meaning is, I am still in the water, I am still in trouble, I am in an emergency situation. This is not conversion hysteria. There is no latent sexual gratification, no self-aggrandizing daydreams or genital pleasure fantasies in the background as in hysteria. The whole sex function is out of the picture here. Like others, I do not like the word conversion because nothing is converted into anything, but I am unable to offer a good term. I call it symbolic type and I do not say that the hysteria is not symbolic, but I say that when you use the term symbol, you do not imply the sexual fantasies.

In World War I, this so-called hysterical type of symptomatology prevailed. It was characteristic that the formation of these behavior fragments was susceptible to contagion, so the man who broke down infected the company.

I understand that this symbol type of acute dyscontrol had become very rare in World War II, just as ordinary conversion hysteria has become very rare in civilian life. Ordinary conversion hysteria has a much more complicated structure because all the sex problem comes in, which is absent here. Psychoanalysis and the understanding of such symbolic behavior fragments are today so widespread that the unconscious intent cannot be satisfied. If a man were to produce these symptoms today, a hundred of his buddies would say, "You are a coward." And that cuts out the possibility of producing such symptoms.

There are, then, two types of dyscontrol. One is the outflow type where this agitation, overactive anxiety, and rage production are taken care of by an outward discharge. The second type is the symbolic behavior, and those who have this symptomatology spare themselves anxiety states. If you act in the sense of anxiety, if you do what anxiety makes you do—namely, defend yourself—you need no longer be afraid. The constant production of anxiety which has to be discharged is due to the fact that no behavior ensues.

Anxiety is a preparatory signal of danger, preparatory for expedience behavior. But if you are incapable of behaving in the spirit dictated by anxiety, if behavior is blocked, then the production of anxiety goes on. On the other hand, if you act in the spirit of anxiety, you can become blind or unable to talk or incapacitated, and you no longer need be afraid. This symbolic behavior fragment, carrying the intention of anxiety to fulfillment by demonstrating incapacitation, saves the person from continually producing fear, and his anxiety and rage can calm down.

Through lack of sufficient filtration and oversensitivity of the autonomic system the individual tends to produce more anxiety than he can dissolve: then you expect a continued anxiety as long as the man cannot do anything about it. The moment he can do something in the spirit of anxiety, when it reaches the executive motor behavior phase, there is a chance for the anxiety to calm down. Even these symbolic types of acute dyscontrol cases may produce nightmares and terror dreams. During sleep the production of anxiety goes on, their symbolic symptomatology ceases, and the anxiety recurs.

The third type of dyscontrol is the inward discharge, the inflow type. This type is the inward discharge of anxiety and rage, followed by the development of conditions such as effort phobia, the psychosomatic group. In general I am just indicating that the essential point is that anxiety and rage, instead of being discharged outwardly through the somatic system, through the skeletal muscles, is here discharged through the autonomic system. It is a visceral elaboration rather than skeletal, muscular elaboration; not outward behavior but dumping the affect into the viscera and thereby upsetting the normal function.

The fourth group of acute dyscontrol is the group that did not develop fresh symptomatology. Rather, dyscontrol precipitates a flareup of their former neurotic symptomatology, whatever it was. For the sake of brevity I call it the *flareup type*.

In my opinion, failure of combat adaptation produces incipient dyscontrol and acute dyscontrol of these four types (outflow type, symbolic type, inflow type, and flareup type). So far the struggle between the desire to serve and the desire to live is still in the balance, neither of these two antagonistic forces having gained a decisive victory.

This state of acute dyscontrol may go over to the third group, the chronic dyscontrol traumatophobia (I am not very proud of this term!). Two factors are involved here: the concept of trauma and the condition becoming chronic. Abraham Kardiner was the first to carry out an investigation of war neuroses from the point of view of adaptation.

So far we have had nothing to say about *trauma*. What we had to say dealt with the varying sensitivity of the autonomic system and the varying combat skill of the soldier in filtrating. The word *trauma*, or *shock*, has a purely historical origin. To my knowledge, Kardiner was the first to try to analyze what a psychological shock is. He interprets pathogenic trauma as a sudden loss of all effective control over the situation "which leaves the lasting damage on the patient's adaptive capacity, his perceptive, coordinative, and manipulative skill, and instills in him a feeling of helplessness."

According to Kardiner's convincing analysis, psychic trauma is an abrupt and transitory stoppage in the individual's efficient personality operation, resulting in inability to meet the demands made on it by a new situation. This psychological reaction does occasionally appear in the wake of physical injury. Multiple instances would be a hysterical fainting spell or paralyzing cry or even the momentary mental paralysis of an incident of trivial embarrassment.

What I would add to Kardiner's description of trauma is the natural vitality of the body and mind, the reparative part of the organism which is responsible for all spontaneous bodily repairs in the wake of damage. We do not know what this quality is which causes automatic, reparative moves to set in. The normal consequence of psychic trauma is that activity immediately sets in for repair of the damage. A trauma becomes pathogenic if there is some need or motive force present that paralyzes spontaneous repair and thereby leaves the individual more or less in a state of paralysis or incapacitation in which he was thrown by the trauma.

That which makes a trivial occurrence into a pathogenic factor is the nonreporting mechanism whereby spontaneous repair is indicated. The healthy reaction to an experience of the latter type, namely, embarrassment, is to make almost automatically immediate efforts to repair that failure. The example of the hysteric, however, introduces the element of the desire to be overwhelmed by the situation, so as to avoid coping with it and also the tendency to shun that situation from then on. In this respect the soldier is in a similar situation. In incapacitation he finds relief from the mounting tension of his inhibited affects and motor impulses, especially if his disability can be made to last for the duration. The nonreporting operations of his emergency control can therefore do nothing better at this juncture than to inhibit the very process that would otherwise mean recovery, and thereby perpetuate the operation.

It cannot be overstressed that this inhibition of repair is a nonreporting anxiety mechanism. While it is in force, the patient is unable to rid himself of a sense of helplessness and discouragement.

If our analysis is correct, the decisive factor in the psychodynamics of the illness is the inhibition of spontaneous repair; that is, a change from the atavistic, enterprising attitude toward life to one of retreat, inertia, and avoidance. Most, if not all human beings contain the possibility of such a development and it would be fruitless to try to tell beforehand how much strain they can stand before withdrawing.

The moment this phobic factor develops, and that can be the case in any one of the four types—any one of these can become chronic—it results in a chronic traumatophobia. This wide area of disturbance created by the overactive state of emergency control finds its central psychological representation in the dread of being further exposed to injury or death. The vague idea of future harm takes shape in the patient's mind as a hurt already suffered. A hurt to come is envisaged on the basis of the hurt already suffered, and this dread of injury becomes a dread of the recurrence of that particular experience.

# Bibliography

RADO, SANDOR. "Achieving Self-Reliant Treatment Behavior," in JULES H. MASSERMAN (ed.), *Science and Psychoanalysis*, Vol. III. New York: Grune and Stratton, 1960.
———. "Adaptational Development of Psychoanalytic Therapy," in S. RADO and G. E. DANIELS, *Changing Concepts of Psychoanalytic Medicine*. New York: Grune and Stratton, 1956.
———. "Adaptational Psychodynamics: A Basic Science," in S. RADO and G. E. DANIELS, *Changing Concepts of Psychoanalytic Medicine*.
———. "An Adaptational View of Sexual Behavior," in PAUL H. HOCH and JOSEPH ZUBIN (eds.) *Psychosexual Development in Health and Disease*. New York: Grune and Stratton, 1949.
———. "An Anxious Mother," *International Journal of Psycho-Analysis*, 9, 1928.
———. "The Automatic Motivation System of the Depressive Behavior," *Comprehensive Psychology*, 2:248–262, 1961.
———. "Behavior Disorders: Their Dynamics and Classification," *American Journal of Psychiatry*, 110:406, 1953.
———. "Between Reason and Magic," paper presented at the 105th Annual Meeting of the American Psychiatric Association, Montreal, Quebec, 1949.
———. "The Border Region Between the Normal and the Abnormal: Four Types," in I. GALDSTON (ed.), *Ministry and Medicine in Human Relations*. New York: International Universities Press, 1955.
———. "The Contribution of Psychoanalysis to the Medical Study of Behavior," *Journal of Nervous and Mental Disease*, 123:421, 1956.

————. "A Critical Examination of the Concept of Bisexuality," *Psychosomatic Medicine*, 2:459, 1940.

————. "Developments in the Psychoanalytic Conception and Treatment of the Neuroses," *Psychoanalytic Quarterly*, 8:427–437, 1939.

————. "Discussion of Dr. Masserman's Paper on Biodynamics," in JULES H. MASSERMAN (ed.), *Psychoanalysis and Human Values*. New York: Grune and Stratton, 1962.

————. "Discussion of Dr. Whitehorn's Paper on Schizophrenia," in PAUL S. HOCH and JOSEPH ZUBIN (eds.), *Psychopathology of Communication*. New York: Grune and Stratton, 1958.

————. "The Economic Principle in Psychoanalytic Technique," *International Journal of Psycho-Analysis*, 6:35, 1925.

————. "Ego Analysis and the Primacy of the Reality Principle," paper read before a special meeting of the Vienna Psychoanalytic Society held in Sigmund Freud's home, Vienna, March, 1931.

————. "Emergency Behavior: With an Introduction to the Dynamics of Conscience," in PAUL H. HOCH and JOSEPH ZUBIN (eds.), *Anxiety*. New York: Grune and Stratton, 1950.

————. "Fear of Castration in Women," *Psychoanalytic Quarterly*, 2:425, 1933.

————. "From the Metapsychological Ego to the Bio-Cultural Action-Self," *Journal of Psychology*, 47:279, 1958.

————. "Graduate Residency Training in Psychoanalytic Medicine," *American Journal of Psychiatry*, 105:111–115, 1948.

————. "Hedonic Control, Action-Self, and The Depressive Spell," in PAUL H. HOCH and JOSEPH ZUBIN (eds.), *Depression*. New York: Grune and Stratton, 1954.

————. "The Institute in Relation to Psychoanalytic Teaching and Research," The New York Psychoanalytic Institute Report for the Academic Years 1931–1934.

————. Lectures at the Columbia University Psychoanalytic Clinic 1945–1955, unpublished record.

————. "Mind, Unconscious Mind, and Brain," *Psychosomatic Medicine*, 11:165, 1949.

————. "Narcotic Bondage: A General Theory of the Dependence on Narcotic Drugs," *American Journal of Psychiatry*, 114, 1957.

————. "Observations on the Development of Psychoanalytic Theory," in PAUL H. HOCH and JOSEPH ZUBIN (eds.), *Current*

*Approaches to Psychoanalysis*. New York: Grune and Stratton, 1960.

———. "Obsessive Behavior," in SILVANO ARIETI (ed.), *American Handbook of Psychiatry*. New York: Basic Books, 1959.

———. "On the Psychoanalytic Exploration of Fear and Other Emotions," *Transactions of the New York Academy of Sciences*, Ser. II, 14:280, 1952.

———. "Pathodynamics and Treatment of Traumatic Neurosis (Traumatophobia)," *Psychosomatic Medicine*, 4:362, 1942.

———. "The Paths of Natural Science in the Light of Psychoanalysis," *Psychoanalytic Quarterly*, 1:683, 1932. (Published in German, 1922.)

———. "Patterns of Motivation in Depression," paper presented at the 12th International Psychoanalytic Congress, Wiesbaden, 1932.

———. "The Problem of Melancholia," *International Journal of Psycho-Analysis*, 9, 1929.

———. "The Psychiatric Aspects of Sweating," *Archives of Dermatology and Syphilology*, 66:175–176, 1952.

———. "The Psychic Effects of Intoxicants: An Attempt to Evolve a Psycho-analytical Theory of Morbid Cravings," *International Journal of Psycho-Analysis*, 7, 1926.

———. "Psychoanalysis and Psychiatry," *American Journal of Psychiatry*, 92:297–300, 1935.

———. "The Psychoanalysis of Pharmacothymia," *Psychoanalytic Quarterly*, 2, 1933.

———. "Psychoanalytic Education: Lessons of the Past and Responsibilities," in JULES H. MASSERMAN (ed.), *Science and Psychoanalysis*, Vol. V. New York: Grune and Stratton, 1962.

———. "Psychodynamics as a Basic Science," *American Journal of Orthopsychiatry*, 16:405, 1946.

———. "Psychodynamics of Depression from the Etiologic Point of View," *Psychosomatic Medicine*, 13:51, 1951.

———. "Psychotherapy: A Problem of Controlled Intercommunication," in PAUL H. HOCH and JOSEPH ZUBIN (eds.), *Pathology of Communication* (Proceedings of the 1956 Annual Meeting of the American Psychopathological Association). New York: Grune and Stratton, 1958.

———. "Rage, Violence, and Conscience," *Comprehensive Psychiatry*, 1:327–330.

———. "Recent Advances of Psychoanalytic Therapy," *Psychiatric Treatment,* Vol. XXI. Baltimore: Williams and Wilkins, 1954.

———. "The Relationship of Patient to Therapist," *American Journal of Orthopsychiatry,* 12:542, 1942.

———. "Schizotypal Organization," in S. Rado and G. E. Daniels (eds.), *Changing Concepts of Psychoanalytic Medicine.* New York: Grune and Stratton, 1956.

———. "Scientific Aspects of Training in Psychoanalysis," The New York Psychoanalytic Institute Report for the Academic Years 1934–1937.

———. "Sexual Anesthesia in the Female," *Quarterly Review of Surgery, Obstetrics, and Gynecology,* 16:24–253, 1959.

———. "Theory and Therapy: The Theory of Schizotypal Organization and Its Application to the Treatment of Decompensated Schizotypal Behavior," in Samuel C. Scher and Howard R. Davis (eds.), *Out-Patient Treatment of Schizophrenia.* New York: Grune and Stratton, 1960.

———. "Toward the Construction of an Organized Foundation for Clinical Psychiatry," *Comprehensive Psychiatry,* 2:65–73, 1961.

———. "The Use of Patients in Graduate Teaching in Psychiatry," *Psychiatric Quarterly,* July, 1959.

———. (ed.) *Zehn Jahre Berliner Psychoanalytisches Institut* (Ten Years of the Berlin Psychoanalytic Institute). With the cooperation of Otto Fenichel and Carl Mueller-Braunschweig; preface by Sigmund Freud. Vienna: Internationaler Psychoanalytisches Verlag, 1930.

———. and George E. Daniels (eds.). *Changing Concepts of Psychoanalytic Medicine.* New York: Grune and Stratton, 1956.

# Index